THE CONSTANTS OF NATURE

θυγατρὶ ποθεινῇ

The Constants of Nature

A realist account

PETER JOHNSON
Balliol College
Oxford

Routledge
Taylor & Francis Group
LONDON AND NEW YORK

First published 1997 by Ashgate Publishing

Reissued 2018 by Routledge
2 Park Square, Milton Park, Abingdon, Oxon, OX14 4RN
711 Third Avenue, New York, NY I 0017, USA

Routledge is an imprint of the Taylor & Francis Group, an informa business

A Library of Congress record exists under LC control number: 97074099

ISBN 13: 978-1-138-34931-5 (hbk)
ISBN 13: 978-1-138-34934-6 (pbk)
ISBN 13: 978-0-429-43635-2 (ebk)

Contents

Figures and tables

Preface

This book is an attempt to resolve certain misunderstandings and ignorance concerning the constants of Nature, which have been at the back of my mind since I was a schoolboy. My inability to cope with the complexities of changing from electrostatic to electromagnetic units, combined with my fascination at a later stage with the precision of measurements of the quantum of circulation provided a fertile ground for woolly thinking. Throw in dimensions, measurement theory and some radical philosophies of science, and one has all the conditions for a thick intellectual fog.

With a better, but not perfect, grasp of these items, I have tried to provide a realist account of the constants in physics as an alternative to the prevailing conventionalist perspective of many philosophers. The discussion first focuses the discussion on the most primitive categories of physical constant which underlie modern science. Subsequently the conventionalist case is examined in depth, and is shown to provide an incomplete account of how constants, and the related concept of dimensions, function in science. Having repudiated the conventionalist challenge, the positive case for a realist notion of constants is then considered. This account is found to be comfortably accommodated by modest realist schools such as the Natural Ontological Attitude (NOA).

There are bound to be errors and omissions in what I have written, but I hope this book helps others to understand this complex and confusing corner of science.

Acknowledgements

I am grateful to the Master and Fellows of Balliol College for allowing me to carry out this research, and to the British Academy for funding it. I am particularly indebted to Dr W. H. Newton-Smith for his insight, guidance and good humour throughout the preparation of this work. A word of thanks is due also to Harvey Brown and John Roberts for their help. Finally I thank my wife and family for their support and patience.

I acknowledge permission of the author, and the editors and publishers of the Journal of Symbolic Logic to quote from *Models and Reality* by Hilary Putnam.

I am grateful to the author and the University of Cambridge for allowing me to include specific passages from *Mind, Language and Reality* also by Hilary Putnam. *The Refutation of Conventionalism* originally appeared in *Semantics and Meaning*, edited by M. Munitz, and I am grateful to the University of New York, the publishers of this work, for allowing me to include specific passages from this essay.

1 Introduction and overview

Contrasting perspectives

Between 1880 and 1950 a good deal was written about the nature of physical quantities, dimensions and, obliquely, physical constants. Much of this interest stemmed from the practical need to understand the issues at stake in the choice of a system of basic quantities to be used uniformly across the scientific community in order to make the results of experiments consistent and comparable. Since the 1950s little has been written in this area, perhaps because the issues were thought to be resolved, and because scientists have settled on the S.I.[1] system of basic measurement quantities.

If there was a prevailing opinion at the end of the 1950s, it was that the choice of quantities, the assignment of dimensions and the nature of constants were entirely matters of scientific convention. Such views were a natural consequence of the operational concept of measurement championed by Bridgman (1926), according to which the conceptual content of a quantity is exhausted by its definition in terms of the carrying out of specified measurement operations in precisely described circumstances. Such a view of measurement clearly had much in common with the philosophical programme of the positivists. These views held sway well into the 1960s, and in the field of measurement they were fully expounded by Dingle (1942, 1943), and most recently by Ellis (1966).

The purpose of the present work is to look closely at the philosophical arguments made to support the customary conventional view of measurement, particularly with regard to constants. It will be argued that these historic accounts provide only a partial understanding of the nature of constants, and that the conventionalism that arises relates only to the numerical representations used to quantify the measurement of quantities. The story of conventional numerical representation needs to be supplemented by an account of the empirical foundations of constants. A modest realist account of constants will be developed under the auspices of Fine's Natural Ontological Attitude (NOA), and this account will be articulated and defended in the context of other prevailing philosophies of science. The intention will not be to defend Fine's particular form of modest realism *per se*, but to describe critically the emergence of NOA and to see whether it forms a suitable home for the empirical notions of constants developed in the first part of the work. It will be argued that NOA can accommodate constants, and that NOA may allow for the possibility that the physical grounding of constants may be underdetermined by tolerating a limited relativism in its account.

To give a sense of the strength of feeling expressed by philosophers and scientists concerning the status of constants, and to illustrate some of the interesting philosophical issues under discussion, it is helpful to contrast perspectives.

The current prevailing orthodoxy of the scientific community is well captured by Barrow, the astrophysicist:

> Real advances in our understanding of the physical world always seem to involve either:
>
> (i) The discovery of a new fundamental constant of Nature,
> (ii) A formula showing how the value of one constant of Nature is determined by the numerical values of others, or,
> (iii) The discovery that a quantity believed to be a constant of Nature is not constant.
>
> .... To most physicists the ultimate goal of their subject is nothing less than the determination of the numerical values of all these universal constants: the demonstration that they can possess only one possible set of self-consistent values, and that this requirement of self-consistency, together with a minimum of symmetry principles, will be enough to determine the structure of the world uniquely. (Barrow 1988 p. 322)

> One of the great goals of fundamental physics is to find the reason for the precise numerical values of the constants that appear in the equations that prescribe the laws of Nature. Many physicists believe that, eventually, we will be able to calculate the values of the fundamental constants, and specify the initial conditions of the Universe by some principle of internal consistency that reveals there to be one, and only one, logical choice for all of them. (Barrow 1988 p. 280)

The view that the values of the constants might be obtainable from theory was also held by Einstein:

> [Einstein] expressed his anticipations concerning the true universal constants ... also in the following way: "In a reasonable theory, there are no (dimensionless) numbers whose values are only empirically determinable." He stressed again, however, that he, naturally, had no proof for this, but that he could not imagine a unified and reasonable theory explicitly to contain a number which the mood of the creator could just as well have chosen differently, whereby a world of a qualitatively different lawlessness would have resulted. (Rosenthal-Schneider in Schilpp 1949 p. 144)

Eddington went further than theoretical deducibility, and spent many years working on *a priori* proofs of the values of constants:

> I believe that the whole system of fundamental hypotheses can be replaced by epistemological principles. Or to put it equivalently, all the laws of nature that are usually classed as fundamental can be foreseen wholly from epistemological considerations. They correspond to a priori knowledge, and are therefore wholly subjective. (Eddington 1939 p. 57)

> My conclusion is that not only the laws of nature but the constants of nature can be deduced from epistemological considerations, so that we can have a priori knowledge of them. (Eddington 1939 p. 58)

While at first sight Eddington's views may seem curious, in fact modern unified field theorists are working along similar lines: Eddington's fundamental theory attempted to integrate quantum mechanics and general relativity by postulating the cosmological consequences of a universe of a finite number of elementary particles, governed by quantum mechanics, and described by his quaternion calculus. Constraints upon the nature of such a system emerged from the simultaneous need to satisfy relativity and quantum mechanics and from constraints imposed by *a priori* features of the mathematical representation Eddington posited. This approach seems similar in outlook to the group-theoretic gauge symmetries that comprise the Standard Model used as the starting point for modern unified approaches.

In contrast to the views of scientists who accorded much importance to constants and their values, we may cite the violently opposing operationalist view of Ellis, one of the natural successors to Bridgman and Dingle:

> We may conclude, then, that simply by adopting different conventions concerning the expression of equations, universal scale-dependent constants may be created or eliminated at will. We cannot, therefore, attach to these constants anything other than a conventional existence; and it is quite absurd to suppose that these constants represent the magnitudes of peculiar invariant properties of space or of matter. (Ellis 1966 p. 125)

Perhaps the best summary of the perplexities posed by constants that give rise to such radically differing views came from Palacios:

> Universal constants have one disturbing feature. They appear in the expressions for the laws of physics without being previously defined either qualitatively or quantitatively. They are independent of the nature of the bodies to which these laws are applied. Further, they are not physical quantities since they always occur with the same value; and to imagine that in another universe they can take other values is an unjustified and useless metaphysical speculation. As there exists only one example of each, if they were physical quantities they would themselves be their own units and their value would be the number one. Nevertheless, they are not mere numbers since their value depends on the system of units adopted to measure the magnitudes which occur in the equations. Finally their existence is in some

> respects precarious since, for example, what has been called the dynamical constant is not mentioned in any physics textbook, whilst the mechanical equivalent of heat, which used to be discussed at great length in textbooks at the beginning of the century, is hardly mentioned in present day works ... In the introduction to the present thesis it was indicated that there is a tendency to reduce the number of universal constants in use. The simplest thing would be to get rid of them all, but as there are not enough disposable units to do this, each author suppresses those which he likes least and a certain amount of published work exists in which, thanks to the suppression of such and such constants, a certain esoteric sense is supposed to be given to the laws of physics so obtained.(Palacios 1964 p. 23)

In the chapters that follow many of the issues raised by these differing perspectives will be explored. Thorough analysis will reveal the extent to which these views are correct, incomplete or misguided.

Summary of principal findings

In advance of detailed reading of the text, it may be helpful to list the principal findings that emerge from this research as a guide and aide-memoire through what is at times a complex and indigestible account.

1 It is possible to distinguish between two separate categories of universal constants: those measured by fundamental means and those given by derived measurement relying on a supporting law.

2 The most primitive fundamental universal constants are the charge, mass and magnetic moments of elementary particles; the most primitive derived constants are c, h, G, e and k.

3 All other universal constants customarily regarded as significant can be obtained from this set of primitive constants.

4 The fundamental universal constants can function as the standard objects within a formal axiomatic system of extensive measurement, and are properties of particles.

5 The derived universal constants can be defined within a formal system of derived measurement and characterise the interactions of particles.

6 The distinction between fundamental and derived quantities is not undermined by substitution of derived for fundamental quantities nor the possibility of alternative representations of fundamental quantities.

7 The conventionality that extends to the dimensional representation of derived quantities does not undermine the status of primitive universal derived constants, which can be grounded in an alternative empirical notion of dimensions.

8 NOA seems to offer a number of advantages compared with traditional realism, internal realism, instrumentalism and constructive empiricism. The potential vulnerability of NOA to problems arising from underdetetermination can be overcome by employing a notion of relativism that finds its origins in Quine's work on the indeterminacy of translation.

9 The choice of alternative empirical systems to ground primitive derived constants represents a case of underdetermination that can be happily accommodated by NOA.

10 NOA provides a modestly realist account of science in which we may embed our notions of primitive constants.

Overview

With the list of key findings in hand, the structure and content of the various chapters fall more easily into place:

Chapter 2 Constants and measurement

In this chapter we review the principal traditional accounts of measurement in so far as they relate to constants. By drawing a distinction between system-dependent parameters and scale-factors, we are able to explain aspects of the physical and numerical systems in which constants are embedded without the confusion evident in the account of Campbell, nor the operationalist dogma of Ellis. There is a readily intelligible account of the physical meaning of constants, which can be formalised in the assignment of single values to system-independent parameters in a systematic account of the numerical representation of extensive quantities based upon the axiomatic scheme provided by Suppes. Important differences exist between fundamental and derived system-independent parameters, which give rise to further questions relating to the numerals and ratios are identified. We argue that no particular importance attaches to composite ratios that turn out to be dimensionless numbers, since it is always possible to use the results of dimensional analysis to turn a dimensioned composite ratio into a dimensionless ratio. The remaining primitive constants can be separated into those obtained by derived measurement and those by fundamental means. Support for this distinction lies in the particulate vs. field aspects of the categories so defined. The account given of primitive fundamental constants is defended against criticisms that it is a meaningless distinction in application and undermined by the possibility of alternative, non-standard representations. Conventionalist arguments against primitive derived constants based upon the theory of dimensions are addressed in Chapter 4.

Chapter 4 Constants, conventionality and dimensions

In this chapter we analyse in detail the arguments that have been made for a conventional status for derived constants. While it is true that constants can be made to appear or disappear at will, and to have whatever dimensions may be desired, these seemingly arbitrary features of constants are entirely aspects of the numerical representation employed, and apply equally to all quantities. It is possible, however, to specify an optimal representation of a formula that does not result in a redundancy of dimensional quantities or of constants. Manipulation of the numerical representation does not affect the underlying empirical systems which may be used to anchor derived constants. A set-theoretic explication of these empirical systems is given in terms of fundamental measurement operations, which precede the assignment of a numerical representation.

Chapter 5 Constants and reality

In this and the succeeding chapter, the account of constants developed is used to test prevailing realist philosophical doctrines such as NOA which have emerged subsequent to the relative demise of convergent realism. The purpose of is to provide a modified realist platform to ground the account of primitive fundamental and derived constants developed in earlier chapters. Realist, instrumentalist and constructive empiricist traditions are reviewed and critiqued, and the emergence of modest realist positions such as NOA is examined.

Chapter 6 Constants and underdetermination

A particular feature of the empirical grounding of primitive derived constants is the possibility of interesting cases of underdetermination arising from the different alternative fundamental measurement systems used to anchor the constant concerned. We may inquire whether this feature is compatible with the adoption of NOA as a suitable realist platform for constants. While more attractive along many dimensions relative to alternatives, NOA initially seems vulnerable to underdetermination. This question is closely analysed, and a degree of relativity in the notion of truth is accepted for the NOA account in order to deal with instances of underdetermination. This relativity is not viewed as injurious, and accommodates easily the underdetermination that arises from the existence of alternative empirical systems used to define primitive derived constants.

Chapter 7 Constants and NOA

The account of constants and an account of NOA which incorporates a limited relativism may, once presented, be swiftly joined to provide a modestly realist underpinning for both primitive fundamental and primitive derived constants, which contrasts strongly with the conventionalist accounts of others. In conclusion, the principal findings of this research are summarised and areas for further analysis are outlined.

Note

1 S.I. (Système International) units are those in the International System of Units adopted in 1960 by the Conférence Générale des Poids et Mesures.

2 Constants and measurement

Introduction

Units and laws

Most accounts of fundamental constants provided by physicists associate constants with the value of *units* or standards within a system of measurement. Cohen, Crowe and Dumond, for instance, in their book *The Fundamental Constants of Physics* (1957), which gives systematic coverage of the most important experiments made to determine the values of constants up to the late 1950's, regarded constants as units:

> One of the most important fruits of physical research has been the discovery that Nature herself has fundamental units such as the charge on the electron, the rest mass of the electron, Planck's constant of action, the speed of light. (Cohen et al. 1957 p. 2)

Similarly, Sanders (1965), in his more recent account of the experimental results believed that constants are natural features of the physical world:

> From the quantitative study of the phenomena of physics has emerged the fact that certain quantities appear in reproducible amounts fixed by nature. Among them may be cited the magnitude of the charge on the electron, the velocity of electromagnetic radiation in free space, Planck's constant, and so on. Quantities of this sort, which are not expressible in terms of each other, are called the fundamental constants. (Sanders 1965 p. 2)[1]

On the other hand, if we turn to accounts of the historic origin of the most celebrated constants, such as the gravitational constant or Planck's constant, or consult a general physics text, we will find that constants are usually defined by what Campbell called a *numerical law* and what we today would call an *equation*. Campbell, for instance, considered Planck's constant to be an excellent example of a universal constant as defined by Planck's law :

$$E = h\nu$$

How may these two different perspectives be explained, reconciled and integrated into an account of measurement?

Synopsis of chapter

In this chapter, we will follow roughly a chronological approach and we will first examine the role of constants in equations, comparing and contrasting the accounts of Campbell and Ellis, who have provided the most explicit and detailed descriptions of the role of constants in measurement.

The accounts of Campbell and Ellis distinguish between types of constant on the basis of the role they play in the numerical representation of laws by equations that relate measured quantities. We will argue that, while thorough, these accounts are incomplete insofar as they failed to recognise distinctly the category of constants of greatest interest to physicists. This separate category of constants will be labelled *system-independent parameters*, to distinguish them from other categories of constants. An example of such a parameter is G, the gravitational constant. The invariance of G may be contrasted with the mutability of parameters which vary with the choice of physical system to which they apply, for example, the density of a substance.

On the way to providing support for this notion, we will consider some of the difficulties encountered by Campbell which resulted from his failure to recognise this distinction. We will also examine closely the arguments of Ellis, who believed that constants arise entirely as a consequence of the conventions we adopt in the choice of the scales we use to measure quantities, and in the choice of the algebraic form of expression of our laws in science. As a consequence of these views, Ellis argued that we can only consider universal constants to be of very limited importance.

Before turning to consider how parameters which do not vary can be embedded in an axiomatic account of the measurement of quantities, we will discuss more precisely the links between the numerical representation of parameters and the physical objects and properties to which these parameters relate.

In the axiomatic account of measurement that we present, we will draw upon the elegant summary analysis provided by Suppes (1963) for the formalisation of measurement. Within this account, we will argue that those parameters which are unvarying and the same for all systems that are measured, should be considered to be the standard objects of a formal measurement system. This will allow us to provide a fairly rigorous account of the most important physical constants that has much in common with the views of scientists. At the heart of this account, however, is a distinction between fundamental measurement and derived measurement, which is subject to scrutiny of its validity in Chapter 3.

The meanings of terms

The most important works on constants and measurement are probably those of Campbell (1920 and 1928), Bridgman (1931), Suppes (1951, 1963 amongst others), Palacios (1964) and Ellis (1966).

The field as a whole is dry, messy and technical. While a number of broad terms and distinctions are shared by these authors, important fine differences exist in the definition and usage of key terms such as *quantity*, *unit*, and *dimension*. Given that it would be lengthy to record and to contrast the complete terminology of each author, we will content ourselves with a brief summary of the major terms and concepts that arise in the work of Campbell, Ellis and Suppes, aiming to highlight more subtle differences as we proceed with our discussion.

The common starting assumption of all these authors asserts that the most basic physical quantities are the numerically orderable properties of physical objects as determined by a well defined measurement procedure.

Campbell, who may rightly be considered the father of formal measurement theory, held that measurement was the assignment of numbers to quantities in virtue of certain laws. His notion of law was broad, and the laws which he applied are more accurately regarded as necessary conditions for measurement to occur.

First, it must be possible to establish a quasi-series in respect of the quantity concerned (Campbell specified the relevant relational definitions). Second, there must be a well-defined measurement procedure for combining objects, which may be represented by an additive binary operation. Finally, it must be possible to create a standard series of objects, so that the measure of a quantity for an arbitrary object will equal that of some member of the standard series. Combining these three sets of requirements, we obtain a set of axioms similar to those first developed by Hölder in 1901.

Measurement which satisfies these requirements does not depend upon the prior measurement of any other quantities. Campbell defined this type of measurement as *fundamental* measurement. Measurement which depends upon the prior measurement of other quantities he called *derived* measurement.

Campbell placed considerable emphasis on the existence of an *additive operation* for quantities which could be fundamentally measured. By an additive operation for a certain quantity, we mean one that allows us to regard each object that possesses this quantity as possessing a certain countable number of measures[2] of that property so that when two bodies or objects are combined, the combined body or object possesses the sum of the numbers of measures possessed individually by the bodies or objects. As a result we expect the formal representation of an additive operation to satisfy the customary distributive and commutative axioms of addition :

1 $A \oplus B > A'$
2 If $A = A'$, and $B = B'$ then $A \oplus B = A' \oplus B'$;
3 If $A \oplus B = x$ then $B \oplus A = x$
4 $(A \oplus B) \oplus C = A \oplus (B \oplus C)$

Campbell called Axiom 1 the First Law of Addition, and took Axioms 2, 3, and 4 to state the Second Law of Addition, which required the fundamental measuring operation to be insensitive to order.

Quantities often support such an operation and those that do are considered to be *extensive* properties. By contrast, qualities are held to be *intensive* properties that do not support such an operation.

Given the close connection between measurement and the additive nature of many quantities, it was a natural step for Campbell to assert that fundamental measurement relates only to extensive quantities which are characterised by an additive combination procedure.

The situation is not, however, quite so tidy. The existence of non-additive operations (for instance for capacitances, and relativistic velocities)[3] argues for a broader category of quantities to be defined, and some properties defined by equations might more naturally be considered qualities, rather than quantities, for example viscosity, permittivity, and self-inductance.[4] Either a change in the definition of extensive quantities (removing the need for a strictly additive operation), or the inclusion in the definition of fundamental measurement of alternative arithmetical operations (to represent the combination procedure), are warranted (see later).

Rather than use the word quantity, Campbell preferred the term *magnitude*. Only those quantities which could be measured by fundamental methods are called *A magnitudes*; all other quantities are *B magnitudes*. Clearly, some A quantities can also be measured by non-fundamental means. By talking directly of quantities as magnitudes, Campbell avoided the need to talk explicitly about the assignment of numbers to quantities, and thereby avoided discussion of what a *scale* is (see later).

Where derived measurement occurs, we rely upon the mathematical *equation* that represents an empirical *law* of physics, to assign measures to a B quantity. When a derived quantity is defined for a particular set of physical systems by the use of an equation, the quantities upon which the derived quantity depends are called *primary magnitudes*. These primary magnitudes will ultimately be reducible to a set of quantities that are fundamentally measured. Note that we may distinguish between situations where measurement is given by means of a defining equation and (i) the quantity thus measured corresponds to a common property of the systems which is empirically discernible, and orderable independently of the equation, as is the case with density and (ii) the quantity thus measured does not correspond to a common property of the systems which is empirically discernible, and orderable independently of the equation, such as, for instance, electric displacement D defined as the product of absolute permittivity and electric field. The former is a *derived* quantity, the latter is a *defined* quantity. Campbell also called a derived quantity measured in this way a *secondary magnitude*. What is primary and what is secondary is not fixed, however, and, in general, is given by the particular application of the equation, since we can use the same equation to define any one of the terms occurring in it: there is no absolute way of determining the independent (primary) and dependent (secondary) variables in the equation.

Campbell eschewed the use of the term *unit*, because often the term is used in a confusing way, conflating the choice of a standard object, the numerical assignment of unity to this object, conversion factors between scales, and dimensions. He preferred to talk of *determining the factor* of a quantity by *choosing the standard* and *choosing the numeral*. Once the standard object is chosen and a numeral is assigned to it, the assignments of all other instances of the quantity are defined. For Campbell, the only arbitrary choice involved in measurement was determining the factor.[5]

According to Campbell, we may choose alternative sets of A quantities with which to express our scientific laws. In the case of any given equation which defines a quantity by derived means, the exponent of a particular A quantity as it occurs in the relevant equation, is defined to be the *dimension* of that quantity. Since we may choose between different sets of A quantities to form the base quantities of our equations, the dimensions of any derived quantity are to be understood relative to the defining equation in question, and are not fixed absolutely.

In our account, the result of a measurement is a *measure* which may be represented as a composite term, consisting of the product of a scalar number, a *value*, and a standard amount of a quantity, which has a vector identity, which we will call (in spite of Campbell) a *unit*. For instance, if we measure acceleration, we will obtain a measure x **a** where x is a value and **a** is the chosen unit. **a** has a specific vector identity in terms of the reference quantities chosen to serve as dimensions. Others have variously called the value, a measure, a magnitude or a numeric; units have also been considered to be notational entities relating scales or to be scalars.

Ellis replicated much of Campbell's account of ordering relations. The only significant modification relates to the strict exclusion of qualities in his definition. Satisfaction of these ordering relations is held to be necessary and sufficient for the existence of a quantity.[6] Like Campbell, his strong operational bias led him strictly to identify different quantities with different measurement procedures. The different quantities that result can only be taken to be equivalent on the basis of similarity in the ordering of the quantity and of a common clustering in usage that occurs for what are, strictly, dissimilar quantity names. With regard to equations, Ellis preferred to talk of *independent* and *dependent* quantities rather than using the primary/secondary terminology of Campbell.

Unlike Campbell, Ellis required measurement to be carried out on a scale. A scale is an assignment rule that always produces the same number for the same object, and does not allow different unequal objects to share the same number (degeneracy). Ellis regarded the use of a scale as a necessary condition for measurement (though we can perhaps imagine certain basic measurements as being possible without the assignment of numbers - consider the physical sorting of objects by an operation, for example grading eggs or ears of wheat). Most scales will be of one of four types: nominal (like football team numbers), ordinal (like Moh's scale of hardness), interval (like the Celsius scale of temperature), or ratio (like our mass and length scales).

Each of these families of scales is characterised by a permissible form of transformation for converting from one scale of this family to another. Interval scales are related to each other by linear transformations: to get from centigrade to Fahrenheit we perform a linear transformation. Ratio scales, on the other hand, preserve relative magnitudes under similarity transformations of the form $f'(x) = \alpha f(x)$ where α is real and positive.

Without providing a rigorous defence for the sufficiency of his requirements for measurement to occur, Ellis was able to provide broad explanatory support for his choices. In distinguishing different types of measurement, Ellis added *elemental* and *associative* categories: elemental measurement occurs when the ordering required for the very existence of a quantity generates a scale (Moh's scale is a good example); associative measurement occurs when a derived quantity is given by the measurement of a single fundamental quantity. A good example of an associative measurement is temperature.

In considering the numerical representation of fundamental quantities, Ellis established the possibility of alternative representations in which arithmetical relations other than addition are used to represent the operation of combining objects. His most famous example is right angle length combination which may be measured either in *dinches* or inches, but if we choose the latter, addition is not the appropriate mathematical representation. Ellis called the choice of representative arithmetic relation, the choice of the *principle of correlation*. Hence, relative to Campbell, Ellis believed measurement involves a greater number of choices: of a combination operation, and a principle of correlation as well as the assignment of a standard object. The customary reason guiding such choices is, Ellis argued, to make the resulting equations as simple as possible, and no a priori justification for our choices can be offered.

Units in Ellis' account, are the names given to scales, by which we are to understand choosing a standard object, fixing its numerical assignment, specifying the measurement procedure and choosing a correlation principle. Dimensions are the names given to families of classes of similar scales, each of which relates to the same quantity and which together constitute the nucleus of scales, defined without reference to other scales, which stands at the centre of our customary systems of measurement. A good example of a dimension, for Ellis, would be mass.

Suppes, like Ellis and Campbell, recognised the distinction between fundamental and derived measurement, providing tidy, axiomatic descriptions of both types, and he also incorporated scales into his account of measurement. He was careful, however, not to fall into the debate concerning the additive nature of the combination operation. Fundamental measurement is defined to occur if it is possible to provide a numerical representation of an empirical system of objects and relations defined on those objects, which is homomorphic to a numerical system comprising a subset of the real numbers and a defined set of numerical relations. This condition can be fulfilled without reference to the physical procedures involved in measuring. Consequently, Suppes attached no particular importance to the existence or non-existence of an additive operation.

Palacios provided a lucid account of the choices available to us in choosing different reference quantities as the *basis* of the dimensional representation of quantities (as will be fully discussed in Chapter 4). He unfortunately chose to talk of primary and secondary quantities where we would talk of fundamental and derived.

Krantz, Suppes et al. (1991) provided a summary of the different uses of terms amongst the principal authors, which we present here in a slightly modified form.

Table 2.1
Comparison of terms

Krantz/Suppes	**Campbell**	**Palacios**	**Ellis**
Measurement Theory			
Fundamental	Fundamental	Direct	Direct
Derived	Derived	Secondary	Derived
Extensive	Fundamental	Primary	Fundamental
Conjoint	-	-	Associative
Algebra of Quantities			
Primary/basic	Primary	Fundamental	Independent
Secondary	Secondary	Derived	Dependent

Parameters and derived measurement

In their accounts of measurement, both Campbell and Ellis explained how new quantities may arise in science from equations which involve quantities which have already been measured. Campbell, for instance, considered the following equation relating to fluids:

$$m = \rho V$$

where m is the mass of a sample of the fluid under standard conditions, V is the volume of this fluid sample and ρ is a property of the fluid under measurement which we call density. Here Campbell identified m and V as the primary variables related by this equation which applies to a particular system characterised by the quantity ρ, which is the secondary variable in the law. The equation, which states a mathematical relation between the functions m and V assigned to particular physical quantities, mirrors a physical relation of *uniform association* between the extensive properties mass and volume which we call *quantities* and which Campbell called *magnitudes*. This uniform association is usually described by saying that the extensive properties are properties of the same system.

According to the criteria established by Campbell for the definition of fundamentally measured quantities (a linear ordering, an additive mathematical representation of the combination of instances of the quantity, and the existence of a standard set of reference objects possessing the quantity), density fails to be such a fundamentally measured quantity (a *fundamental* or *A magnitude* in Campbell's terminology; *directly measured* in Ellis'), because the combination of two liquid samples does not satisfy the axioms of addition for the representation of density.

Using the above equation, however, individual liquids may be ordered by the term ρ, which Campbell and Ellis both called a *constant* but which I shall call a *system-dependent parameter*. The system dependence in the example arises from the variation of ρ with different systems i.e. liquids. The order of ρ so established coincides with that arising from an empirical investigation of density using the definition that A is denser than B if a body can be found which floats in A and sinks in B (Campbell 1928 p. 82). The existence of the ordering and supporting equation allowed Campbell to bestow the category of *B magnitude measured by the derived process* on the density parameter ρ. Ellis similarly, called the quantities so defined either *derived* or *associative* measurements.

A curious feature of both accounts, is that ρ is not in general constant in spite of being so called.[7] It has the same value only for a particular set of systems, for which an empirical law relating other, fundamental quantities and ρ holds. This is the nature of the system-dependency of ρ.

Parameters, scale factors and constants

The use of the term parameter is not pedantic: it reflects the genuine difference that exists between those constants that reflect a common physical feature in laws describing different sets of physical systems which obey those laws, and those constants that arise merely from a choice of measurement scales.[8] Such *scale factors*, as I shall call them, typically arise from the uniqueness characteristics of ratio-scales, which are used for most measured quantities, up to the level of a similarity transformation $S' = kS$ (as elegantly demonstrated by Suppes 1963).

Campbell considered parameters and scale factors to be the same thing, both of which he covered by the term 'constant'. As a consequence, he had difficulty explaining the role of a term like a in the empirical law describing thermal expansion:

$$y = a + bx + cx^2$$

For, according to Campbell, we can describe any equation entirely in terms of (1) *variables* (e.g. x, y), (2) *formal constants* (such as the squaring factor ^{2}) which specify the mathematical form of the law, and (3) *constants* which are symbols which denote indeterminate numerals. If we equate constants with scale factors, the terms b and c can be regarded as scale factors introduced by the choice of standard objects for x and y, whereas a cannot. Are we then to consider that a is a formal constant, as opposed to being simply a constant, since there are no further variables like x and y giving rise to a scale factor ? If yes, does this mean that formal constants are not invariable in certain circumstances, which would undermine their definition and the distinction Campbell drew between formal and other constants? As Campbell put it:

> Accordingly we have either to admit that there may be more constants in a law than are necessary to allow for change of factor, all these constants actually changing with the factor; or we have to admit that formal constants may fitly be represented by indeterminate numerals and may therefore represent magnitudes. In either case the simple relation between constants and secondary magnitudes from which we started would have to be abandoned. (Campbell 1928 p. 87)

We can avoid this difficulty by not forcing a dichotomy between formal constants and scale factors i.e. by realising that system-dependent parameters and scale factors are distinct. In this equation a is a system-dependent parameter and neither a scale-factor nor a formal constant. What gives rise to the identification of scale factors and system dependent parameters, is that system-dependent parameters are typically B (derived) quantities measured according to a scale. This means that whenever we introduce a system-dependent parameter into an equation, we can also introduce a system-independent scale factor corresponding to the choice of scale for the measurement of that parameter at the same time, just as we can do for the variables x and y (See page 27). The fact that parameters and scale-factors are so linked does not mean, however, that they are to be equated with each other.[9]

Ellis, unlike Campbell, did draw a clear distinction between scale-dependent and system-dependent constants i.e. between scale factors and system-dependent parameters:

> We are now in a position to say more precisely what is meant by derived measurement. Derived measurement is measurement by the evaluation of the single system- and/or scale-dependent constants which occur in numerical laws expressed in standard form. (Ellis 1966 p. 118)

Unfortunately, as we will see, Ellis tended to focus on the mathematical representation of quantities, as opposed to their physical referents and as a consequence, while recognizing the distinction between scale-factors and parameters, robbed the latter of their substantivality.

When are parameters quantities?

At the heart of all measurement is a linkage between an empirical system of objects and relations, and a representational system of numerals and numerical relations. Parameters have both a physical and representational aspect: how can we be sure these aspects are congruent? Is the definition of parameters as constants in equations sufficient grounding for them to be held to be quantities i.e. properties of objects which can be numerically ordered by a well-defined measurement procedure?

Campbell himself, identified a separate category of *defined* quantities, distinct from fundamental and derived quantities, which arise whenever we specify any arbitrary function of a set of variables which represent other quantities. How do we know in the case of a parameter defined by a particular equation, that the parameter is anything more than a mathematical construction of the defined kind? What is the referent of the parameter?

Campbell specified the general conditions giving rise to the derived measurement of constants, understood to be quantities:

> In a numerical law with n variables, n constants are needed in general to allow for changes of factor. We have to associate with each variable $x, y, z, \ldots$ a multiplicative factor a, b, c and write the law
>
> $$y = f(ax, bz, \ldots).$$
>
> In one special case, however, only a single constant is needed to allow for the changes in the factor of any number of variables; this is when the law can be written in the form

$$y = a.x^m.z^n ....$$

> In the general case, all constants will be secondary magnitudes, if and only if the classes of systems subject to the law form an n-dimensional series, composed of n one-dimensional series, each characterised by a variation of one of the constants. In the special case the single constant will be a secondary magnitude, if the classes form a one-dimensional series characterised by the variation of that constant. (Campbell 1928 p. 84)

In support of these requirements, Campbell offered numerous examples, but he gave no formal consideration to the necessary satisfaction of the linear ordering relations which is required if the constants in these equations are to be quantities themselves. He did not allow us to be sure that system-dependent parameters are in fact properties of systems and not simply mathematical definitions.

Furthermore, Campbell believed that certain constants as they appear in laws do not correspond to quantities: when the constants are system independent, but uninteresting, or in the case of constants in empirical laws. In recognition of the inadequacy of his account, Campbell confessed:

> That constants are so often important secondary magnitudes, quite as important as the primary magnitudes from which they are derived, is a fact which we have to accept without explanation, as part of the perpetual miracle of laws in general and of numerical laws in particular. (Campbell 1928 p. 85)

Ellis, on the other hand, asserted a direct link between constants derived from equations and quantities, at the price of a reduced physical significance for constants in general. Because procedures can be devised, using the equation which defines a constant, to assign a linear ordering of values to the constant, the constant will satisfy the conditions Ellis deemed to be sufficient to be a quantity. The result follows from his starting assumption that any derived law can be expressed in *standard form* (this is the special form referred to by Campbell $y = a.x^m.z^n....$): [10]

> Let us suppose that
>
> $$C\, s^a t^b u^c ... = k$$
>
> is a numerical law expressed in standard form with respect to the classes of scales *[S], [T], [U]*, ... and pertaining to the systems of a class *[A]*. Let any system A_i belonging to *[A]*, and any set of scales S_1, T_1, U_1, ... belonging to *[S], [T], [U]*, ... be chosen. Then if the appropriate measurements are made, the value of *k* for the system A_i may be determined. Now it is clear that this procedure may be repeated for the various systems of the class *[A]*, and the appropriate values of *k* determined. We have, therefore, a determinate rule for making numerical assignments to the systems of *[A]*; hence we may say that we have a scale for measuring these systems. Moreover, the *k*-order must be a linear one. Hence we must have a scale for the measurement of some quantity possessed by the various systems of the class *[A]*. (Ellis 1966 p. 119)

Thus, for Ellis, there was no distinction to be made between parameters and derived quantities nor between derived and defined quantities. His position is, however, open to objection both on technical grounds and because it leads to problematic results. Turning to the technical aspects first.

Ellis offered but one example of how to reduce a given equation involving several constants to one involving related quantities defined on new scales linked by a single constant which can be linearly ordered. It is not clear that this can always be done, in particular, for differential equations higher than first order (consider simple harmonic motion, where the general solution requires two constants to be specified), and Ellis offers no general proof of his result. We may charitably suppose that multi-dimensional scales provide a solution, but this is far from obvious.

Second, if we do have a law, characterised by a single constant, which relates to a series of measurements of quantities defined on sets of similar scales, the resulting equation will be expressible in standard form provided the function describing the law is differentiable. The linear ordering of the constant and its recognition as a derived quantity according to Ellis' criteria then follows. It is open to us to challenge the assumption of differentiability.

Differentiability requires limits to be well defined, which in turn requires continuity and the use of real numbers. This assumption is commonly made for the purposes of derived measurement, but is in fact not warranted on the basis of measurement alone, which requires only a dense ordering of rational numbers.[11]

Considerations of continuity blinded Ellis to the fact that we may employ discrete, rational functions and values for both variables and constants. This permits constants obtained by derived measurement to be single-valued for a particular set of scale choices and for particular systems, opening the door to important physical constants that have universal applicability. We may also entertain all manner of discontinuous functions that give rise to values of constants that are not linearly ordered: an example would be a cyclic or angular law where the value of a derived physical parameter may repeat regularly, having the same value for different sets of systems. Without questioning Ellis' assumptions, it is all the easier to concur with the reduced role he advocates for the overly broad category of constants that he supported.

Turning to the broader philosophical issues raised by Ellis, let us consider what happens if his procedures for the derived measurement of a constant are met. Consider the case of constants that arise from nominal scales: for instance imagine partitioning the earth into sectors on the basis of latitude; to each sector we might assign a number; we might then determine g as a function of the sectoral number. Given the corrections that are normally used to account for the fact that the earth is not an inertial frame, we might expect to find some useful correlations between the measured value of g and the sectoral numbers assigned. These correlations might be formulated as an equation which relates g and the sectoral numbers and which gives rise to a constant. Nonetheless, in most cases we will probably be reluctant to consider the sectoral number or the derived constant to be a "genuine" quantity. Other situations may be devised where the connection between equations and system-dependent constants do not naturally give rise to the recognition of a quantity.[12]

It may be argued that quantities defined by derived means are well-gounded even if we cannot offer any independent empirical support, such as the existence of an ordered series or quasi-series, for them. One might assert that derived quantities which lack a physical anchor, are properties of the quantities which feature in the equation, but are not the properties of the objects themselves which are used in derived measurement.Thus, for example, we could consider density to be a property of mass and of volume which are themselves properties. As properties of properties, these quantities would have a different status.

Alternatively, if we accept that an equation provides the means for establishing a linear ordering, and that this counts as a measurement procedure, then those quantities defined by equations are indeed derived quantities. All constants are thereby derived quantities; there is no distinction between derived and defined quantities. We may address our concerns about the genuine physical grounding of certain constants which we believe are physically significant by delineating a subset of derived quantities, called *parameters* for which an adequate physical referent can be provided. This reference arises from the physical relationships between the properties of a physical system mathematically represented by the equation.

The structure of the empirical system may be captured formally as a set of well defined physical relations and operations between objects. In Chapter 4 we will outline how this might be done to provide an empirical account of certain primitive constants. In general, we require a correspondence, formally modelled as a homomorphism, to exist between the empirical system and the numerical system which represents it. System-dependent parameters are embedded in the structure of the empirical systems of objects, relations and operations. Corresponding to each parameter, there is a mathematical function defined by the corresponding physical equation in the numerical system. As an example, density could be considered to be formally identified with equivalence classes of objects formed under an appropriate set of weighing and floating operations. A representation theorem establishing a homomorphism between this empirical system and the numerical system based upon the customary equation $\rho = m / V$ could be established. (See the end of Chapter 2 and Chapter 4). The assertion, which is not proven in the general case, is that for each system-dependent parameter, it is possible to provide a formal representation theorem which establishes a homomorphism between the empirical system which gives rise to the equation in which the derived quantity occurs, and a numerical system comprising a subset of the reals and a defined set of numerical relations.

We must also recognise that occasionally we are able to identify quantities which vary between systems for which we do not have a satisfactory equation and which are not fundamentally measurable (the early theories of heat and temperature, such as those of Dalton, would be an historical example). In these situations, a structured empirical system may exist (for example, an ordered series of heated objects), without an adequate mathematical representation. We can accommodate this situation by recognizing the existence of one or more system-dependent parameters, even in the absence of derived measurement procedures involving an equation.

To make these distinctions concerning derived measurement and parameters clear, we may represent them graphically:

Figure 2.1
System-dependent parameters and derived measurements

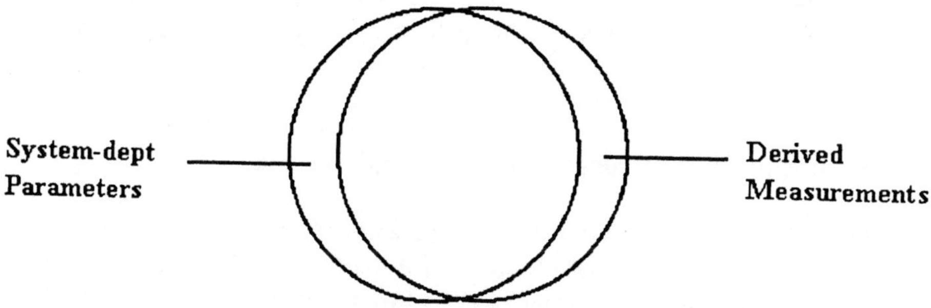

As a further step we may identify a subset of system-dependent parameters where the dependency is zero: system-independent parameters:

Figure 2.2
System-independent parameters

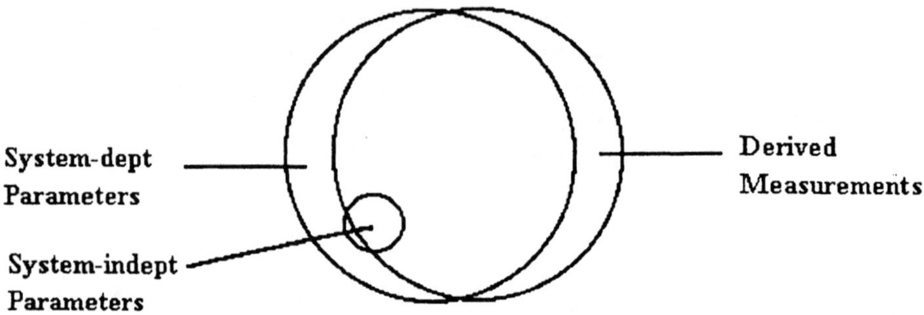

Let us look more closely at this situation where the parameter characteristic of a particular law does not vary as we change from one *class* (Campbell) of objects, or *system* (Ellis) to another. Is this a matter of significance?

System-independent parameters and universal constants

Campbell believed that on some occasions, a parameter that does not vary with the choice of system has great significance (for instance Planck's constant as cited above), but he had difficulty specifying when we should pay attention to such a parameter. In particular, he did not explain convincingly how to distinguish these situations from more spurious instances of system-independent constants such as scale factors which arise from the adoption of a particular standard for measurement. Consider the equation for Ohm's Law

$$E = I R$$

where we consider E, the potential difference across an Ohmic conductor, and I, the current flowing through the Ohmic conductor, to be variables, and R to be a parameter, which depends upon the Ohmic conductor in question i.e. R is system-dependent. The values of R which occur in the equation, will in turn depend upon the choice of unit, R' say, against which the value of R is determined. This means that R is unique only up to the choice of scale factor, and that in general we may write

$$E = k\,I\,R'$$

or, upon substitution of the letter R for R',

$$E = k\,I\,R$$

where k is a scale factor which is not system dependent. In Campbell's and Ellis' parlance k is a *universal scale-dependent constant*. What grounds are there for the assertion that k is not significant, and why does such reasoning not apply to constants such as G ?

Such scale factors can always be introduced for both fundamental and derived quantities. For instance, if we have discovered a law for accelerating bodies relating the fundamental quantities of force and mass, such that the force impressed upon a system is proportional to its mass, we may represent this by

$$(f) \propto (m)$$

where the brackets indicate that we are talking about measures of force and mass. If the measure *(m)* is equal to m units of mass, and we assign a value k_2 to a unit of mass, and similarly k_1 to a unit of force then the corresponding equation, which relates the values associated with each measure is given by

$$k_1 f = k_2 m$$

where k_1 and k_2 are scale factors associated with each of the fundamental quantities. Alternatively, we may write

$$f = k_3 m$$

In the case of derived quantities, let us consider a quantity y defined by an equation in standard form involving x_1, ...x_n other quantities, then

$$y = x_1^{\alpha} \ldots . x_n^{\nu}$$

If we now introduce a universal constant k , we may define

$$y' = k\,x_1^{\alpha} \ldots . x_n^{\nu}$$

Hence $$y' \,/\, y = k$$

But since y and y' refer to the same measure

$$y \mathbf{u} = y' \mathbf{u'}$$

where **u** and **u'** are the units of the scales for measuring y and y'. Hence

$$k = y' / y = \mathbf{u} / \mathbf{u'}$$

So the occurrence of the spurious constant[13] k is equivalent to a change of unit.

As a practical example of the occurrence of scale factors, we may consider the technical system of units, often preferred by engineers, where the unit of force is defined as the weight of a unit mass. In the metric version, because 1 kg-force = 9.81 N, we must replace the usual equation for Newton's second law

$$f = m\, a$$

by

$$f = 1 / 9.81 \,.\, m\, a$$

In the imperial technical system, a different scale factor is required: one pound-force equals 32 poundals, and we must write[14]

$$f = 1 / 32 \,.\, m\, a$$

The choice of these particular scales has made the results of measurement inconsistent with the traditional formulation of Newton's second law, and the choice of units is than said to be *incoherent* (the derived unit of force is not equal to the product of unit mass and unit acceleration, which are *reference*[15] units in the SI system). Fortunately, Palacios showed that these parasitic coefficients can be eliminated if we develop a coherent set of units, where the units of reference quantities are assigned the value unity, and the equations for derived quantities are taken to hold *exactly* for the measures of the primary variables that occur in them (i.e. they would not permit the introduction of k above). More simply expressed, we can eliminate spurious scale factors by setting them all equal to one.[16]

For Campbell, the situation was much less simple, because he had, as we have described, failed to separate scale factors and parameters. In order to discriminate between spurious universal constants and instances of system-independent parameters, Campbell invoked other means of measurement and the expectations of scientists:

> If the systems subject to the law, though they form a single class in respect of its constants, form many clearly distinguishable classes in some other respect, and especially if these distinguishable classes form an ordered series such as might be expected to generate a magnitude, then the law and the constant in it are likely to be extremely important.... An obvious example of such a universal constant is Planck's h. (Campbell 1928 p. 85)

Ellis, on the other hand, was not afraid to grasp the bull by the horns and, on the grounds of consistency, robbed universal constants, both scale factors and system-independent parameters entirely of their significance:

> We may conclude, then, that simply by adopting different conventions concerning the expression of equations, universal scale-dependent constants may be created or eliminated at will. We cannot, therefore, attach to these constants anything other than a conventional existence; and it is quite absurd to suppose that these constants represent the magnitudes of peculiar invariant properties of space or of matter. (Ellis 1966 p125)[17]

In reaching his conclusion, Ellis drew upon the vanishing qualities of universal constants, as well as their capricious appearances. Given the power of his conclusions, his argument deserves closer scrutiny.

Ellis on universal constants

In order to make a universal scale-dependent constant appear in a given numerical law, Ellis repeated the procedure illustrated above:

Given

$$f(s,t,u, \ldots) = k$$

Ellis wrote:

> Let d be the name of the quantity of which k is a measure, and let *[K]* be the class of similar derivative scales defined on the basis of this law. Then instead of expressing the law with respect only to *[S]*, *[T]*, *[U]*, ..., let us express it with respect to *[S]*, *[T]*, *[U]*, ...and *[K]*. Then, clearly, we must write
>
> $$f(s,t,u, \ldots) = ck,$$
>
> where c is a purely scale-dependent constant. Hence, if the law has the required universality, it follows at once that c is a universal constant. (Ellis 1966 p. 122)

While the introduction of c is unproblematic mathematically, Ellis' account failed to distinguish between scale factors like c, which are universal and scale-dependent, and parameters like R or k which may turn out to be universal and system-independent.[18] This distinction is hidden but implicit in Ellis' description of the situation: he asserted that k is a measure of , i.e. represents formally, a quantity d. This is not true of c, which does not represent any physical quantity, but is, rather, a feature of the numerical representation that we have conventionally chosen for the quantity d. R, on the other hand, does represent a quantity, a system parameter, and we can imagine that R might be the same for all systems.[19]

Turning to the elimination of a universal scale-dependent constant, Ellis considered the example of Newton's law of gravitation:

$$f = G\, m_1 m_2 \,/\, r^2,$$

where G is a universal scale-dependent constant. To eliminate G, we need only express the law with respect to, say, *[M]* and *[L]*. Then we should have that

$$f' = m_1 m_2 \,/\, r^2,$$

where f' is a scale- and system-dependent constant which may be taken to measure the force acting between the gravitating bodies on a derivative scale dependent only on the choice of mass and length scales. G is thus successfully eliminated from this particular law (Ellis 1966 p. 124)

This elimination is not, of itself, problematic because, as Ellis himself recognized, the elimination of G will, if we are not careful, give rise to a new universal constant in other laws. In this way, it might be held that the total number of universal constants in physics cannot be reduced. Ellis believed this is wrong:

But the case is stronger than that. Many universal scale-dependent constants can in fact be eliminated *without remainder* simply by the adoption of new conventions. (Ellis 1966 p. 124)

To support this claim, Ellis returned to the example of Newton's law of gravity, and to demonstrate the error he committed, I quote the whole of his argument:

Let us consider the case in more detail. For convenience, let us adopt the c.g.s. (centimetre, gram, second) system of measurement. Then, according to the law (31) $[f' = m_1 m_2 / r^2]$, f' must be measured in g.^{2}cm.$^{-2}$ (by the usual conventions). Hence, when we come to express the second law of motion with respect to these particular scales, we must write

$$f' = k\, m\, a, \qquad (32)$$

where k is a universal scale-dependent constant determined in the units g. cm.$^{-3}$sec.^{2}.

However, if instead of using the law (30) $[f = G\, m_1 m_2 / r^2]$ to define a derivative scale of force, we had used it to define a derivative scale of mass, then no universal constant would have appeared in the second law. In place of (31) $[f' = m_1 m_2 / r^2]$, we should have

$$f'' = m'_1\, m'_2 / r^2. \qquad (33)$$

And in place of $[f' = kma]$, we should have

$$f'' = m'\, a, \qquad (34)$$

m'_1 and m'_2 being system- and scale-dependent constants defined via $[f'' = m'_1\, m'_2 / r^2]$ and f'' being a system- and scale-dependent constant defined via $[f'' = m'\, a]$. In the c.s.

(centimetre, second) system, m' would be determined in the units cm.^{3}sec.$^{-2}$ and f'' in the units cm.^{4}sec.$^{-4}$. The reader can easily verify that this leads to no 'dimensional' anomalies. (Ellis 1966 p. 124)

Problems with this account are immediately evident if we consider the form of Newton's second law as given by Ellis in (34). As he explains above, both m' and f'' are constants for a given system. This means that the value of a must also be a constant, as opposed to a variable for a given system. Stripped of its generality, it is hard to see why we would bestow the title of law upon (34). What has gone wrong?

Through a notational slight of hand this argument runs together two separate analyses. First, consider the solution of the following pair of equations:

$$p = u\,a$$

and

$$p = u_1 u_2 / r^2$$

where the subscripts denote particular instances of the quantity u, and r and a have their customary meanings. The solution to these equations is identical to that proffered by Ellis: p and u will have the same dimensions as f'' and m'. As a mathematical derivation, this result is acceptable, but whether these equations have physical significance is a separate matter. There are no commonly known physical quantities defined by these equations. Ellis, as an avowed operationalist, should have been aware of the need to establish the linkage between p and u, and f'' and m', i.e. force and mass.

Turning to the second line of approach adopted by Ellis: if we distinguish different uses of the same physical law [$f = G\, m_1 m_2 / r^2$] to define, first, a derived scale for force (f') and then a derived scale for mass (f''), by the use of $'$ to indicate derived quantities, we shall have:

First

$$f' = m_1 m_2 / r^2 \qquad \text{where } f' = f / G,$$

then

$$f'' = m'_1\, m'_2 / r^2 \qquad \text{where } m'_1 = m_1 \quad m'_2 = m_2 .$$

The same substitutions, however, must be made consistently, and so we also find:

$$f' = k'\, m\, a, \qquad \text{and}$$

$$f'' = k'\, m'\, a \qquad \text{where } k' = 1 / G.$$

The latter result clearly contradicts, Ellis' result (34). Without these consistent substitutions, however, there is no formal link between f , f', and f'' ; the notation is deceptive. There is no more a logical link between f' and f'' in Ellis' account than between f and p in mine. How do we know that m' is mass? We do not and we make an error if we assume that equation (33) is a derivative scale for mass, as Ellis asserted, rather than for some other quantity, which I have defined as u. This mixing of analyses would have been more transparent if Ellis had used f' rather than f'' in equation (33).

We obtain the same conclusion if we put

$$m'_1 = \sqrt{G}\, m_1$$

This yields

$$f = m'_1\, m'_2 / r^2$$

which we may denote as f''. It remains the case that $f = ma$, so substituting the correct identities:

$$\begin{aligned} f'' &= m\,a \\ &= k\,m'\,a. \\ &= m'\,a' \qquad \text{if} \qquad a' = a/\sqrt{G} \end{aligned}$$

In this case, why should we consider a' and a, and m' and m to be the same quantities?[20]

Our findings are also supported by the findings of dimensional analysis. It is always possible to restate a given law of standard form in such a way that the constant occurring in this law is dimensionless and can numerically be set to unity, thereby disappearing. To do so, however, requires specific dimensions to be assigned to the other quantities occurring in the law. If this constant-stripping assignment is the one which is conventionally made, as is the case with Newton's second law of motion, which involves no constant, then other "non-Newton-II" laws, involving these other quantities will in general give rise to dimensioned constants. If we adjust, however, the dimensions of these quantities in a "non-Newton-II" law, to which we have previously by convention assigned a dimensioned constant, so that the constant in this law is dimensionless, then the algebraic relations required for the dimensional assignment to give rise to a dimensionless constant in the second Newtonian law of motion will no longer be met. The constant in this second Newtonian law will no longer be dimensionless and it will appear explicitly in the statement of the law. Of course, this dimensioned constant can always be assigned a numerical value of unity by adjustment of the scale factor associated with it, but this amounts to disguise, not elimination.

As we shall see in Chapter 4, the only circumstances where we can eliminate a constant are where we are prepared to eliminate one of the dimensions which we use to represent physical quantities. While this may be held to be an economy, it leads to spurious mathematical results, and has no ontological bite, since such manoeuvres are more accurately described as suppression rather than elimination. Ellis did not suggest he was prepared to accept such a conclusion, and even had he done so, as an operationalist he would still have been left with the problem of continuity of reference for mass measured fundamentally and measured by his choice of equation for the derivative measurement of mass (the $m = u$ problem above).

Ellis' conclusions are unfounded: there exist system-independent universal constants that have a physical significance, which we shall term system-independent parameters. In reaching his conclusions, Ellis was misled by the aspects of convention that relate to the mathematical representation of physical quantities into believing that the same aspects of convention pertain to the physical quantities themselves.

Formalist foundations

In order to provide a more rigorous underpinning for the notions we have advanced, we may turn to the axiomatic account Suppes' provided for fundamental and derived measurement.

Fundamental system-independent parameters

Turning first to fundamental measurement, let us define an empirical relational system $\Psi = \langle A, \leq_m, \leq_q, \leq_l, \oplus_m, \oplus_q, \oplus_l, \ldots \rangle$, where A is the set of elementary[21] particles, and $\leq_m$ and similar relations are those linear ordering relations corresponding to the measurement of fundamental ('A') quantities such as mass, charge, length[22] (for instance $\leq_m$ here denotes the relation 'is equal or less in mass than') and $\oplus_m$ and similar relations are the binary operations of combination appropriate to each of the fundamental measuring procedures involved for mass, charge, length etc. The reason for choosing elementary particles as the empirical objects of our system, is that elementary particles are identical and immutable. Many of their physical properties are system independent.

Suppes' established that a numerical representation will exist that is homomorphic to Ψ defined on $\mathfrak{R}$ a subsystem of the numerical extensive system comprising real numbers under the arithmetic relations $\leq$ and $+$, provided the quantities m, q , l etc. obey the customary axioms for extensive properties:

1 If $a \leq_m b$ and $b \leq_m c$, then $a \leq_m c$
2 $(a \oplus_m b) \oplus_m c \leq_m a \oplus_m (b \oplus_m c)$
3 If $a \leq_m b$, then $a \oplus_m c \leq_m c \oplus_m b$
4 If not $a \leq_m b$, then there is a c in A : $a \leq_m b \oplus_m c$ and $b \oplus_m c \leq_m a$

5 Not $a \oplus_m b \leq_m a$
6 If $a \leq_m b$, then there is a number n such that $b \leq_m na$ where the notation na is defined recursively as follows: $1a = a$ and $na = (n-1)\, a \oplus_m a$. (Archimedean axiom)

Campbell defined extensive measurement as the measurement of fundamental quantities which support the existence of an additive operation, and hence fundamental quantities satisfy these axioms by definition. Suppes, himself, declared that he attached little significance to the existence of an additive operation, and avoided being drawn into a discussion of the differences between extensive and intensive properties (Suppes 1963 p. 16). He did, however, rely on the existence of an additive operation in his outline of a representation proof. We shall return to the links between fundamental quantities and the existence of additive operations in Chapter 3. For the moment, it suffices to assume that these axioms are satisfied with regard to the fundamental quantities we wish to measure.

The type of numerical representation which Suppes established is one of many possible representation types that might be established for this empirical system, as he himself acknowledged. Alternative types of representation give rise to alternative arithmetics, as is exemplified by Ellis' discussion of "dinches" as an alternative measure of length. If we restrict ourselves for the moment, however, to a standard arithmetic model, then the permissible transformations linking alternative numerical representations of the same type are similarity transformations. If we denote the homomorphic mapping function (*numerical assignment* in Suppes' terminology) between the extensive empirical and numerical relational sytems by f_m etc., then we may define fundamental scales for the quantities m, q, l by the ordered triples $\langle \Psi, \Re, f_m \rangle$, $\langle \Psi, \Re, f_q \rangle$, $\langle \Psi, \Re, f_l \rangle$ etc. Let $\langle \Psi, \Re, f_m \rangle$ be a scale, and g_m be any function having the property that $\langle \Psi, \Re, g_m \rangle$ is also a scale. Then f_m and g_m are related by a similarity transformation:

$$f_m(a) = k\ g_m(a)$$

where k is a positive real number. This means that the standard representations of an extensive system define a set of ratio scales that are unique up to a similarity transformation by a positive real number k, hence k corresponds to what we have been calling a scale factor. Note that k, strictly, is a characteristic of a similarity function $f(x)$ from the set of real numbers to the set of real numbers such that $f(x) = kx$, and is a feature of the mathematical representation that has been established. It is not to be confused, as it was in Campbell's account, with a separate conventional choice of a standard object, called e in Suppes' proof, which is required to be made in order to determine the numerical assignment f that gives rise to the homomorphism. Suppes assigned the value 1 to the equivalence class of objects defined by *e* for the quantity in question i.e. $f([e]) = 1$. Alternative values could equally well have been assigned. In our scheme, *e* is to be identified as a system parameter, to which we assign a value. As distinct from *k*, *e* is a feature of the empirical system.

We may now propose that we select those system-independent parameters shared by all particles which are capable of being measured fundamentally (i.e. which, for the moment, we assume can be additively combined in an extensive measurement system) as the standard objects of our extensive empirical system of elementary particles under fundamental measuring operations. As an example, we could take the rest mass of the proton as the standard object of an extensive system of fundamental mass measurement defined on elementary particles. To this standard object we could assign a number representing its mass. This procedure would allow us to assign a single value to a system independent parameter, the mass of a proton, which has physical significance. As a result we might characterise the value of those universal constants which are quantities subject to fundamental measurement as *the single value that is assigned in the mathematical representation of the associated fundamental extensive measuring system to the relevant system-independent physical parameter.*[23]

Perspectives of Campbell and physicists

Support for this line of thinking can be found in Campbell, who himself suggested that system-independent parameters may usefully serve as standards:

> The most definite standards of the widest accessibility would be the classes of classes of systems characterised by universal constants; if a substance is chosen as a standard, questions such as whether it is pure or at the prescribed temperature may still arise; but if a constant is truly universal, the only question is whether a law of a given form is obeyed. Unfortunately no method of derived measurement based on a law involving only such universal constants as are usually recognised is comparable in sensitivity with the best fundamental measurements; the choice of such classes of classes as standards would fail to fulfil the first condition which must determine such choice, namely the establishment of the greatest possible agreement between different workers. (Campbell 1928 p. 109)

Campbell's concerns about sensitivity need not prevent us in the adoption of universal constants (system-independent parameters) as standard objects of fundamental measurement. In those situations where we assign a value of unity to the system-independent parameter, we may say that the associated universal constant can be used as the name of a scale (for instance the scale of atomic mass).

This type of approach is clearly behind much of the thinking of physicists, when they talk of universal constants in terms of fundamental physical units. Petley (1985) remarked for instance:

> Measurements of dimensional physical quantities that are made in science and technology are normally expressed in SI units. This system of units is essentially a practical one in which each unit has a convenient magnitude for the proverbial man or woman in the street to use, but overall they do not have a natural basis. Consider how one would communicate an estimate of one's size and mass to someone on a remote planet in a distant galaxy. It is clear that metres and kilograms would not be very useful for this purpose. There are, however, physical quantities which come rather closer to being the natural units of science, and these are termed the fundamental physical constants. They include the velocity of electromagnetic radiation, the electronic mass and charge and a number of other constants. (Petley 1985 p. 1)

These accounts are confused to some extent in their mixing together of scale factors, system parameters, constants and dimensions under the general heading of choosing a unit. Following the approach we have outlined, however, it is possible to make reasonable sense of these remarks.

In summary, we can take them to assert that the physical objects that give rise to universal constants that are fundamentally measurable can, at least hypothetically, be selected as standard objects in an extensive measurement system, and values can be assigned to these objects via an initial assignment, or via the application of a scale-factor if we wish to change the mathematical representation of the fundamental quantity by choosing a different scale. In this sense, the assignment of values to universal constants can be loosely understood in some sense 'to define fundamental physical units'.

Ellis pointed out, fairly, that the choice of a unit for a scale, which he regarded as the same as naming the scale, in fact requires other additional choices to be settled: namely those involving the choice of measurement procedure, since different procedures may be available for the same physical quantity, and the choice of type of mathematical representation (what Ellis calls the *principle of correlation*). In Chapter 3 we shall return to discuss further these questions in relation to a taxonomy of fundamental constants.

We may also note, importantly, that both Campbell and Ellis discussed constants uniquely in the context of derived measurement. Neither contemplated the existence of system-independent parameters that can be fundamentally measured.[24] This oversight largely explains their failure to attribute greater substantivality to the basic constants researched by physicists.

If we extend our account to embrace fundamental measurement, we may depict the situation graphically as follows:[25]

Figure 2.3
Parameters and measured quantities

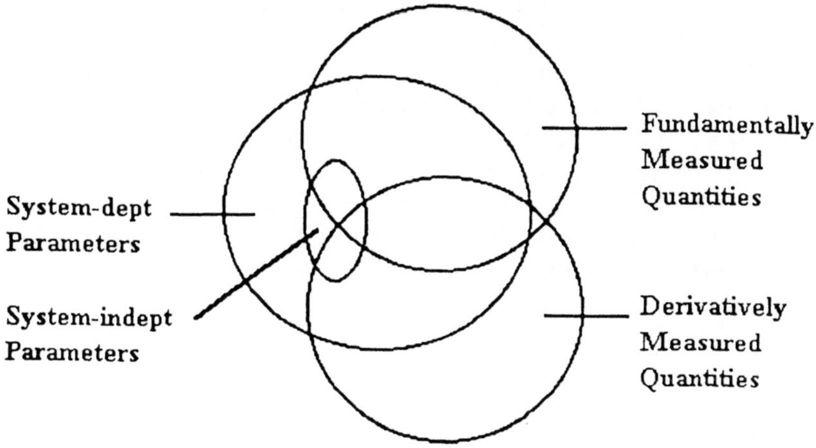

Derived system-independent parameters

Not all constants (system independent parameters) can be measured by fundamental means. Those that cannot be so measured are defined by an equation that gives rise to derived measurement. Planck's constant is a good example of such a constant. In the case of these constants, we can adopt the formalism provided by Suppes for derived measurement.[26] A derived measurement system $\Xi = \langle B, f_1, f_2 \ldots f_n \rangle$ comprises a non-empty set of objects B and $f_1, f_2 \ldots f_n$ numerical-valued functions defined on B or on Cartesian products of B with itself. Thus in the case of density, Ξ would be the triple $\langle B, m, V \rangle$, where m is the numerical assignment for mass and V is the numerical assignment for volume. Let g be a numerical-valued function on B or on Cartesian products of B with itself, and let $\mathcal{L}$ be an equation relating $f_1, f_2 \ldots f_n$ and g, then we may define a derived scale $\langle \Xi, \mathcal{L}, g \rangle$ where g is the derived numerical assignment for objects in B.

In the case of density, $\Xi = \langle B, m, V \rangle$ and the equation is $\mathcal{L}(m, V, \rho)$ defined for every b in B:

$$\rho(b) = m(b) / V(b).$$

The triple $\langle \Xi, \mathcal{L}, \rho \rangle$ is then the derived scale for density.

While Suppes' formalism, and the approaches taken by Campbell and Ellis do not require each of $f_1, f_2 \ldots f_n$ to be the numerical assignment of a quantity measurable by a fundamental procedure, we shall assume, without loss to our argument, that this is the case. For, wherever we have an equation $\mathcal{L}$ which employs derived quantities as primary variables (i.e. $f_1, f_2 \ldots f_n$ do not necessarily relate to fundamental quantities) we will transform this equation by replacing each of $f_1, f_2 \ldots f_n$ by $h_1, h_2 \ldots h_m$ until we obtain an equation $\mathcal{L}'$ which contains only fundamental quantities as primary variables. The underlying physical relation between the objects of B and between the extensive properties which may be fundamentally measured, will be the same for $\mathcal{L}'$ and $\mathcal{L}$.

Turning to system-independent parameters that are measured by derived methods, we may define these universal constants by means of a derived scale comprising elementary particles (including photons), the equation in which the parameter occurs, and the numerical assignment to the parameter, which will be single-valued i.e.

$$g(b) = k \text{ for all } b$$

As with fundamentally measured system-independent parameters, the assignment of a value to a system-independent derived parameter will change if we switch to another scale on which to measure the parameter, consistent with the customary introduction of a scale-factor as a feature of the chosen mathematical representation.

If $f_1, f_2 \ldots f_n$ give rise to ratio scales, i.e. satisfy the customary axioms of an extensive empirical system and support the standard arithmetic representation, then g will also give rise to a ratio scale. Not only will alternative derived numerical assignments g' be related to g by a similarity transformation, but the derived numerical assignment g'' arising when $f_1, f_2 \ldots f_n$ are transformed to similar scales $f_1', f_2' \ldots f_n'$ will also be related to g by a similarity transformation. Thus, in Suppes' terminology the derived scale will be a ratio scale in both narrow (i.e. change of scale factor associated with k) and broad senses (i.e. change of scale factors associated with $f_1, f_2 \ldots f_n$).

According to these definitions of derived measurement, we may characterise the value of those universal constants which are quantities subject to derived measurement as *the single value that is assigned in the mathematical representation of the associated derived measuring system to the relevant system-independent physical parameter*.

If we assign the value of unity to $g(b)$, we will, as in the case of universal constants fundamentally measured, be able to name the scale upon which the derived quantity is measured in terms of the associated universal constant. We may also loosely say that universal constants that are quantities measured by derived means may 'define the derived physical units' of a scale for the measurement of that quantity.

When units are so assigned, one important assumption needs to be highlighted: that the same systems of similar scales are used for the measurement of fundamental quantities which occur in the equations $\mathcal{L}, \mathcal{L}'$ etc. which define derived system-independent parameters. This requires us to use the same set of fundamental A quantities as the primary variables in $\mathcal{L}, \mathcal{L}'$ etc., the same numerical assignment and choice of standard objects, and the same types of numerical representation (principles of correlation). If we assume as a matter of convention, that the same standard types of numerical representation will be used, the restrictions on standard objects and assignments may be relaxed since similarity transformations and scale factors will give rise to interchangeable numerical assignments $f_1, f_2 \ldots f_n$ and $f_1', f_2' \ldots f_n'$ which correspond to the choice of different standard objects and scales. It will still be the case, however, that the choice of fundamental A quantities will be the same for all derived system-independent parameters.

The assumption of shared A quantities is equivalent to assuming the same dimensional basis in terms of selected A quantities for the derived system-independent parameters. A change of the dimensional basis, what Ellis calls a change of the central independent scales in our scale system, would alter the dimensional assignments of derived system-independent parameters, and inconsistent bases would cause conflicts. For example, constants (system-independent parameters) that are ratios of other constants, might be expressed inconsistently in terms of dimensions, they might for instance cease to be dimensionless, because the defining equations for the constituent constants might be different. We may express this conventional assumption by stating that we express all our defining equations relative to an equivalence class of similar scale systems. This equivalence class is defined by an equivalence relation *shares the same scale centrality*. We shall return to this aspect of conventionality in detail in Chapter 4.

Differences between fundamental and derived parameters

One key difference between universal constants measurable by fundamental and derived means is that in the case of the latter it is not strictly necessary to choose a standard object which instantiates that constant.[27] The system-independent parameter captured by the derived measurement may be taken to be a property of the quantities to which numerical values are assigned by the numerical assignments $f_1, f_2 \ldots f_n$, rather than to be the property of an object. The numerical assignment given to this parameter may be strictly considered only to characterise the physical relationship of uniform association which exists between the extensive properties which give rise to $f_1, f_2 \ldots f_n$.[28] In cases where the system parameter defined by the equation is not system-independent, the parameter may be taken to characterise the association of the extensive properties captured by the equation which are shared by classes of objects for which the equation holds.

As an aside, we may note that for practical reasons we may choose to define a standard object for a derived scale, but in so far as this actually involves the denotation or specification of an object, this object is implicitly being chosen as the standard for the scales of the quantities which are capable of being measured fundamentally, and which give rise to the numerical assignments $f_1, f_2 \dots f_n$ involved in the definition of $\mathcal{L}$. Campbell gave an account of when such choices are to be made, but he also recognised situations involving the assignment of numerals in the case of a derived scale where the recipient of the assignment is either a scale-factor, or a universal system-independent constant, i.e. a system-independent parameter (Campbell 1928 Note 2 p. 131). In the latter case, it is immediately evident that no standard object, as opposed to value, is assigned to the system-independent constant. Ellis similarly recognised that the units, taken to be defined by the selection of a standard object, measuring procedure and principle of correlation, of derived scales always, and of fundamental scales occasionally, may be dependent upon the choice of units for other independent fundamental scales. We shall return to discuss this further in Chapter 3.

In order to provide a more adequate account of the referents of parameters, in particular derived universal constants, we may equate derived quantities with the features or structure of an empirical system of objects, relations and operations for which a representation theorem is not directly provided by Suppes' formalism for derived scales as suggested on page 20. Instead of explicating derived measurement in terms of the numerical assignment functions given to fundamental quantities, we can posit a more direct homomorphism between (i) the empirical system that gives rise to a system-dependent parameter measurable in terms of certain fundamentally measured quantities, and (ii) the numerical system used to represent it. If a representation theorem can be provided for the empirical systems that characterise derived measurement as an alternative to the Suppes formalism for derived measurement, which more strictly speaking is for derived measurement, we may accord derived constants a similar status to that of fundamental quantities: properties of objects. An outline of how this could be done for primitive[29] derived constants is provided in Chapter 4.

The significance of parameters

If it is charitable to assume that the formalism provided does support the existence of system-independent physical parameters which are single valued, we still need to address the question of the significance of such numbers.

Campbell suggested that system-independence does not necessarily confer significance:

> When a constant is not a secondary magnitude, because its value is the same for all the systems subject to the law, the law is usually of very narrow range; both law and constant are unimportant, and will probably not be recognised in any treatise. (Campbell 1928 p. 85)

Campbell gave a qualitative criterion for significance based upon the existence of interesting distinguishing properties of different classes of system to which the law applied.

> Planck's law defines a constant, which is actually the same for all the systems subject to that law. But these systems are divided on other grounds into many well-marked classes, some of which form series; there are the classes of chemically simple and chemically complex substances, the class of the elements forming a series of atomic number, and so on. It is the fact that all these distinguishable classes form a single class for the purpose of the law that makes the law and its constant so important. In the same way, the constant c is the same for all classes of radiation; the gravitational constant G the same for all classes of substances.
>
> A universal constant, then, is distinguished from an unimportant constant that merely fails to be a secondary magnitude, because the systems that it characterises can be classified in an important manner apart from the law. (Campbell 1928 p. 86)

Unfortunately, Campbell did little more than replace *significance* by *importance*. He also failed to provide an example of a system-independent parameter that is not significant.

Latent heats and atomic numbers may be examples of universal constants of limited significance, but for our purposes let us attach some significance to any system-independent physical parameter that is single-valued, which we call a universal constant, or on occasion, where the context permits, simply a constant. If this largesse is acceptable, we may then turn to consider in Chapter 3 the relative status and significance of different universal constants.

Summary

In this chapter we have reviewed the principal traditional accounts of measurement in so far as they relate to constants. By drawing a distinction between system-dependent parameters and scale-factors, we have been able to explain aspects of the physical and mathematical systems in which constants are embedded without the confusion evident in the account of Campbell, nor the operationalist dogma of Ellis.

There is a readily intelligible account of the physical meaning of constants, which can be formalised in the assignment of single-values to system-independent parameters in a systematic account of the mathematical representation of extensive quantities based upon the axiomatic scheme provided by Suppes. Important differences exist between fundamental and derived system-independent parameters, which give rise to further questions relating to the relative significance of different constants.

Notes

1 As we shall see in Chapter 4, this latter remark is not strictly correct. For an adequate representation of quantities in modern physics, we need five reference quantities. Since there are more than five primitive constants, some can be expressed in terms of others.

2 See p. 12 for an explication of the term measure.

3 Campbell discussed such operations himself: see Campbell (1920 pp. 292-3).

4 Campbell indeed considered these properties of objects to be qualities (1920 p 283).

5 This is not strictly true: Campbell considered the possibility of alternative non-additive representations but failed to identify a quantity which could be measured by two genuinely distinct procedures that supported different representations. *Apparently measurement is actually unique except for the arbitrary choice of unit because there is only one way of combining two systems in respect of the property under consideration which obeys the first law of addition.* (Campbell 1920 p. 294).

6 Qualities do not satisfy Campbell's First Law of Addition and Ellis excludes them.

7 Campbell himself remarked, that if we establish the equation $x = f(y, a, b)$: *The distinction between the variables and the constants is simply that the propositions, of which the truth defines the form of the function f, involve only x and y and not a and b. Accordingly, if the possibility of a change in a and b is admitted by writing them as algebraic symbols and not as numerals, the terms variable and constant are slightly misleading* (Campbell 1920 p. 339).

8 Sedov (1959) uses parameter in a similar fashion: *A mechanical system and the state of its motion are determined by a number of dimensional and non-dimensional parameters and functions* (1959 p. 21).

9 In particular, we may note that we would in general expect the parameter to be system-dependent and the scale factor to be system-independent but dependent upon the choice of scale.

10 It is possible to show that an equation which retains the same form under a change of scale factor must be expressible in standard form.

11 Campbell rejected continuity for physical quantities. See Campbell 1928 p. 24 and p. 214: *Mathematical continuity is a conception inapplicable to magnitudes.* His account of an additive operation also presupposed countability.

12 Ellis himself acknowledged this conclusion: *But it is doubtful whether there is anything which could be described as a nominal scale for the measurement of a quantity. Nominal scales have indeed been described. But these scales cannot be said to be scales for the measurement of anything, except, perhaps, sameness and difference* (Ellis 1964 p. 359).

13 Guggenheim (1942) called these spurious constants *definitional constants.*

14 In America, engineers regard a 'pound' as a unit of force, replacing the unit 'lb-force'. The unit of mass then becomes a 'slug', equal to 32 lbs in the traditional 'mass' system of units.

15 The notion of reference quantities will be fully explained in Chapter 4.

16 We may not always want to do this in some circumstances e.g. considerations of spherical symmetry have led to the introduction of a factor of $1 / 4\pi$ in rationalised systems of electromagnetic units.

17 Even Focken, an operationalist par excellence and ardent disciple of Dingle, did not draw such radical conclusions, identifying carefully a category of experimental (as distinct from definitional) constants (Focken 1953).

18 Here we assume that k is a genuine quantity, i.e. d.

19 The distinction is also reflected in the fact that c is dimensionless, whereas k is dimensioned.

20 Wilson was aware of some of these difficulties: *Let us compare the convention which introduces the mass M' with another mass substitute. We adopt the Newtonian formula* $F = G M_1 M_2 / r^2$ *where G is the gravitational*

constant, and introduce a new quantity M", to serve the purposes of mass, defined by M" = GM we thus find, ..., for the dimensions of M", M" = L^3 T^{-2}. *This mass, or substitute for mass, called gravitational mass, is referred to by Clerk-Maxwell in his Treatise, and Dr Brown [Burniston Brown 1941] attaches importance to it. Is it really so important? or is it in any sense of fundamental significance? Clearly there are more conventions than one which enable us to define a mass substitute whose dimensions are derivable from length and time. I find nothing to say in favour of the gravitational substitute except its practical convenience for astronomers* (Wilson 1942 p. 32).

21 By elementary particles understand the particles which orthodox scientists believe constitute matter, such as protons and electrons. Such objects naturally comprise the empirical systems which gives rise to the constants we measure, but are not to be held as "elementary" in some deeper, metaphysical sense.

22 While the fundamental particles are points, they may still function as the objects of spatial relations to define distances e.g. orbits.

23 In similar fashion Campbell wrote (1920 p. 370): *Before any measurement of the fundamental magnitude can be made the system that has unit magnitude must be realised and made the subject of experiment.*

24 Campbell wrote (1920 footnote p. 346): *all universal constants are purely theoretical conceptions*; and (1920 p. 395): *All the universal constants, if they were concepts, would be derived magnitudes, with the possible exception of the mass of an electron.*

25 The possibility of alternative numerical representations of unorthodox operations allows the inclusion of fundamental measurements which may not be measured derivatively and which may not correspond to a system parameter.

26 As we shall discuss in Chapter 4, more strictly speaking, Suppes' account provided a formalism for defined, as opposed to, derived measurement.

27 For instance Focken (1953 p. 23) writes: *there is a difference between the unit of a derived magnitude and that of a fundamental magnitude; and before any measurement of the fundamental magnitude can be made the system that has unit magnitude must be realized and made the subject of experiment. But in order to measure derived magnitudes it is not in the least necessary that the system which has unit magnitude should be realized. We never realize a rod which has unit Young's modulus or a fluid that has unit viscosity.*

28 Implicitly, we are suggesting that Suppes' formalism applies strictly to *defined* measurements i.e. where a quantity is defined by an equation, as opposed to a situation where experiment reveals the existence of a *derived* quantity which is found to be measurable in terms of certain other fundamental quantities.

29 For the sense of 'primitive' here see Chapter 3 *Primitive particle and field constants*.

3 The taxonomy of constants

Introduction

In the previous chapter, a framework was provided for the analysis of constants, which are held to be system-independent parameters. If, in principle, we accept for the moment the existence of these parameters, which are to be regarded as quantities (or qualities perhaps in some cases), we may then inquire how constants may be classified and distinguished from one another. The purpose of this chapter is to provide a coherent account of the differences that do exist between the various constants that feature in our most prized physical theories. In particular, we shall be concerned to establish whether some constants are more significant than others, and whether, in some appropriate way, certain constants can be reduced to others.

Synopsis of chapter

We will present a typical list of fundamental constants, based upon the compilation of Kaye and Laby (1986)[1], which will form the basis of our categorisation. Separate categories of constants will be defined, beginning with mundane constants, numerals, and ratios. These categories are discarded for the purposes of philosophical investigation because they lack generality.

Composite constants, which may be reduced to complex instances of more primitive constants, will be identified. We will argue that no particular importance attaches to composite ratios that turn out to be dimensionless numbers, since it is always possible to use the results of dimensional analysis to turn a dimensioned composite ratio into a dimensionless ratio and vice versa.

Pure ratios will similarly be identified and eliminated from consideration since their values are entirely dependent on the existence and use of shared measurement scales for the quantities concerned.[2]

The remaining constants can be separated into those obtained by derived measurement and those obtained by fundamental means, and this distinction is supported by the particulate and field aspects of these distinct categories.

The distinction between fundamental and derived measurement, which is critical to this account, is defended against criticisms that it is a meaningless distinction in application and undermined by the possibility of alternative representations of quantities. Conventionalist arguments attacking primitive derived constants based upon the theory of dimensions are addressed in Chapter 4.

Mundane constants, numerals and ratios

Mundane constants

At the end of Chapter 2, we asked whether system independence conferred significance. Lacking a clear criterion to apply, we agreed to a temporary enfranchisement of all system independent parameters. Table 2 shows the consequences of this largesse.

Table 3.1
System-independent parameters

Name	**Formula**	**Value**	**Units**
Densities			
Elasticities			
Viscosities			
Heat Capacities			
Refractive Indices			
etc.			
Speed of light in vacuum	c	299792458(1.2)	m s^{-1}
Permeability of vacuum	μ_0	12.5663706144	10^{-7} H m^{-1}
Permittivity of vacuum	ϵ_0	8.854187818(71)	10^{-12} F m^{-1}

Fine-structure constant	$[\mu_0 c^2/4\pi] / e^2 hc$	7.2973506(60)	10^{-8}
Elementary charge	e	1.6021892(46)	10^{-19} C
Planck constant	h	6.626176(36)	10^{-34} J s
Avogadro constant	N_A	6.022045(31)	10^{23} mol^{-1}
Atomic mass unit	u	1.6605655(86)	10^{-27} kg
Electron rest mass	m_e	9.109534(47)	10^{-31} kg
Proton rest mass	m_p	1.6726485(86)	10^{-27} kg
Ratio of proton mass to electron mass	m_p / m_e	1836.15152(70)	
Neutron rest mass	m_n	1.6749543(86)	10^{-27} kg
Electron charge to mass ratio	e / m_e	1.7588047(49)	10^{11} C kg^{-1}
Magnetic flux quantum	Φ_0	2.0678506(54)	10^{-15} Wb
Josephson frequency voltage ratio	$2e / h$	4.835939(13)	10^{14} Hz V^{-1}
Quantum of circulation	$h / 2m_e$	3.6369455(60)	10^{-4} J s kg^{-1}
Faraday constant	F	9.648456(27)	10^{4} C mol^{-1}
Rydberg constant	R_∞	1.097373177(83)	10^{7} m^{-1}
Bohr radius	a_o	5.2917706(44)	10^{-11} m
Classical electron radius	r_0	2.8179380(70)	10^{-15} m
Thomson cross section	σ_e	0.6652448(33)	10^{-28} m^2
Free electron g-factor	μ_e / μ_B	1.0011596567(35)	
Free muon g-factor	μ_μ / μ_B	1.00116616(31)	
Bohr magneton	μ_B	9.274078(36)	10^{-24} J T^{-1}

Electron magnetic moment	μ_e	9.284832(36)	10^{-24} J T^{-1}
Gyromagnetic moment of protons in water	γ'_p	2.6751301(75)	10^{8} s^{-1} T^{-1}
Gyromagnetic moment corrected	γ_p	2.6751987(75)	10^{8} s^{-1} T^{-1}
Magnetic moment of protons in water in Bohr magnetons	μ'_p / μ_B	1.52099322(10)	10^{-3}
Proton magnetic moment in Bohr magnetons	μ_p / μ_B	1.521032209(16)	10^{-3}
Ratio of electron and proton magnetic moments	μ_e / μ_π	658.2106880(66)	
Proton magnetic moment	μ_p	1.4106171(55)	10^{-26} J T^{-1}
Magnetic moment of protons in nuclear magnetons	μ'_p / μ_N	2.7927740(11)	
Magnetic moment corrected	μ_p / μ_N	2.7928456(11)	
Nuclear magneton	μ_N	5.050824(20)	10^{-27} J T^{-1}
Ratio of muon and proton magnetic moments	μ_μ / μ_π	3.1833402(72)	
Muon magnetic moment	μ_μ	4.490474(18)	10^{-26} J T^{-1}
Ratio of muon mass to electron mass	m_μ / m_e	206.76865(47)	
Muon rest mass	m_μ	1.883566(11)	10^{-28} kg
Electron Compton wavelength	λ_c	2.4263089(40)	10^{-12} m

Proton Compton wavelength	$\lambda_{c.p}$	1.3214099(22)	10^{-15} m
Neutron Compton wavelength	$\lambda_{c.n}$	1.3195909(22)	10^{-15} m
Molar volume of ideal gas at s.t.p.	V_m	22.41383(70)	10^{-3} m^3 mol^{-1}
Molar gas constant	R	8.31441(26)	J mol^{-1} K^{-1}
Boltzmann constant	k	1.380662(44)	10^{-23} J K^{-1}
Stefan constant	σ	5.67032(71)	10^{-8} W m^{-2} K^{-4}
First radiation constant	c_1	3.741832(20)	10^{-16} W m^2
Second radiation constant	c_2	1.438786(45)	10^{-2} mK
Gravitational constant	G	6.6720(41)	10^{-11} m^3 s^{-2} kg^{-1}

Many of the constants listed, while of considerable practical value, are of little interest philosophically: densities, elasticities etc.

In addition to system-independence, we require that the parameter in question have the widest applicability: in other words, the systems to which it relates must form a very large category of system. The systems must be general.

> Invariability then is one essential element in the relation established by any law which has importance for science; but it is not the only element....The observations between which the invariable connection is established must be so general that we are sure that they will occur again; and the more general they are and the more likely they are to occur again, the more important and valuable will be the invariable relation. Generality, therefore, is as important an element of the relation of laws as invariability. (Campbell 1920 p. 69)

As an example of specificity, Palacios gave Hooke's law applied to a wire of length l and cross-sectional area a subject to a force f. The equation describing this law makes use of a system-independent parameter (Young's modulus) but because the value of this constant is specific to each type of wire, the lack of generality means it is of little value.

Campbell considered many constants in empirical laws to belong to this category of mundane constants, where they would remain until a more fundamental theoretical account could be given for their values. These thoughts are echoed in Bunge:

> And it is hoped that all specific constants will eventually become derivative, i.e. analyzed in terms of a few fundamental constants, because specific constants characterize macro systems which we expect to understand in terms of fundamental theories regarding micro systems. (Bunge 1966 p. 35)

Like laws which vary in their generality partly as a function of the explanatory role they play, the constants that characterise our most cherished theories, if they are to have a wide explanatory role, should be of great generality. According to Bunge:

> Fundamental theories contain no specific constants. Thus Newtonian mechanics contain no constant at all; Newtonian gravitation theory contains only G, and Einstein's gravitation only ℵ (analyzable but not definable in terms of G and c); non-relativistic quantum mechanics contains only h, and quantum electrodynamics c, h, e. The reason for the absence of specific constants in fundamental theories is that they deal with comprehensive classes of physical systems, not with specific systems like the CdS crystal or a position measurement device. (Bunge 1966 p. 35)

Ellis did not draw this distinction between universality and generality. Because the systems, to which a law applies, must meet certain specifications if the law is to be applicable, Ellis argued that the parameter designating the systems is system-dependent. He asserted that consequently there are no universal system-independent constants of interest, only scale-independent universal constants.

Hidden in Ellis' account was an ambiguity in the notion of "dependence". A parameter depends upon the system concerned in so far as the parameter is identified only for certain systems (those that meet the specification), but does not depend upon the system, in the sense that the nature and value of the parameter are determined by other properties of the system. Dependency in this second sense, is usually established by some physical link between the properties of a system and a parameter.

Ellis was led to underestimate the significance of system independence of the second sort. It is, indeed, significant that certain parameters apply to the broadest categories of system, and have unique values which are independent of the constitution of the systems.

Numerals

Returning to Table 2, we may next identify a category of constants which are disguised numerals largely of computational significance: Avogadro's constant (N_A), which gives the number of molecules in a mole of a gas at standard temperature and pressure, the Faraday ($N_A e$), the molar gas constant ($N_A k$), the molar volume of an ideal gas at s.t.p. and the atomic mass unit (one twelth the mass of a ^{12}C carbon atom). These constants are not strictly system-independent parameters but scale-factors which allow us to establish new scales of measurement for mass and charge and temperature suited for the applications that typically arise in a research laboratory.[3] From a philosophical perspective, these constants are of limited interest, and should not strictly be included in a table of fundamental constants.

Composite constants

Having eliminated these computational factors, we may turn our attention to a second category of constants, which appear to have a lesser philosophical status: those dimensioned composite constants that are ratios of other, more basic constants. In this category, we would include: e/m_e, Φ_0, h / e, $2e / h$, $h / 2m_e$, h / m_e, R_∞, a_0, r_0, σ_e, μ_B, μ_N, γ_p, γ'_p, λ_c, $\lambda_{c.p}$, $\lambda_{c.n}$, σ, c_1, c_2.

The significance of these composite constants appears to arise from their use in successful theories and models: quantum electrodynamics, the theory of the atom, the theory of the nucleus, and thermodynamics. Each constant captures a common characteristic of a family of physical systems: charged particles in electric or magnetic fields, atoms and nuclei, radiative particles. This aspect of commonality supports the explanatory role of these constants, many of which reflect the application of classical concepts to the world of particles, for example the Bohr radius, the classical electron radius, the Thomson cross-section and magnetic moments. The linkage to classical concepts is provided by the use of the same dimensions for the constant as its classical analogue e.g. length, area etc.

As Bunge put it:

> Scme universal constants are typical of macrophysics (e.g. k and R), others of microphysics (e.g. e and h), and finally others are level independent (e.g. c and the gravitational constants G and ℵ). In other words, some universal constants are more universal than others and therefore the theories characterised by them are more comprehensive than others. (Bunge 1966 p. 35)

The existence of these constant physical parameters is reflected in their repeated occurrence in the numerical laws and theories in these domains. The consistency of theory in these areas allows us to assign a common definition to these constants, even though they appear in several numerical laws. In this category, we also include the fine-structure constant, α, which contingently turns out to be dimensionless as a consequence of the customary dimensional basis we conventionally choose for current theories.

From an ontological point of view, these composite constants are defined as ratios, and as such are the mathematical representation of a relationship holding between certain quantities belonging to physical systems. They are thus the property of quantities i.e. second-order properties. Campbell included such composite constants among the class of *defined magnitudes*:[4 5]

> If x, y, z, etc., are numerals representing any magnitudes, measurable either by the fundamental or the derived method, characteristic of the same system, then any function of these numerals (in the algebraic sense) is also a numeral characteristic of the system... Most magnitudes defined in this way without reference to numerical laws to which the system is subject would be of no importance whatever, but some of them may have an importance arising either from numerical laws in which they are constants but applicable to other systems, or from laws applicable to the systems but in which they are not constants.
>
> Defined magnitudes may thus be measured, in the literal sense of our definition of measurement, because they may be represented by numerals that are assigned in virtue of laws; but they are distinguished from other magnitudes because these laws, while they justify the assignment of some numeral to them, do not fix the particular numerals that are to be assigned. They vary in degree from pure defined magnitudes, which have little or no importance derived from laws, to magnitudes so completely confirmed (as we shall say) by laws which give importance to them that they are barely distinguished from secondary magnitudes arising from derived measurement. (Campbell 1928 p. 94-5)

As examples of defined quantities, Campbell cited pressure and distance, neither of which are strictly measured by derived or fundamental means.

Having identified this distinction, Campbell devoted no further discussion to defined quantities, noting that the important distinction is that between quantities which can be measured without the prior measurement of other quantities, and those that cannot, i.e. the fundamental vs. derived distinction.

If we accept that derived measurement also occurs whenever we define an equation (see Chapter 2 page 17 onwards), as opposed to a set of experimental procedures for measuring the other quantities involved in the law, defined measurement becomes a subset of derived measurement. Most defined measurements will not correspond to system-dependent parameters, which, as we have discussed, largely overlap with derived measurements. Occasionally, as is the case with pressure, a suitable causal explanation can be given to warrant the inclusion of the defined measurement amongst system parameters. Usually this is not the case (e.g. e/m) and we will consider these composite constants to be defined quantities and of secondary importance. Before returning to the fundamental / derived distinction, we must next turn to a second category of ratios, that of dimensionless constants.

Dimensionless ratios and the Π theorem

A separate category of dimensionless ratios may also be discerned in Table 2. In this category, two instances of the same quantity are compared, and since conventionally these two instances are measured on the same scale, the corresponding ratio will be dimensionless.[6]

Examples of this type of dimensionless ratio are: m_p / m_e, μ_e / μ_B, μ_μ / μ_B, μ'_p / μ_B, μ_p / μ_B, μ_e / μ_p, μ'_p / μ_N, μ_p / μ_N, μ_μ / μ_p, m_μ / m_e. All of these constants involve the relative magnitude of properties of particles, either to each other, or to a theoretically derived analogue such as the Bohr magneton.

Much importance has been attached to these dimensionless ratios, and various speculative projections have been made concerning the impact of changes in these ratios for the purposes of anthropomorphic arguments. Nonetheless the ratio of two commensurable quantities is not of itself an item of significance.

From an ontological perspective, we may consider that these ratios only have significance as a property of the mathematical representation chosen for the quantities in question: the ratios are formally defined by the numerical assignment functions relating to the quantites in question, but there is no concurrent physical relation involving the quantity featuring in the ratio, as was also the case with the dimensioned ratios already distinguished. These dimensionless ratios represent a particular example of *defined magnitudes*, as explained above. If we change the representation, these values change.[7]

In attaching little significance to the actual value of these ratios, we do not thereby imply that little significance attaches to the concept of relative magnitude. We can agree with Bridgman with the central anchoring role played by the conservation of relative magnitude in our system of ratio scales, while attaching little importance to the actual values of relative magnitudes. This means we do not assign an *absolute significance to relative magnitude*, in Ellis' words[8], but recognise nonetheless the importance of the notion and measure of relative magnitude in arguments relating to scale invariance and similitude.[9]

The fine-structure constant α has been considered particularly noteworthy because it is dimensionless other than by the simultaneous occurrence of quantities of the same kind. Many scientists and natural philosophers have wondered why it has the value it does, roughly 1/137. In fact, no particular significance attaches to this ratio as opposed to others, for two reasons. First, the actual value given to α may be arbitrarily changed by choosing alternative scales, either other, incoherent, ratio scales for the quantities that define α, or more radical alternative scales of the type described by Ellis.

Second, any composite constant can be stated in dimensionless terms if we are prepared to reformulate the equation that gives rise to it. Let the quantity m be measured by derived measurement given by an equation in standard form[10] involving the variables s_k, and the scale-factor C, i.e.

$$m = C\, s_1^{a1} .\, s_2^{a2} . . . s_r^{ar}$$

then

$$\log (m / C) = \Sigma a_k \log s_k \qquad (k = 1 \text{ to } r),$$

where the dimensions of *m* in terms of s_k are a_k. Without loss of generality we may replace m / C by m', and write

$$log\ (m') = \Sigma a_k\ log\ s_k \qquad (k = 1 \text{ to } r).$$

This definition gives only the dimensions of m' in terms of the variables associated with it in some definite equation. If we now further generalise the definition, to give us greater choice of variable, the distinction between m' and s disappears and we may write the form of the law as:

$$\Sigma a_k\ log\ s_k = 0 \qquad (k = 1 \text{ to } r).$$ [11]

If we then select certain quantities as reference quantities, for instance p, q, ..., in terms of which we conventionally specify dimensions (e.g. mass, length and time), and if the dimension of s_k in terms of p is written k_p, we obtain:

$$\Sigma_k a_k\ log\ s_k = \Sigma_k a_k\ (k_p\ log\ p + k_q\ log\ q + ...) = 0$$

$$= log\ p\ (\Sigma_k a_k k_p) + log\ q\ (\Sigma_k a_k k_q) + ... = 0$$

This in general implies that:

$$\Sigma_k a_k k_p = \Sigma_k a_k k_q = ... = 0 \qquad (k = 1 \text{ to } r).$$

These equations stipulate that the sum of the indices of each of the reference quantities p, q, ... etc. sum to zero. To recover the form of the law defining m', we require that these equations have a solution. For this, it is sufficient, but not necessary, that the dimensions k_p are known for all but one of the s_k (i.e. for all but s_r), and that no two quantities s_k should have the same dimensions in terms of p, q, ..., and that the dimensions of all the s_k should not be the same for two dimensions p, q.[12] In general s_r will be dimensioned depending on the known dimensions k_p of s_k.

If s_r is the coefficient that corresponds to m', and m' is a constant which we require to be dimensionless, then :

$$\Sigma_k a_k k_p = \Sigma_k a_k k_q = ... = 0 \qquad (k=1 \text{ to } r\text{-}1)$$

This will not in general be the case, since we have assumed that the dimensions of all the a_k (k=*1* to r-*1*) are already known, and that they generate non-zero summations. Since the choice of the reference quantities p, q, ..., in which we express dimensions, is a matter of convention, we may choose, however, to set the dimensions l_p of the variable s_1 so that the summations are zero. The result will be to generate the above equation so that r_p, r_q is zero and hence m' is dimensionless. The forcing of the dimensions of s_l is equivalent to introducing a dimensioned constant in the equation which defines s_l , in exactly the same manner as the elimination by Ellis of a constant in Newton's law of gravity gave rise to the appearance of a new constant in Newton's second law. By introducing this constant into the revised derived law for s_l, we can again obtain dimensional homogeneity for this law.

This result is a specific application of a more general theorem of dimensional analysis, known as *Buckingham's Π theorem*. According to this theorem, if variable A_1 depends upon the independent variables A_2 , A_3 , ... A_n , then their functional relationship can be set equal to zero in the form:

$$f\ (A_1\ , \ A_2\ , A_3\ , \dots A_n) = 0\ .$$

If these n variables can be described in terms of m dimensional reference quantities, then the Π theorem states that they can be grouped in n - m dimensionless terms π_i that are called "pi-terms" - that is:

$$g\ (\Pi_1,\ \Pi_2,\ \dots,\ \Pi_{n-m}) = 0\ .$$

Each π term will contain m + 1 variables, only one of which needs to be changed from term to term, the m reference quantities occurring in each of the pi-terms.

A typical example of the use of this theorem is the analysis of complex dimensional relationships in fluid mechanics. For instance, consider the case of fluid motion, where it is possible to group the important variables into three groups: four linear dimensions that define channel geometry and other boundary conditions; a rate of water discharge and a pressure gradient that characterize dynamical and kinematic flow properties; and five fluid properties (density, specific weight, viscosity, surface tension and elastic modulus). The total of eleven variables (n), can be expressed in terms of three dimensions (m); accordingly, a functional relationship can be written involving eight π terms (n-m). The problem is reducible to the solution of simultaneous linear equations to determine the exponents of the π terms that will render each term dimensionless i.e. $\pi_i = L^o\ M^o\ T^o$ in which $L^o\ M^o\ T^o$ refers to a dimensionless combination of length, mass and time, the three fundamental units in which each variable is measured. The use of the Π theorem in conventionalist arguments concerning the status of constants will be examined in detail in Chapter 4 , but we can use it here to render α dimensionless.

Imagine that we discover experimentally that the energy of a body is proportional to its relativistic mass, and that we represent this law by the equation

$E = m$, we shall find

$$[E] = [M] \qquad \text{and} \qquad [h] = [T][M].$$

If we regard force as a derived quantity defined by Newton's second law with the dimensions $[M][L][T]^{-2}$, then the Coulomb force has the same dimensions so

$$[e^2/4\pi\epsilon_0] \quad = \quad [M][L]^3[T]^{-2}$$

and hence α has the following dimensions[13]

$$[e^2/4\pi\epsilon_0 hc] \quad = \quad [L]^2[T]^{-2}$$

The possibility of rendering any particular derived constant into a dimensional or dimensionless form, means that no especial significance is to be attached to the fact that α turns out to be dimensionless[14] under the conventional assignments of dimensions that physicists currently make. For this reason, it seems more appropriate to class α with composite constants, rather than with those constants that are definitionally dimensionless (on the assumption that we measure instances of the same quantity on the same scales).

Sedov (1959) came to a similar conclusion concerning dimensionless quantities by considering the possibility of using specific measures, rather than absolute measures, for the measurement of quantities. For example, we might measure acceleration in terms of *g* rather than in newtons. By doing so, our values for acceleration become independent of the choice of reference units, typically mass, length and time units, for the measurement of *g*: the value of the acceleration is dependent only upon the choice of scale for acceleration.

Using specific measures has the same effect as introducing a new reference quantity into the representation : namely, acceleration. It is as though acceleration were a fundamental quantity. We have replaced the customary derived quantity, defined by an equation involving mass, length and time, by what seems to be a new fundamental quantity. In this way, acceleration, as it appears in any equation, will have its own dimension, [acceleration]. Acceleration will be a reference quantity, and will function as a primary quantity (i.e. independent variable) in the equations in which it appears.[15]

In carrying out this procedure, we must bear in mind, however, that although acceleration behaves representationally as though it were a fundamental quantity, whether it is or not, is separately and independently determined on the basis of the existence of a suitable combination operation and the satisfaction of the axioms for extensive measurement. This is an empirical matter which was overlooked by Dingle and Focken when they declared the distinction between fundamental and derived measurement a matter of convention.[16] The fact that we can make *h*, or any other derived quantity, behave like a fundamental quantity with its own dimension, does not make it one. To assume it does, is to confuse the "primary/secondary quantity" distinction with the "fundamental/derived quantity" distinction.

If we measured one of the derived quantities in the expression for α specifically, α would no longer be dimensionless. In fact we could use specific measures for each of the derived quantities to obtain the following dimensions for α:

$$[e]^2[\epsilon_o]^{-1}[h]^{-1}[c]^{-1}$$

We concur with Sedov:

> The concepts of dimensional and non-dimensional quantities are therefore relative. Each quantity is measured in certain units. When these units of measurement are identical in all systems the corresponding quantities are called non-dimensional. Dimensional quantities are defined as those for which the units of measurement can vary in experimental or theoretical investigations. Here it is irrelevant whether or not the investigations are actually carried out. It follows from this definition that certain quantities can be considered dimensional in some cases and non-dimensional in others. (Sedov 1959 p. 3)

While not significant philosophically, the fact that certain quantities are dimensionless is very useful for the presentation of data, computation etc. This usefulness was designed in from the beginning, however, and arises from the choices we make of reference quantities, the particular form of equations and the Π theorem. It ought to be no surprise that α is dimensionless given the application of the Π theorem to the equations used to describe atomic systems and our choice of mass, length and time as reference quantities. The application of the Π theorem produces α as a dimensionless π term.

All four categories of constants identified so far have subordinate status: they are either of limited generality, computational or formulaic abbreviations or ratios. Commitment to them does not disturb our starting ontological neutrality. The existence of such constants is a contingent consequence of the existence of more basic categories of constants from which they are derived.

Primitive particle and field constants

Returning to Table 2, we may identify two final categories of constant which correspond to system-independent physical parameters which are measured either by fundamental or by derived means.

The category of fundamentally measured constants comprises e, m_e, m_p, m_n, m_μ, μ_e, μ_p, μ_μ. Interestingly, these A quantities relate to the properties of particles which are subject to electromagnetic and gravitational interactions.

The remaining constants are characterised by derived measurement in an equation or differential equation: G , c , h and ϵ_0 (or alternatively μ_0). Boltzmann's constant k will be considered separately later. These B quantities characterise coupling aspects of the interaction of the particles (G and ϵ_0), or coupling aspects of the properties of particles (h links wave and particle phenomena, c relates time and space intervals). Insofar as the A constants relate to particles, these derived B quantities seem to relate to fields. Once these quantities would have been considered properties of the vacuum. Levy-Leblond has developed a partially similar view:

> Let me start by proposing a classification of physical constants into three types. This, hopefully, may bring some order in the otherwise rather incongruous lists offered by the standard tables. By order of increasing generality, I will thus distinguish:
>
> A) Physical properties of particular objects; for instance, the masses of the fundamental particles, their magnetic moments, energy widths of unstable ones, etc.
>
> B) Constants characterizing whole classes of physical phenomena; these are mainly the coupling constants of the various fundamental interactions, such as e associated with electromagnetism, or G with gravitation, or still the Fermi constant for weak interactions.
>
> C) Universal constants, such as c or h, which enter the most general theoretical framework available, independently of particular objects or specific interactions. (Levy-Leblond 1977 p. 189)

The distinction between types B and C is not well founded, and relies in part in the customary elimination of a number of traditional classical constants that occurs as a consequence of the use of defining laws which eliminate some dimensions (see *Dimensional proliferation and reduction* in Chapter 4).

It may be argued that not only is the derived/fundamental quantity distinction helpful in our taxonomy, but that it also allows us to confer greater significance on those constants measured by fundamental means. The argument would be that derived B quantities rely on the prior measurement of fundamental quantities, and they may also reflect a choice of qualities or features of space-time that we recognise in order to develop a framework of laws defining the behaviour of elementary particles: this choice may seem to some degree conventional. For these reasons, we might be persuaded to accord a lesser ontological status to these B entitities. We may also inquire whether primitive derived constants are qualities or quantities.

Qualities or quantities

Campbell thought that in general the distinction between quantities measured by fundamental and derived means, reflected a distinction between quantities and qualities:

> We shall see later that no accurate and important distinction can be drawn between the magnitudes that are measured by the fundamental method and those that are measured by the derived. But there is a way of distinguishing them that is approximately accurate; it is generally true, in spite of important exceptions, that magnitudes measured by the fundamental process are quantities, and that those measured by the derived are qualities. (Campbell 1928 p. 14)[17]

Ellis, on the other hand, attempted to exclude qualities from his system of measurement by imposing a modal condition on the binary ordering relation which requires that it be possible for objects to stand in a "greater than" or "less than" relation in respect of the property concerned: this condition is generally only met by quantities.[18] As a result, all measurement relates to quantities not qualities.

If we consider normal language usage, however, it may seem that Ellis' modal condition does not rule out numerically orderable properties of objects, which many would more naturally hold to be qualities.

To defend his case, Ellis cited colour and shape as examples of qualities for which he believed it was hard to conceive of $A >_R B$. But what about a quality such as sweetness? Is this a quality of a substance or a quantity? Clearly, I could establish an ordering, which might be improved over time by polling expert tasters. On this basis, sweetness would satisfy Ellis' requirements for being a quantity, though we would typically consider sweetness to be a quality. (Note that such quantities do not necessarily give rise to an additive combination operation). Does this mean sweetness is a quantity for Ellis?

In the case of sweetness, we might not in fact be able to assign a scale of numbers, so let us consider another example, where this is possible. In conjoint marketing studies individuals are asked to rank order composite products which combine subsets of possible product features (in the auto industry a shiny car, four doors, fuel economy, and sporty looks might be an example of the conjoint presentation of possible product features, some of which are qualities). Based upon the orderings given for various product permutations, individual preferences (utilities) are assigned for each separate product feature, including qualities, and by means of a mathematical transformation (the logit transformation), aggregated consumer preferences for product features are converted into additive feature purchase probabilities on a zero to one scale. In this way, starting from consumer preferences, it is possible to define certain values (the partial utilites and purchase probabilities) and an ordering relating to the features, including qualities, of the products.

Furthermore, these attributed values conform to certain empirical laws: there are direct links between expected product market shares and conjoint attribute utility scores, which may be formulated as equations. This suggests that certain of the marketing variables relating to quality features are in fact derived quantities according to Ellis' characterisation of measurement.

In light of these considerations, the distinction between qualities and quantities appears to be one of degree not kind. Qualities are not usually quantified, and difficulties may inhibit ordering, but in other situations, procedures and assignment rules can be specified to define an ordering. We might allow that quantities are properties which are orderable, according to Campbell and Ellis' axioms, but recognise that certain qualities (for example, opacity or perceived loudness) also meet these criteria.

Campbell also argued that a further distinction can usefully be drawn between qualities and extensive properties.[19] He highlighted the fact that qualities, which largely coincide with his derived B magnitudes, do not enjoy the additivity that is traditionally taken to be characteristic of extensive properties.

> For a very large proportion of B-magnitudes derive their theoretical importance from the very fact that they are not additive or capable of fundamental measurement; they are qualities of substances, which remain unchanged when the quantity of the substance is altered. (Campbell 1928 p. 100)

In the case of the derived system-independent parameters, G , c , h and ϵ_0, all considered until now to be B quantities, this distinction between additive extensive quantities and non-additive qualities, appears good. It is hard to see how, for instance, gravitational constants can be combined or added: G , c , h and ϵ_0 are more intelligibly understood as qualities or features of spacetime or the vacuum to which we can assign a numeral, in virtue of the law which describes the behaviour of objects in a spacetime or vacuum characterised by this quality or feature. Their values do not increase if we add more to the amount of substance to which they apply (viz. a bigger spacetime or more extended vacuum). We could then consider these constants, more precisely, to be derived B *qualities*, which are system-independent parameters measured by derived means.

Bunge lends some support to this line of argument. He distinguished two categories of constants: referential (such as e and c) and non-referential, such as Boltzmann's constant k and Planck's constant. The former were held to be the special values of a unique physical variable, the latter are simply numbers.

> This structural difference matches a deep semantical difference: the numbers refer to no physical system, they are non-referential proportionality constants, whereas the special values of the magnitudes are properties of classes of physical systems. Thus Boltzmann's k is not the k of a class of substances or even of an arbitrary substance, while e is the charge of an arbitrary member of the class of electrons. In other words, unlike e, k is not a particular value of a function defined on a set of physical systems. (Bunge 1966 p. 37)

Bunge's basic message is that some constants refer to objects (physical systems), some do not. While a distinction between these two types of constant has some foundation, simply assigning a number to the supposed non-referential constants conflicts with our account. We might modify Bunge's views, however, to suit our framework, by taking the reference for constants that do not refer to objects to be fields and interactions. We cannot agree with Bunge, either, that *c* refers to a physical system or set of systems. Individual objects or systems possess velocity, but the value of this velocity is frame (i.e. system) dependent and never equals *c*. We take *c* to be a feature of the linkages between space and time, defined by the equation for electromagnetic propagation.[20] We conclude that the two categories of primitive constants have different referents: objects and fields/interactions.

To summarise the story so far: the categories in our classification of constants might be seen to correspond neatly to the distinctions Campbell observed in the measurement of quantities: empirical factors, computational scale-factors, dimensionless numerals (what Campbell called similarity magnitudes), defined quantities, derived quantities and, in pole position, fundamental quantities. Unfortunately, the story is not so simple. Given that many fundamentally measured quantities can also be measured by the derived process, how can we attach significance to the fundamental/derived distinction for our categories of constants?

The fundamental/derived distinction

Critics may challenge our account because of its reliance on the distinction between fundamental and derived measurement. A particular aspect of our account is that we have relied upon the fact that scales for fundamental A quantities require the existence of standard objects instantiating the extensive quantity concerned, (derived B quantities do not in general require a standard object for the construction of a scale of measurement). The most fundamental constants are then identified with these standard objects, providing a view of these constants as physical units which appeals to scientists. Measurement of the basic fundamental quantities thus seems to provide a realist hook on which we could hang our notions of system-independent physical parameters.

It may be argued, however, that the fundamental/derived distinction is not meaningful because:

1 All fundamental quantities can also be measured by derived means (such measurement was called *quasi-measurement* by Campbell), and hence the attribution of referent objects to primitive fundamental constants and not to primitive derived constants is suspect. Fundamental quantities would then merit

only the same ontological status as derived quantities (which, as we shall in Chapter 4, some philosophers regard as entirely conventional).

2 Alternative unusual mathematical representations permit all derived quantities to be fundamentally measurable (though these quantities will not be additive quantities), and so object referents must also exist for these derived quantities.

If we were to accept that no meaningful distinction could be made between fundamental and derived quantities, we could maintain a view of constants as "units" in the sense in which Ellis uses this term: constants would be a label for the dimensions of derived scales used for a particular quantity, the choice of correlation principle (type of numerical representation) and of scale factor. In other words, constants would describe the particular choice of equation and mathematical representation chosen to represent quantities. Consider an equation:

$$k = f(x, y, z)$$

where x , y , z are measured on sets of similar scales [X] , [Y] , and [Z]. For a particular choice of scales, we have

$$k_1 = f(x_1, y_1, z_1)$$

and if the law is in standard form

$$k_1 = x_1^{\,a} y_1^{\,b} z_1^{\,c}$$

For a second choice of scales related by similarity transformations, assuming a standard correlation principle

$$x_2 = \mathrm{p}\, x_1 \;; \qquad y_2 = \mathrm{q}\, y_1 \;; \qquad z_2 = \mathrm{r}\, z_1$$

and

$$k_2 = x_2^{\,a} y_2^{\,b} z_2^{\,c} = \mathrm{p}^a \mathrm{q}^b \mathrm{r}^c k_1$$

Now k is a derived quantity which could be measured on a class of similar scales [K] , for this is the very way Ellis defines derived measurement. Instead of scale K_1 , however, we may choose to call the same scale by the complex unit name of $X_1^a\, Y_1^b\, Z_1^c$, and we may assign the value of unity to k_1 when $x_1 = x_0$, $y_1 = y_0$, $z_1 = z_0$. In this way, we do not require a standard object for the [K] family of scales, we simply assign a number to k and a complex unit name $X_1^a\, Y_1^b\, Z_1^c$, naming the scale for the measurement of f. We thereby deny any absolute physical significance to k , according it instead only a relational significance. The assignment of a number to k is what Ellis meant by a constant. On this interpretation, Planck's constant arises from Planck's scale of Energy/Radiation Frequency. All measurements on this scale yield the same value, which we conventionally assign the numeral 6.626 x 10^{-34} Js, and which is the ratio of the two quantities energy and frequency for a universe of wave and particle systems. Such a constant is universal, but its value depends on the numerical assignment chosen. Ellis called it a universal scale-dependent constant.

Taking points 1 and 2 above together, a sceptic might say all fundamental quantities may be derived and all derived quantities may be fundamental. In such circumstances, no special ontological significance could be ascribed to fundamental constants as opposed to derived. In addition, the status of derived constants would be without ontological significance because they can be manipulated, replaced and eliminated by changes in measurement conventions. This second attack on the substantivality of primitive *derived* constants will be examined in detail in the next chapter.

Let us consider here the arguments raised by these two points, as far as they relate to primitive *fundamental* constants, noting that they do not assume any change in the number of dimensions that we use in our laws, but assume merely that we may choose to measure the quantities we take as reference dimensions, such as mass length and time, by derived means not fundamental.

In assessing the threat posed by these arguments, let us first consider the precise nature of the variables involved in the equations used to define, in quasi-measurement, a derived scale of measurement for a fundamental quantity such as length. We will be interested to see whether in the special case of quasi-measurement a derived scale requires a standard object.

Standard objects and the form of derived laws in quasi-measurement

Imagine that we inhabit a world characterised by a minimal length parameter defined operationally for an extensive system of measurement. All lengths, which are actually measured in this world, are a rational multiple of the parameter, either a whole number or a fraction of this parameter. Perhaps this mimimal length is given by the size of some basic particle. In these circumstances, we could accommodate this fundamental length constant within our framework, considering it to be the standard object in a fundamental extensive system of length measurement. This account, however, stands to be entirely overthrown if there is not a firm basis to the distinction drawn between quantities measured by fundamental and derived means. If length can be measured unproblematically by derived means, Ockham's razor says there would be no need for a standard object, and hence no need for the system-independent parameter associated with it.

One immediate response is to suggest that, although any particular standard object is dispensable, any new system of derived length measurement also requires a standard object, S, to which we make a numerical assignment in order for a workable scale to be established. Let us call this response the New Object Gambit, initially assuming that the value of unity is assigned to the standard object S (this is not a critical assumption, but merely convenient). The length of this standard object must be related to the constant of minimum length by a ratio. In so far as any numerical assignment implicitly, if not explicitly, allows room for a scale-factor, we may so choose the scale factor to correspond to the ratio of the standard object to the minimum object.[21] This allows us to amend the numerical assignment given to S. By this means we may effectively reconstruct the original fundamental scale, and we may consider that the new standard object is merely a convenient aggregation of the original standard object characterising the minimum length parameter, rather like the Faraday or Avogadro's Number. The new standard object substitutes for the minimum length object. Although we may have grounds of convenience or efficacy for changing to the new derived system of measurement, the ontological significance is nil. But let us consider again, more closely, whether derived scales in quasi-measurement in fact require standard objects?

Campbell suggested they do:

> The total number of factors to be determined is equal to the total number of magnitudes, both A and B. (Campbell 1928 p. 115) [22]

In order to determine the factor of a magnitude, we must both select the standard object and assign a numeral to it. This seems to imply that derived, B quantities require standard objects to be selected. In our hypothetical world, this means that even if length is not a fundamental A quantity, it still requires a standard object (like S).

While Campbell might be able to argue this is indeed the case, it is only on the basis of a curious notion of what an object is. Campbell included both classes and classes of classes as objects, which allowed him to assert that the fixing of factors for B magnitudes does involve the selection of a standard object (sometimes a class of classes). In fact, these classes and classes of classes are no more than a way of identifying particular scale factors, which as we may recall, are confusingly called universal constants by Campbell. Campbell's procedure is thus essentially the same as that of Ellis described on pages 59 and 60, where we fix a precise value k_1 to the scale factor k.

Campbell gave a more correct account when he observed that:

> B magnitudes, then, like A magnitudes, must have their factors determined. And their factors, like those of A magnitudes, can be determined either directly by choosing an individual standard or indirectly by choosing a universal constant. (Campbell 1928 p. 115)

In those situations where a derived system of measurement is established, and a standard object is directly chosen, making this choice is a practical matter and is not, from a philosophical point of view, at all necessary. *Derived scales do not require standard objects*. It then seems that if quantities, hitherto measured by fundamental means, are measured derivatively, we should make only a limited ontological commitment to the standard objects of measurement systems for these quantities. This conclusion casts a shadow over our account of constants.

An example

An example may serve to make these arguments more intelligible. Let us consider the derived measurement of length by light signals. Three separate forms of the equation may be distinguished:

1 Conventional fundamental scale of length with standard object.

x	=	c	t
Fundamental		Derived	Fundamental
A quantity		B quantity	A quantity
Primary variable		Secondary variable	Primary variable.

In the conventional measurement of length, we would explain the equation describing the propagation of a light signal, in terms of the two fundamental quantities, length (or more correctly, distance) and time which function as primaries in the equation which defines a derived quantity c, which turns out to be system-independent, and is therefore a universal constant of significance for Campbell, given that it might have been expected to vary for different systems.

Usually, standard objects would be used to define the scales for x and t, and this would provide a route for the development of our account of constants.[23]

2 Alternative derived scale of length I : the new object gambit

x	=	k	t
Derived		Derived	Fundamental
B quantity		B quantity	A quantity
Secondary variable		Primary variable	Primary variable.

One may propose the above form for the equation relating to the propagation of light. By analogy, consider the flight of an arrow from a standard bow. We might take k to measure some distance covering property of either light or arrows : it would be a derived, B quantity. In the case of an arrow, we might actually measure distances in *arrow-flights*, and it is conceivable that we might establish a reference standard in a laboratory corresponding to this length.

Given this might be so, the fact that the value of $k = c$ presents practical problems of presentation, need not deter us from logically asserting that in this case, also, we would need to establish a standard length object for our scale to work. If this is correct, we will be able to maintain the usefulness of the fundamental/derived distinction as applied to our account of constants, and we will require a standard object for this derived scale of length.

Unfortunately, this is not the case. (Let us set aside the use of k as an indirect means of assigning a standard object to the scale of time, which is without significance as we have discussed in note 23 below). In order for k to function as a derived magnitude, as opposed to being simply a scale-factor, with an assigned standard object that is anything more than a practical convenience, we require that k be capable of independent definition as a secondary variable (since it is a B quantity) in another equation other than the one above. This law would provide a separate account of the measurement of arrow-flights. Unfortunately, no other law is available.

We might consider alternatively that k is in fact an A quantity, measured by fundamental means, but this would merely make the analysis of length as a derived quantity depending on *one* fundamental quantity, by reference to this particular simple equation, inappropriate and would not provide a solution to our difficulties. We would be obliged to consider a different example of quasi-measurement involving two quantities (here time and distance) where one of the fundamental quantities (here distance) is measured according to a law involving the other fundamental quantity.

3 Alternative scale of length II : no standard objects for length

The physical basis for determining distance by reference to the transmission of light might be expressed by saying that the distance between two points is proportional to the time it takes a light signal transmitted from one point to reach the other. The full form of the mathematical representation of this physical relation would be:

X	x =	T	t
Scale factor	Derived B quantity Secondary variable	Scale factor	Fundamental A quantity Primary variable.

The two scale factors could be replaced by a single factor without loss of generality. Campbell, as we have noted, calls these scale factors *universal constants*, and Ellis calls them *universal scale-dependent constants.* For Campbell, each is associated with a class of systems, or a class of classes of systems which obey the law of light propagation or permit the fundamental measurement of time interval respectively. In fact, they do not need to be associated with any object, since they are just features of the mathematical representation of the quantities concerned reflected in the choice of assignment functions, as is made apparent in Ellis' treatment. While we may wish to select a standard object for length, no such object is required in the process of quasi-measurement. If we are to establish a significant distinction between those constants measured fundamentally and those measured by derived means, this distinction must find its basis in the fact that certain quantities are *capable of being* fundamentally measured, rather than the fact that they *are* so measured.

Argument against the significance of quasi-measurement

While initially compelling, to conclude, because we could provide measurements for fundamental quantities using derived scales, that there are no standard objects corresponding to such fundamental quantities, is to be seduced by the mathematics of the situation at the expense of the physics.

That, in our interconnected world, fundamental quantities feature in scientific laws involving other quantities, is an empirical fact. The use of equations to represent the quantities in empirical laws allows us a certain economy in expression and computation. Taken to the extreme, we may choose to make do with a very small number of quantities which can be used to derive other quantities. This choice, however, does not eliminate the standard objects of the quantities we have chosen to measure by derived means which might otherwise be treated as fundamentally measured.

The world might have been different: *no such empirical laws permitting the derived measurement might have existed.* Nonetheless, we might still encounter quantities capable of being measured fundamentally, possessing their own standard objects. In Chapter 2, when we provided a more formal account of derived measurement, we defined a derived scale as a triple $\langle \Xi, \mathcal{L}, g \rangle$. Any derived scale for a fundamental quantity, critically assumes we are able to define a law $\mathcal{L}$ which provides a numerical assignment for the value of a fundamental quantity of an object in the derived measurement system Ξ in terms of other quantities already defined. *Such a law may not be available.*

Where we encounter situations where a quantity, which may be measured fundamentally, is measured by derived methods, we must ask ourselves, whether this is (i) merely a numerical convenience, and not ontologically significant, because the primary quantities in the relevant equation must ultimately obtain their numerical values by a process which assumes the measurement of the fundamental quantity under discussion by fundamental means, or is (ii) a genuine situation where the quantity considered fundamental, for instance force in Newton's second law, can indeed also be derived from a law which ultimately only makes recourse to other distinct fundamental quantities.

The latter situation genuinely contains empirical information about nature, akin to the information conveyed by the equivalence of inertial and gravitational masses. It turns out that a quantity which can be measured fundamentally, force, can also be measured according to a law we have discovered about the world. The two measurement procedures, fundamental and derived, produce the same classification and ordering of forces. That there is such a law is a fact about the world.

Note, separately, that if a representation theorem can be provided for the empirical systems that characterise derived measurements as an alternative to the Suppes formalism for derived measurement, derived quantities would then be clearly seen to be features of the empirical systems in question, not of the mathematical representation. An outline of how this could be done for primitive derived constants is provided in Chapter 4. In these circumstances, the fact that force is both a fundamental and derived quantity would give us valuable and distinct information about the empirical system of objects under consideration, in terms of the coexistence of an extensive combination operation for force (arising from the fundamental measurement of force), and of a structural feature (arising from the derived measurement of force) of the systems of objects relating their mass and their acceleration. In this way, we might consider force measured fundamentally, and force measured by derived means, to be *both* properties of the empirical system (rather than the latter being a property of properties), and yet maintain that the distinction between fundamental and derived quantities is valid and meaningful.

We may recognise the pattern of the argument of our critics: arguments that apply to the mathematics of the situation, are used to establish truths about the physics. Because the numerical systems we employ in physics involve mathematical representations where a quantity may be defined by more than one numerical assignment function, choice and economy permit the streamlining of our methods of representing a large number of physical quantities. As a result certain quantities, according to our choices, may be given a lesser status, including certain fundamental ones (represented instead by derived quantities via an available law). This argument is then carried over from the numerical systems we employ to apply to the empirical systems upon which the representations are based. This argument by transference is not legitimate, since it assumes an identity has been established between a quantity that is capable of being measured fundamentally and by derived means, which is the very point under discussion. Even if, like Dingle (1950), we reject a realist foundation, we must recognise that the identity of a quantity obtained from different measurement procedures is an empirical fact, and as such the distinct nature of a fundamental quantity cannot be brushed aside simply by the choice of particular mathematical representations.

Non-standard representations

The distinction between fundamental and derived quantities is also under threat from non-standard representations of the numerical assignments given to measured quantities. Such non-standard representations need not be far-fetched, as is the case for Ellis' *dinches*, nor pathological.

Consider the measurement of resistance for resistors wired in parallel (or series connected capacitors). The wiring together of additional resistors can be taken to correspond to the combination operation that characterises an extensive measurement system. We can assign values to the resistors A and B of a and b respectively i.e. $f(\mathrm{A}) = a$, $f(\mathrm{B}) = b$, and define

$$1/f\ (\mathrm{O(A,B)}) = 1/a + 1/b$$

The value of B in terms of some combination of A's could be determined by a Wheatstone Bridge arrangement. This mathematical representation will not lead to difficulties and the values assigned to the resistance of particular objects will be consistent with those obtained from the more customary series-combination of resistors. The reciprocal of resistance is conductance, and the combination operation for conductance and its mathematical representation would be addition. Resistance defined by the parallel combination operation however, would not accord with the standard representation of the combination operation by addition.[24] If we restricted our definition of fundamental measurement to those extensive systems which involved additive quantities, resistance (assuming we were not aware of the series combination of resistors) defined by parallel combinations would be a derived measurement. This suggests that we should adopt less stringent requirements with regard to the mathematical representation of the combination operation, but new problems will arise if we do so.

In his discussion of the representation and uniqueness theorems for measuring systems, Suppes restricted his analysis to non-deviant empirical systems and combination operations. In discussing representations of the combination operation other than addition, such as exponentiation (which gives rise to power rather than similarity transformations between scales), he also considered only tidy, well behaved alternatives. The reason is that a more general account is hard to provide:

> The first fundamental problem of measurement may be cast as the problem of showing that *any empirical relational system that purports to measure (by a simple number) a given property of the elements in the domain of the system is isomorphic (or possibly homomorphic) to an appropriately chosen numerical relational system* ... The second aspect of the representation problem needing amplification concerns the phrase "appropriately chosen numerical relational system" which appears in the last statement of the representation problem. The representation problem is not adequately solved if the isomorphism is

established between a given empirical system and a numerical system employing unnatural or "pathological" relations. In fact, if the empirical system is finite or denumerable (i.e. has a finite or denumerable domain) some numerical system can always be found that is isomorphic to it. It is of no great consequence therefore merely to exhibit some numerical system that is isomorphic to an empirical system. It is of value, however, to exhibit a numerical system that is not only isomorphic to an empirical system but employs certain simple and familiar relations as well. A complete or precise categorization of the intuitively desirable relations is unfortunately somewhat elusive, so for this reason the statement of the representation problem refers mainly to an "appropriately chosen" numerical system.(Suppes 1963 pp. 7,8)

Both Dingle[25] and Suppes did not require that a fundamentally measurable quantity satisfy the axioms for extensive measurement. We can imagine constructing bizarre combination operations for a set of objects, which satisfy the axioms given for extensive systems, that give rise to non-standard representations involving homomorphic numerical systems (essentially, any unique assignment of numbers to the objects would do). Notionally, at least, these would count as fundamental measurements. This could be done generally for derived quantities with suitable, exotic operations and non-standard assignments. Given the homomorphic mapping to empirical systems that is established by the representation theorem, we could claim that the quantities arising in this representation have reference, and are as well grounded philosophically as Campbell's more familiar A quantities. This would undermine the distinction we have employed throughout the taxonomy of constants presented.

The solution lies in the definition of a boundary which adequately delineates acceptable alternative representations. Campbell investigated this question explicitly, and suggested a way forward: we may allow only those alternative representations which are isomorphic to the standard additive arithmetical representation.

Consider a pair of scales $\langle \Psi, \mathfrak{R}, f \rangle$ and $\langle \Psi', \mathfrak{R}, f' \rangle$ where $\Psi = \langle A, \leq_x, \oplus_x \rangle$ and $\Psi' = \langle A, \leq_x, \oplus_x' \rangle$, and where $\oplus_x$ is an alternative fundamental measuring operation and where $\oplus_x'$ is the customary fundamental measuring operation, then we require

$$f'(A_1 \oplus_x' A_2) \quad = \quad f'(A_1) \quad + \quad f'(A_2)$$

where

$$f'(A_1) \quad = \quad \phi(f(A_1)).$$

If we define

$$\xi(f(A_1), f(A_2)) \quad \equiv \quad f(A_1 \oplus_x' A_2)$$

then

$$f'(A_1 \oplus_x' A_2) = \phi(f(A_1 \oplus_x' A_2)) = \phi(\xi(f(A_1), f(A_2)))$$

and the condition we seek is

$$\phi(\xi(f(A_1), f(A_2))) = f'(A_1) + f'(A_2)$$

If

$$f(A_1) = x \qquad f(A_2) = y$$

the condition is

$$\phi(\xi(x, y)) = \phi(x) + \phi(y)$$

Ellis' example of dinches for instance satisfies this requirement if

$$\phi(x) = x^2 \qquad \xi(x, y) = \surd(x^2 + y^2)$$

Similarly, we can accommodate relativistic velocities if

$$\phi(x) = \log((1 + (x / c))/(1 - (x / c)))$$

$$\xi(x, y) = (x + y)/(1 + (xy / c^2))$$

Since the derivative of ϕ in these cases is positive (i.e. ϕ is monotonic increasing) the order of A is preserved under the transformation of scale. Generally, we do not consider that we are measuring different quantities on the two scales: the equality relation for the two procedures is the same, which means that in the case of length, for instance, two equal lengths measured by one procedure, are also equal according to the second procedure, since the quantity measured by the two procedures is the same.

If we consider measuring capacitance using series and parallel combination operations, we may seek to provide a scale transformation ϕ for the single quantity capacitance measured by the two procedures on two scales. Thus we may establish

$$\phi(x) = 1/x \qquad \xi(x, y) = xy/(x + y)$$

but here the derivative of ϕ is negative, and the transformation from one scale to the other reverses the ordering. In the case of resistance and conductance, Campbell rejected this particular transformation (Campbell 1920 p292), and maintained that resistance and conductance were two distinct quantities, because of the order reversal. The case of capacitance suggests that he was wrong to do so, for although the order is reversed, the ordering is preserved.[26]

We now have the means to define which alternative representations are acceptable. Our definition accommodates both Ellis' and more familiar reciprocal quantities in physics. Our approach allows fundamental measurement scales with variable but well-defined and well-behaved metrics (as best seen in the relativistic velocity example). In each instance, there is an alternative combination operation that gives rise to the non-additive aspects of the representation.

It may seem that our result conflicts with the uniqueness of isomorphic ratio scales to the level of a similarity transformation. This is not in fact the case, since the isomorphism so established related numerical systems corresponding to an empirical system comprising a single common combination operation $\oplus_x'$. Here we require the representations associated with two empirical systems involving two different operations $\oplus_x'$ and $\oplus_x$, to be isomorphic. As a result, some of the permitted scales will be ordinal scales, which do not preserve ratios (and therefore do not support a similarity transformation), but which have other structural features reflecting the well-defined nature of their metric.[27]

It may be argued that to draw the line here is arbitrary, and that pathological representations should not be ruled out. This largesse does violence, however, to even the most minimal accounts of measurement. Even Dingle required a 'precisely specified operation' for measurement to occur. We rule out the pathological on the grounds that they are not well defined, and any notion of *quantity* must involve more than the arbitrary assignment of numbers to objects. By relying upon the transformation constraints specified for alternative procedures, we are thus able to reject the general threat posed to the distinction between fundamental and derived quantities by the possibility of alternative representations.

Boltzmann's constant

At first sight, Boltzmann's constant seems not to fit the schema of primitive derived constants because k does not appear to relate two fundamental extensive quantities. W, the number of possible final states of lowest entropy, is not additive: when we combine two systems with values of W of W_1 and W_2, we do not obtain a system with value $W_1 + W_2$ but with value $W_1 W_2$. The appearance of a logarithmn in the equation for k appears to make the situation worse.

In fact, this is an example of the use of a non-standard alternative representation, which is not additive, but which is isomorphic to the standard representation. If we were to measure the quantity W on a scale defined by transforming the original scale in the following way

$$\phi(x) \quad = \quad \log(x)$$

and where the representation of the original combination operation is given by

$$f\,(A_1 \oplus_x A_2) \quad = \quad f\,(A_1)\, f\,(A_2) \;=\; x\,y$$

then the combination $(A_1 \oplus_x A_2)$ will be represented on the new scale by

$$\begin{aligned} \phi(f\,(A_1 \oplus_x A_2)) &= \phi(x\,y) \;=\; \log(x\,y) \\ &= \log(x) + \log(y) \\ &= \phi(f(A_1)) + \phi(f(A_2)) \end{aligned}$$

Since the order is preserved and the new system is isomorphic to the old, we may assert that the new scale measures the same quantity. In other words, the new scale will have a standard additive interpretation. Hence, if W is measured on this scale, the combination operation will be additve and k will link the quantities entropy $[S]$ and disorder, which is captured by $[W]$, similar to the way that h links energy and period. Convention dictates, however, that we customarily write

$$S \quad = \quad k\,W' \quad \text{where} \quad W \quad = \quad \log W'$$

We may also note that these quantities strictly relate to the properties of groups of objects, whereas the quantities associated with the other primitive derived constants are the quantities of individual objects.

Summary

In this chapter, we have proposed a taxonomy of constants which highlights their ontological significance. Many constants are only of significance for classificatory or computational reasons, or on the grounds of conciseness. The most primitive constants fall into two categories: the first most basic category identifies constants as the values of the system-independent parameters which characterise the objects in a fundamental system of extensive measurement; the second category identifies another category of constants as the values of the system-independent parameters in various derived systems of measurement. Constants of the first group relate to the properties of elementary objects; of the the second, to the coupling properties of interactions and fields.

This taxonomy relies heavily upon the distinction between fundamental and derived quantities. Criticisms can be levelled against the way the distinction confers greater ontological significance on fundamental quantities. The possibility of measuring all quantities by derived means, and the existence of alternative representations suggest that derived and fundamental quantities should be accorded equal status (that hitherto given to derived quantities). It may then be argued (Chapter Four), that this status is entirely conventional.

These critical arguments fail to distinguish, however, between aspects of the numerical systems used to represent quantities, and aspects of the empirical systems in which the quantities are embedded. The fact that certain quantities can be measured fundamentally, is an empirical finding about the world logically independent of the way we chose to represent them. That measurement by fundamental means entails the existence of a standard object, supports our account that the primitive object-related constants (at least) are substantive, not conventional. Alternative representations can be accommodated within our account provided they lead to isomorphic measurement structures, and need not give rise to a notion of fundamental measurement that is so broad as to undermine its significance relative to derived measurement.

Notes

1 Rossini (1974) has provided an historical summary of the compilations of the fundamental physical constants, and the work of Cohen and Taylor, included in Kaye and Laby, may be considered definitive.

2 We can also manipulate values by inconsistent use of scale factors, and by using alternative scales which do not preserve absolutely relative magnitudes e.g. dinches.

3 Avogadro's number is also the reciprocal of the sum of the masses of the electron and proton, and hence may be held to be a composite constant

4 As opposed to derived magnitudes.

5 Dingle and Focken made a similar distinction when they split physical equations into those that express definitions and those that express experimentally established physical relations: the former give rise to defined, the latter to derived measurements.

6 We note with Campbell, that we could, in fact, choose to use different scales for the two instances, even though they are instances of the same quantity. We might also chose a derived scale and a fundamental scale for the same quantity.

7 For instance, if we use non-standard representations, such as dinches, the numerical value of relative magnitudes change. Rather than possessing single-values, relative magnitudes are dependent upon the choices of scales, in particular the choice of the principle of correlation.

8 Ellis (1966 p 141).

9 The conservation of relative magnitudes under changes of scale (where all the scales share the same principle of correlation) gives rise to the concepts of dimensions and dimensional homogeneity.

10 Standard form i.e. a monomial function is required if the law is to be invariant under a change of scale (similarity transformation).

11 We may set k = 1, r as opposed to k = 1, r+1 without loss of generality.

12 These conditions arise from the requirement that the highest rank determinant associated with the solution of these equations is non-zero.

13 This result contradicts Palacios' findings. He stated (Palacios 1964 p. 43) *contrary to what holds for null vectors, quantities of zero dimension have great significance in physics. First, if a quantity has zero dimension in one basis, then it has zero dimension in all other bases, even in the insufficient ones.* This discrepancy is explained by the fact that we have not obtained α as the dimensionless Π product of a set of laws governing atomic phenomena. Had we done so, and had we investigated the representations of the laws in various vector spaces, which we systematically collapse, we would have obtained Palacios' result because of the implicit, if not explicit, use of $x=ct$ in our derivation i.e. [L] = [T].

14 Throughout this chapter we speak of dimensions in traditional terms regarding them as coded descriptions of the numerical tranformations that ensue from changes of unit amongst reference quantities. In Chapter 4 we discuss a separate concept of dimension arising from the structure of empirical systems of objects and operations. The fact that certain quantities are dimensionless in terms of this new concept may be considered a significant empirical finding.

15 Campbell was aware of these transformations. In discussing ρ as a primary variable in the law $\rho = mV$, he observed: *And just as the fundamental magnitude volume has been changed into something very like a derived magnitude, so the derived magnitude density has been changed into something very like a fundamental magnitude. For by refusing to realise a unit of volume, we have converted the statement that the standard substance has unit density from a result of experimental measurement into a definition that cannot be proved or disproved. The selection of a certain substance as possessing unit density is precisely analogous to the selection of a certain body as possessing mass. But again it must be remembered that the*

resemblance is not complete. the important fact always remains that volume can and density cannot be measured in terms of the unit by a fundamental process; unless volume could be measured as volume, the law defining density could never be established; while density can never be measured as density, but only by measuring something that is not density (1920 p. 381).

16 To be fair to Dingle, he defined fundamental measurement to be measurement where the measure of a quantity is unaffected by changes in the assignment of units to any other quantity i.e. representationally. Dingle would therefore agree that specific measurement is fundamental measurement, even though no suitable extensive operation existed. Thus Dingle did not speak of what we mean by fundamental measurement when he said the distinction between fundamental and derived measurement was conventional, and if we always allow the possibility of specific measurement to substitute for derived measurement, his statement makes sense (according to his definitions). We may still legitimately ask, however, why his definition of fundamental measurement was not grounded in extensive operations.

17 In his earlier work (1920), Campbell established a closer correspondence between qualities on the one hand, and, on the other hand, the satisfaction or the non-satisfaction of the axioms of extensive measurement: *We feel that the amount of substance in a body is something which is increased by combining two bodies, while the properties of the substance are something which are not changed at all by any combination of two similar bodies; accordingly we feel that properties for which a process of addition can be found which satisfies the first law of addition represent the amount of some kind of substance, while those for which the law is always false represent the quality of a substance, In general we desire to be able to place a property in one or other of these two classes, either the class of amounts or quantities of substance, or the class of qualities of substance. Accordingly, if we find a property such that no process of addition can be found which fulfils all those laws, so that the property is excluded from one class, we always try so to define the property so that it falls into the other class, inclusion in which implies that 1+1 = 1. It is not mere accident that there is a large class of physical properties of which this proposition is true; besides density, there are viscosity, solubility, dielectric constant and a host of others; they are all the result of deliberate intention; they have been deliberately defined so that they are the same for any combination of similar bodies as for the component bodies.*

18 Russell distinguished similarly between extensive properties, where equality and sum may be defined, and intensive properties where equality and inequality only are possible.

19 Campbell took these latter to be those quantities which could be measured by fundamental means.

20 Bunge's views in fact seem a little inconsistent in that he considers a number of magnitudes such as field strengths, spin, and strangeness to be directly referential, but not directly measurable. What is the difference, one may ask, between spin and *h*, given both are defined by equation?

21 In claiming there is a new standard object we are implicitly following Campbell in attributing some type of ontological status to the constant (i.e. scale factor) involved in the new measurement system.

22 Determining a factor means choosing a standard object and assigning a numerical value to it.

23 Note, however, that it would nonetheless be possible to define the standard object and numerical assignment for either *x* or *t* if standards assignments had already been made for *c* and *t* or *x* (respectively). This is the *indirect* assignment of a standard object to x or t, but is without significance, given that *c* in principle cannot logically be assigned an object or numeral before *x* and *t* because it is a derived, not a fundamental, quantity.

24 Campbell himself recognised that conductance was fundamentally measurable in Campbell (1942b p. 763).

25 Dingle said: *A measurement is any precisely specified operation that yields a number* (1950 p. 11). Given the minimality of this definition, it might be objected that even a change in scale-factor amounts to a change in operation, and therefore gives rise to a different quantity.

26 Campbell was not entirely consistent on this point. He remarked, for instance: *It may be noted that it would make little difference if F ' (a) were always negative in place of positive; the order of F (a) would then be the inverse of the order of a: but we regard two magnitudes as practically the same if the order of one is simply the inverse of the order of the other: such pairs of magnitudes are resistance, and conductance, or density and specific volume...accordingly in what follows no distinction will be made between a derived magnitude and its reciprocal; both will be called the same derived magnitude* (Campbell 1920 p. 366). See also Campbell 1928 pp. 10 and 26.

27 Logarithmic scales, for instance, always attribute the same interval to a doubling, or tripling etc. of a given value.

4 Constants, conventionality and dimensions

Introduction

In the previous chapter, we identified a group of primitive constants, some obtained by fundamental measurement, some by derived means.

Those primitive constants, such as the mass and the charge of an electron, which are fundamentally measurable are associated with certain physical objects which may function as standard elements in a fundamental system of measurement as discussed in Chapter 2. We have defended this account of the status of *fundamentally* measured constants against operationalist attacks.

Primitive *derived* constants, which we will examine in this chapter, are not similarly associated with objects. Lacking the means thereby to hook into the fabric of the physical world, primitive derived constants such as Planck's constant, the speed of light and the gravitational constant have been considered by some philosophers to be of little ontological significance, arising merely as a consequence of the choices of representation we have made in physics.

We will challenge this view, and analyse in detail the accounts of the dimensions of quantities which give rise to it. We shall be concerned, in particular, to identify those elements of the mathematical representation of scientific laws, which are features of the representation alone, and which do not mirror structural aspects of the physical world.

Synopsis of chapter

The nature and history of the conventionalist case is reviewed, and the implications for the account of constants which has been proposed, are summarised.

Using the results of linear algebra and of vector spaces, the methods of dimensional analysis, in particular Buckingham's Π theorem, which give rise to the conventionalist case, are analysed. The use of different permitted reference quantities to change dimensional formulae, and to increase or reduce the number of derived dimensional constants is considered in detail.

From a technical standpoint, dimensional manipulation will not eliminate the use of all significant dimensioned derived quantities, and any reduction in the number of primitive derived constants, can only be achieved by a reduction in the adequacy of the representational system chosen.

It is argued that the conventionality that pertains to the representation of measured quantities, does not carry over to the empirical systems which give rise to those quantities. Much confusion has arisen in the discussion of dimensions from the failure to distinguish the empirical and representational aspects of the situation.

To complete the account, an empirical notion of dimension is explicated, to supplement the notion of dimension which arises from representational considerations alone. Using this empirical footing, we are able to provide a satisfactory account of the status of primitive derived constants, which is not conventionalist, and which to a large degree coincides with the notions of experimental physicists and cosmologists.

The conventionalist case

Campbell, Bridgman and Ellis identified a strong measure of convention[1] in the choice of the quantities we use to anchor our systems of measurement, scales and units (i.e. scale names and dimensions). Campbell saw this as a choice *amongst* the fundamental A magnitudes which we select in our most basic physical laws, and which are used to define the dimensions of other quantities:

> It is therefore entirely misleading to assert that any magnitude has definitely and uniquely any specified dimensions. It is only permissible to assert that it has specified dimensions in terms of a specified complete set of standard magnitudes or, more generally, that the assignment of dimensions to a specified class of magnitudes (which has to be selected with care) fixes the dimensions of all other magnitudes. Yet we find that our text-books assign in perfect unanimity definite dimensions to some magnitudes and never suggest that this assignment is not unique; for example, all expositions agree in giving to volume the dimensions 3 in terms of length and 0 in terms of all other magnitudes. What are we to make of such statements ? I see no alternative but to reject them as simply false in spite of their weight of authority. (Campbell 1928 p. 125)

> The choice of standard magnitudes is much wider than is sometimes suggested. There is no special virtue in the usual choice of mass, length and time. All the conclusions that follow by dimensional analysis when these three are chosen would follow equally if many other sets of three standards were chosen; thus force, volume and acceleration would serve equally well as standards. Nor is the limitation to three standards necessary or even desirable; the method would have a wider scope if there were more standards. (Campbell 1928 p. 255)

Along similar lines Bridgman stated:

> It is particularly to be emphasized that the dimensions of a primary quantity as defined above have no absolute significance whatever, but are defined merely with respect to that aspect of the rules of operation by which we obtain the measuring numbers associated with the physical phenomenon. (Bridgman 1931 p. 23)[2]

> It is by many considered that a dimensional formula has some esoteric significance connected with the "ultimate nature" of an object, and that we are in some way getting at the ultimate nature of things in writing their dimensional formulas....To this view it is repugnant that there should be two dimensional formulas for the same physical quantity. Often a reconciliation is sought by the introduction of so-called suppressed dimensions. Such speculations have been particularly fashionable with regard to the nature of the ether, but so far as I know, no physical discovery has ever followed such speculations; we should not expect it if the view above is correct. (Bridgman 1931 p. 24)

Ellis described the same notions in terms of the *centrality* of our scale systems: we can make our systems more or less centred depending upon the number of quantities which are chosen to be measured on a family of similar independent scales, characterised by a simple unit name, which Ellis termed a *dimension*. In the limit, Ellis suggested we could have single-centred scale systems.

There is a difference, however, between the views of Campbell, who placed the conventionality in the choice made between alternative sets of fundamental quantities, and Ellis, Dingle and others, who considered it a conventional matter as to which quantities in a series of equations are regarded as fundamental and which are derived.[3]

For the purposes of dimensional analysis, both fundamental and derived quantities can be handled and manipulated mathematically in the same way. Since any fundamentally measured quantity can also be measured by derived means, it is then an easy step to assume that whether a variable in an equation is fundamental or derived, is entirely a matter of choice.

In fact, the reader will recall from Chapter 2 that Campbell clearly distinguished between the roles of individual variables in an equation (some are held to be *primary*, others are held to be *secondary*), as well as between the methods that gave rise to the measurement of the quantity (*fundamental* or *derived*). Since scientists typically use certain fundamental quantities as the primary variables in equations, looseness of language has encouraged authors such as Dingle (1942a) and Focken (1953) to blur these distinctions and to assert that it is a matter of convention as to which quantities are derived and which are fundamental.[4]

> (4) Magnitudes are of two kinds - *fundamental* and *derived*. A fundamental magnitude is one whose value is unaltered by any change in the process of measurement, or in the chosen unit, of any physical quantity other than the one to which it refers. A derived magnitude is one whose value is in general altered by such a change.

> (5) The number of fundamental magnitudes is arbitrary. (Dingle 1942a p. 322)[5]

As we have seen, it is a matter of fact, which quantities are capable of measurement by fundamental means (and hence how many fundamental quantities there are), and which of measurement by derived means. In any particular instance, we may choose to measure a particular quantity in a certain way, if more than one method is possible, but this choice does not imply that certain quantities, which are not capable of being fundamentally measured, can be made so by convention.[6] The number of fundamental quantities is not arbitrary; the number of primary quantities is.[7]

More properly, we should state that, where we are concerned with dimensional formulae, which quantities are primary and which are secondary, is a matter of convention. In most circumstances, however, no confusion will arise in employing the term *fundamental* quantity (when in fact we mean a particular quantity has been chosen as a *primary* variable in the equations which we are using to establish the dimensional formulae of other secondary variables), but where it may, we will use the more modern terminology of Isaacson and Isaacson (1975), and will talk of *reference* quantities.[8]

The historic debate

If we consider a simple equation such as that representing Newton's second law

$$f = ma$$

we may take *force* to be a fundamental or a derived quantity in this equation. If we choose the latter, we customarily, assign the dimensions [MLT^{-2}] to force; if we choose the former, then we would consider force to have the dimension [F], and we would be obliged to introduce an additional constant into the above equation to ensure dimensional homogeneity ($[k] = [F][T^2][L^{-1}][M^{-1}]$).

The question naturally arises as to whether the dimensions we have given belong to the quantity "force" as it arises in Newton's second law, or whether they belong merely to the equation representing Newton's second law. Realists might further inquire as to which were the true or real dimensions of force. If we review the main physical and philosophical journals between 1880 and 1945, we will find many discussions of these questions, in particular with respect to the nature of electromagnetic quantities.

Two main positions developed: on one side it was maintained that the dimensions of a physical quantity were a unique and intrinsic property of that quantity. The view is lucidly put forward by Tolman (1917):

> The fact that it has become usual to pick out the units for derived quantities in the way indicated has sometimes led to an unfortunate confusion as to the real significance of dimensional formulae. Thus there has grown up the practice of speaking of the dimensions

of a unit when what is really intended is the dimensions of the quantity involved. It certainly seems best, however, to use the dimensional formula of a quantity as a shorthand restatement of its definition in terms of the fundamental kinds of quantity. The dimensional formula is thus a symbol for the physical nature of the derived quantity and a recapitulation of the necessary relation between different kinds of quantity rather than the statement of a relation between units which we find convenient. (Tolman 1917 p. 249)

More recently Douglas expressed similar views:

> The dimensions of a body, or of a system, are the measurable properties which can be used to describe its physical state ... Dimensions are properties which can be measured, and units are the standard elements in terms of which these dimensions may be measured numerically to describe quantitatively a given situation. (Douglas 1969)

According to these views, in which a dimensional formula for a quantity might be taken to be some sort of genetic code or chemical formula for the quantity, no two quantities should have the same dimensions, and no quantity should have more than one dimensional formula (Lanchester1936). It was argued that only if the dimensions of quantities possessed this significance, could equations in physics be held to be meaningful.

The requirement for dimensional homogeneity in the equations of physics, first enunciated by Fourier (1822), but echoing earlier thoughts found in Newton and Galileo, was a requirement that we compare like with like.

> It should be noted that each physical quantity, known or unknown, possesses a dimension proper to itself and that the terms in an equation cannot be compared one with another unless they possess the same dimensional exponent. (Fourier 1822 §160)[9]

Without such a constraint, the equations of physics could be likened to nonsensical equations such as "2 dogs + 4 hens = 6 boats". As Moon and Spencer (1949) remarked:

> A basic principle of dimension theory, stated by Fourier in 1822 and by Maxwell in 1863, is the principle of *dimensional homogeneity*: if two terms in an equation of physics have the same dimensions, they can be added. But no one seems to have remarked that this law cannot possibly hold universally unless there is a 1:1 correspondence between designation symbol and concept. In the l, m, t system, the principle holds sometimes but not always; and it is these exceptions that make traditional dimensional theory so treacherous and unsatisfactory a tool. (Moon and Spencer 1949 p. 173)[10]

The alternative point of view held that dimensions were encoded description of the changes required in computation which arise when the unit of measurement of a primary quantity is changed. This view was forcefully developed in the seminal work on electromagnetism by Clerk Maxwell (1892), and was made yet more explicit by Williams (1892):

The dimensional formula of a physical quantity expresses the numerical dependence of the unit of that quantity upon the fundamental and secondary units from which it is derived, and the indices of the various units in the formula are termed the *dimensions* of the quantity with respect to those units. When used in this very restricted sense, the formulae only indicate numerical relations between the various units. (Williams 1892 p. 237)

More recently, Campbell, Focken, Duncanson, Duncan and Dalzell have expressed the same view.[11] As we have discussed, Ellis (1966) also adopted a similar position: dimensions are held to be the name of a class of scales defined by an equivalence relation ("shares the same transformation function as") generated by one or more similarity transformations which relate the numerical assignments that arise according to the choice of different member scales from the family of central scales at the centre of our measurement system. This means the scales share units with the same mathematical monomial structure, and the units for different scales from the same class may be exchanged for each other by a monomial function of the scale factors defined by the similarity transformations that relate to the choice of different individual versions of the central scales at the centre of our measurement system to each other. Mathematically, dimensions are then composite similarity functions to transform between complex scales defined in terms of particular choices of central scales. In short, this is a more sophisticated version of the unit view of Williams.

Under the "unit-transformation" view of dimensions, the homogeneity of equations was taken to be an operational constraint imposed by our need to be able to derive consistent mathematical results independent of the choice of a particular set of units made by any given group of scientists. The dimensionality of quantities themselves, as opposed to that of units of measurement, was regarded as a piece of metaphysical humbug. As Planck succinctly put it:

To inquire into the 'real' dimension of a quantity has no more meaning than to inquire into the 'real' name of an object. Many unfruitful controversies in physical literature, particularly those concerning the electromagnetic system of measurement, would have been avoided, had this circumstance always been properly appreciated. (Planck 1916 p. 46)

Two particular observations lent weight to the conventionalist cause. First, there are clearly a number of instances where physical quantities are accorded the same dimensional formula (irrespective of whether this is metaphysical code or shorthand for various unit transformations). A well known example is torque and energy, which are both traditionally given the dimensions $L^2 M T^{-2}$.[12] This specific instance can be resolved by a finer dimensional specification involving vector lengths L_x L_y L_z as shown by Huntley (1952) and others, but other quantities continue to share the same dimensional formula (e.g. potential and kinetic energy).

Second, it is possible to show that workable physics may be obtained from a variety of different choices of reference quantities in which dimensional formulae are expressed, depending upon the choice of the defining equations for derived quantities.

Maxwell (1892), for instance, developed dimensional formulae for all electromagnetic quantities in terms of the classical reference quantities for mechanics: mass, length and time. This was, no doubt, because he believed in an ultimate mechanical explanation of all phenomena, as was reflected in the prevalence of ether theories at the turn of the century. Unfortunately, Maxwell's choice resulted in the confusing dual systems of electrostatic and electromagnetic units. Other choices of reference quantities, to include for instance charge or magnetic monopoles, give rise to different systems of units, such as the Gaussian and Heaviside-Lorentz systems (see Dresser 1971). Under the system developed by Giorgi, for instance, it was possible through the suitable choice of values for the dielectric and permeability constants of empty space, to measure both electomagnetic and electrostatic quantities in terms of the defined units of the SI system.

In the lengthy debates as to the most appropriate choice of reference quantities, it became clear that both the number and identity of the reference quantities could be changed, provided consistent units, which did not give rise to spurious additional scale factors, and the number and values of constants were suitably specified (discussed in greater detail later). For instance, Bridgman wrote:

> Many persons will object to the dimensional formulas given for these electrostatic quantities on the ground that we arbitrarily put the dielectric constant of empty space equal to unity, whereas we know nothing about its nature, and therefore have suppressed certain dimensions which are essential to a complete statement of the problem. This point of view will of course not be disturbing to the reader of this exposition, who has come to see that there is nothing absolute about dimensions, but that they may be anything consistent with a set of definitions which agree with the experimental facts. (Bridgman 1931 p. 78)

The same conclusion was also reached with regard to thermodynamic quantities, where a similar debate had taken place as to whether the appropriate set of reference quantities were mechanical only or included temperature, heat or both.

A number of authors took it upon themselves to advocate the choice of one particular set of reference quantities over another. Tolman (1917), for instance argued that there were five necessary and sufficient reference quantities in physics (length, time interval, mass, quantity of electric charge and entropy), corresponding to the five different types of concept (space, time, matter, electricity, and "degree of run-down-ness") which characterise physics. Interestingly, Tolman explicitly required the reference quantities to be extensive, insisting, for instance, upon the choice of entropy as a reference quantity, rather than the more usual choice of temperature.

As an alternative, Duncanson (1940) recommended four quantities, (mass, length, time and charge) because an electrical quantity was required to obtain a fully adequate solution of the laws of electromagnetism, and since it was not possible to measure or define a single, individual charge (as opposed to, say, a pair of charges), charge was the logical choice as a fourth "indefinable" quantity.

Burniston Brown (1941), maintained, on the other hand, that a system with only the two reference quantites of length and time was to be preferred because the process by which numbers are introduced as symbols for certain aspects of nature, always involves the measurement of a length and of a time (using pointers on dials etc.).

The resolution of these conflicting claims was provided by Dingle (1942a), who maintained a strict operational interpretation of measurement. He explained how the choice between competing dimensional systems was a matter of convention, and how in any particular instance, there are probably practical and experimental reasons for making particular choices. Dingle's position was closely aligned with that of Bridgman, a pioneer of dimensional analysis, who similarly maintained a pragmatic attitude to the question.

Both Bridgman and Campbell recognised the conventional aspect of dimensional allocations dependent upon the choice of equation for each derived quantity, but it was left to Dingle to investigate the consequences of extreme positions, where at one end, all quantities are reference quantities, and at the other, we only have one reference quantity.

Where we proliferate reference quantities and dimensions, we are obliged to introduce a very large number of new dimensional constants each discovered by experiment, essentially one for each quantity previously held to be derived. While we may still obtain useful numerical results and predictions from the equations of physics, it is cumbersome in the extreme to do so.

If we reduce the set of reference quantities to only one, a large number of degeneracies arise in the solutions of equations because quantities which are normally dimensionally distinct are given the same mathematical representation. The example of a pendulum given later will make this clear. A single-reference system, while manifestly simple for calculation, lacks the rich descriptive complexity of a system with a greater number of reference quantities.

> The net result of these considerations, then, is that if we wish to give the greatest scope of usefulness to the principle of dimensional homegeneity, we must choose sufficient fundamental[13] magnitudes to prevent two or more magnitudes from having the same dimensions, but not so many that indeterminable "constants of nature" are forced into our equations. (Dingle 1942a p. 338)

Dingle concluded that for most purposes, a system with three, four or five reference quantities, met the computational and descriptive needs of physicists, but there is no logical precedence of any given system over another. The sting was thereby drawn from the various competing accounts of reference quantities: each account is acceptable, representing a particular convention. Dingle's views were well articulated, coincided with the views of a number of physicists who shared an operationalist philosophy, and have held sway virtually unchallenged since he expounded them. Ellis (1966) clearly shared the same philosophical assumptions.

Let us accept the broad thrust of the conventionalist platform for the moment, and consider how such views impinge upon the number and nature of the fundamental constants we have identified.

Conventional dimensions and constants

First, let us explain what is meant by conventionalism.

In his book Space and Time, Reichendach distinguished between definitions which served to reduce one concept to other concepts, and *coordinative definitions* which relate concepts to objects.

> Defining usually means reducing a concept to other concepts. In physics, as in other fields of inquiry, wide use is made of this procedure. There is a second kind of definition, however, which is also employed and which derives from the fact that physics, in contradistinction to mathematics, deals with real objects. Physical knowledge is characterized by the fact that concepts are not only defined by other concepts, but are also coordinated to real objects. This coordination cannot be replaced by an explanation of meanings, it simply states that *this concept* is coordinated to *this particular thing*. In general this coordination is not arbitrary... But certain preliminary coordinations must be determined before the method of coordination can be carried through any further; these first coordinations are therefore definitions which we shall call *coordinative definitions*. They are *arbitrary*, like all definitions; on their choice depends the conceptual system which develops with the progress of science. (Reichenbach 1958 p. 14)

Reichenbach reasoned that the principle of the distant congruence of measuring rods was a matter of definition, and that consequently the determination of the geometry of a physical space depended upon a preceding coordinative definition. Poincaré had likewise argued that no matter what observational facts are found, the physicist is free to ascribe to physical space any one of the mathematically possible geometrical structures, provided she makes suitable adjustments in the laws of mechanics and optics and consequently in the rules for measuring. The choice of geometry and physics seemed to be a matter of convention with no possibility of establishing the truth of one set of conventions over another (unless we posit unknowable facts, which is unlikely to be an acceptable philosophical premiss). The conventions involved need not be trivial semantic equivalents, as the substantive debate concerning the conventionality of distant simultaneity in special relativity attests, but the implication is that the choice of convention is without ontological significance.

Within the framework we have developed, we may understand the choice of representation of an empirical system to be a choice of co-ordinative definition, and hence to be a matter of convention. This choice might be a trivial one (as, for instance, in the selection of a standard object), or a significant one, as in the case of alternative principles of correlation such as dinches, or alternative sets of reference quantities. It is important to distinguish, however, between choices in the way we choose to represent an empirical system, and choices between equivalent empirical systems which are not isomorphic, and which provide incompatible but epistemologically equal accounts of the world. The latter we hold to be a case of underdetermination. In the arguments that follow, our intention will be to establish that the existence of alternative empirical systems which define primitive derived constants, gives rise to a case of underdetermination which is not damaged by the fact that alternative conventional choices exist for the representation of these primitive derived constants.

Given the possibility of conventional choices in the coordinative definitions of physics, a number of philosophers of science have developed a conventionalist view of many aspects of science. Conventionalism is the doctrine which asserts that there are alternative, inconsistent accounts of the physical world which are equally well grounded in workable physics, and equally compatible with all available empirical evidence. If a choice is to be made between alternative accounts this can only be done by fiat or by some methodological or pragmatic principle: in the absence of such guiding constraints, the accounts themselves do not provide the means whereby we are able to discriminate between them.

In the particular context we are discussing, conventionalism asserts that there are alternative dimensional formulae for physical quantities, that we have no *a priori* ground for choosing one formula over another, and that the formulae lack any absolute significance.

The conventionalist attack is in principle damaging in four ways to the account of primitive derived constants we have provided.

First, the dimensions of any given derived constant are not fixed. If we choose a different set of reference quantities, or a different set of equations to define derived quantities, then the dimensions of a derived constant will change.

Second, individual derived constants can be eliminated through manipulation of the number of reference quantities.

Third, the reduction of the reference basis to a single quantity, suggests that the number and significance of primitive derived constants will be reduced en bloque. Perhaps there will only remain a single arbitrary constant associated with the single reference quantity.

Finally, the conventionalist approach clearly conflicts with any account that attributes a substantive, non-operational notion to constants, especially primitive derived constants.

To see that such a challenge is not a fiction, we need only cite the work of Lewis (1921):

> A new empirical law usually involves one or more constants, and if the law appears to be general and fundamental these constants are called constants of nature. The discovery of every such constant is indeed a milestone in the progress of science. Nevertheless, to call these quantities natural constants is a characteristically human attempt to shift responsibility.

> Adopting an old-fashioned phraseology, there is nothing nature abhors more than an arbitrary number which possesses no intrinsic meaning ... If we accept the view that is set forth in this paper, and consider every physical constant indicates some flaw in our scientific system, it becomes as useful a scientific service to eliminate them as to discover them. (Lewis 1921 p. 266)

Fortunately, the precise impact of dimensional and reference choices may be understood using the Π theorem, attributed to Buckingham (1914), but first developed by Vaschy (1896) and Riabouchinsky (1911).

Buckingham's Π Theorem

As we have discussed in Chapter 3, according to this theorem, any equation in physics which relates n physical quantities, which may each be defined by a monomial function of the form $X^a Y^b Z^c$.., where X, Y, Z .. are k reference quantities chosen from n, must be expressible as an arbitrary function of n-k dimensionless terms, called "Pi terms", formed from monomial combinations of the k reference quantities in such a way that each of the n-k derived quantities occurs only once in each term.

For example, consider the case of the period of a simple pendulum.

Figure 4.1
A simple pendulum

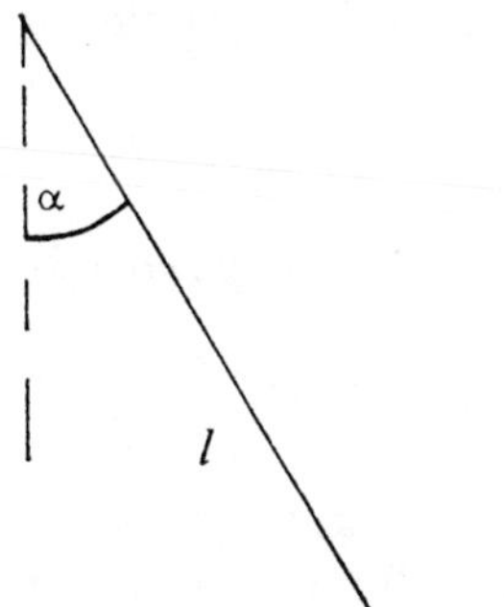

The only force which affects the motion of the pendulum is the weight of the pendulum $w = mg$. Consequently, the period t of oscillation will be determined by the mass m, l the length of the pendulum, and the angular amplitude α of the oscillations, which is a dimensionless ratio.[14] If we express the dimensional exponents of the explanatory variables as a matrix, we obtain:

	t	l	m	w
L	0	1	0	1
M	0	0	1	1
T	1	0	0	-2

Since there are four unknown variables and three independent reference quantities, there will be only one monomial Π term involving t and w , m, and l, raised to the powers p, q, and r respectively. The period will be given by the product of this Π term and an unknown function of α. To ensure dimensional homogeneity, we require that $w^p\, m^q\, l^r\, f(\alpha)$ has the opposite dimensions to t.[15] This means:

$$p + r = 0 \qquad p + q = 0 \qquad 1 - 2p = 0$$

$$p = \tfrac{1}{2} \qquad q = -\tfrac{1}{2} \qquad r = -\tfrac{1}{2}.$$

Consequently Π is given by:

$$\Pi = t\sqrt{(w/ml)}$$

or, since $w=mg$:

$$\Pi = t\sqrt{(g/l)}$$

and, taking into account α, we obtain the complete solution:

$$t = \sqrt{(l/g)}.f(\alpha).$$

This result is in accordance with the known solution to the problem:

$$t = 2\pi\sqrt{(l/g)}(1 + \alpha^2/16 + \ldots).$$

This method of dimensional analysis arises from the requirement that the equations of physics be invariant (to the level of a scale factor) under changes of scale. Mathematically, we may express this requirement in the following way:

A real function $f = f(x_1, x_2, \ldots, x_n)$ of the n real variables x_n is said to be unconditionally homogeneous if, when we multiply each of the variables x_i by a real factor k_i, the function f is given by:

$$f(k_1x_1, k_2x_2, \ldots, k_nx_n) = g(k_1, k_2, \ldots, k_n)\, f(x_1, x_2, \ldots, x_n)$$

where $g(k_1, k_2, \ldots, k_n)$ is known as the homogeneity factor and $k_1, k_2, \ldots, k_n$ are mutually independent factors.

According to the theory of homogeneous equations applied to dimensional analysis, the following results may be derived, (which first appeared in a far-sighted article by Mrs Ehrenfest-Afanassjewa (1926), which was rather hastily[16] dismissed by some of the leading physicists of the day, most notably Campbell and Bridgman).

1 Every continuous unconditionally homogeneous function is a monomial (in other words the equations of physics have standard form, e.g. $x_1^p x_2^q x_3^r$);

2 If an equation $x_n = f(x_1, x_2, \ldots, x_{n-1})$ which defines a variable x_n as a continuous function of the other variables $x_1, x_2, \ldots, x_{n-1}$, is conditionally homogeneous, and if the conditional equations are given by:

$$k_{m+1} = k_1^{\alpha_{11}} \ldots k_m^{\alpha_{m1}} \qquad \text{etc.}$$

$$k_n = k_1^{\alpha_{1r}} \ldots k_m^{\alpha_{mr}} \qquad \text{and } r = n\text{-}m$$

then:

$$x_n = x_1^{\alpha_{1r}} \ldots x_m^{\alpha_{mr}} \, \mathrm{F}(\Pi_{m+1}, \ldots, \Pi_{n-1})$$

where

$$\Pi_{m+1} = x_{m+1} / (x_1^{\alpha_{11}} \ldots x_m^{\alpha_{m1}}) \qquad \text{etc.}$$

$$\Pi_{n-1} = x_{n-1} / (x_1^{\alpha_{1r-1}} \ldots x_m^{\alpha_{mr-1}}).$$

Alternatively, we may write:

$$\mathrm{F}'(\Pi_{m+1}, \ldots, \Pi_n) = 0.$$

This more formal mathematical result is simply Buckingham's Π theorem: the m variables $x_1, x_2, \ldots, x_m$ are the reference quantities employed, and $x_{m+1}, x_{m+2}, \ldots, x_n$ correspond to secondary, derived quantities obtained from the reference quantities according to the conditioning equations. We can express the equation involving all these variables as a function F' of the r (= n-m) Π terms, which are each dimensionless as can be seen by inspection of the conditioning equations.

The same conclusions may be reached from group-theoretic considerations (the dimensional space of quantities may be taken to define an affine group under linear transformation) as shown by Birkhoff (1960), or from calculus using a Taylor expansion, as was outlined by Bridgman (1931), or from generalised algebraic considerations (Langhaar, 1951). Greater physical intuition, though at the expense of some rigour, may be gained from the accounts of Moon and Spencer (1949) and Corrsin (1951), and Thun (1960), who formulate the proof in a vector space.

The space is spanned by the m independent unit vectors which correspond to the chosen reference quantities, and all other derived quantities may be decomposed into these reference vectors as shown in Figure 5. The orientation of the vector representing any given quantity is defined by its dimensional formula, and its length represents higher or lower powers of the basic dimensional formula.

Figure 4.2
Vector representation of quantities

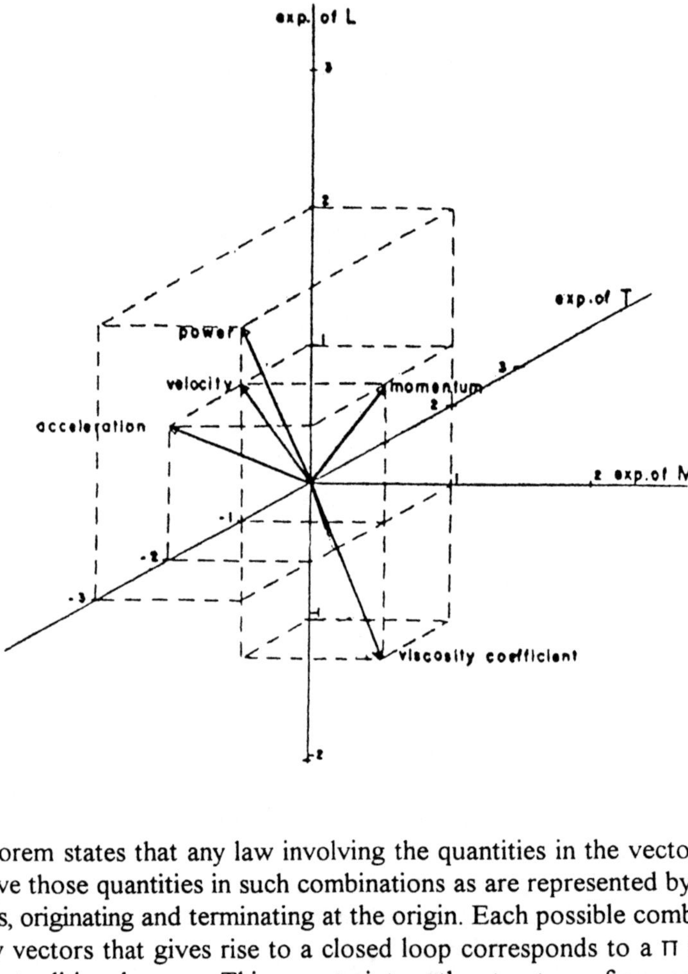

The Π theorem states that any law involving the quantities in the vector space must involve those quantities in such combinations as are represented by closed vector paths, originating and terminating at the origin. Each possible combination of quantity vectors that gives rise to a closed loop corresponds to a Π term as obtained by traditional means. This constraint on the structure of any equation, is that of scale invariance which implies dimensional homogeneity.[17]

In the vector space, we may select a new set of basis vectors corresponding to a new set of reference quantities, which may be monomial combinations of other quantities. Mathematically, we may represent this change of basis by a rotation of axes in the vector space, and customary matrix algebra may be applied (See Thun (1960)). As a simple example, we may transform quantities from the 3-vector space spanned by M, L and T to the 3-vector space involving force, L and T, by means of the following matrix operation:[18]

$$\begin{bmatrix} 1 & 0 & 0 \\ -1 & 1 & 0 \\ 2 & 0 & 1 \end{bmatrix} \quad \mathbf{Q}_{MLT} \quad = \quad \mathbf{Q}_{FLT}$$

For instance, energy which is represented as ML^2T^{-2} in the M, L, T basis is transformed as:

$$\begin{bmatrix} 1 & 0 & 0 \\ -1 & 1 & 0 \\ 2 & 0 & 1 \end{bmatrix} \begin{bmatrix} 1 \\ 2 \\ -2 \end{bmatrix} = \begin{bmatrix} 1 \\ 1 \\ 0 \end{bmatrix}$$

so in the new reference basis FLT, energy has the dimensional formula FL.

When dimensional analysis is undertaken by physicists and engineers, they attempt to specify the *n* quantities which may occur in the equation which describes a physical phenomenon. Included in these quantities will be certain fundamental quantities, usually some derived quantities and also physical constants i.e. system parameters, which are treated mathematically as variables in exactly the same fashion as any of the other quantities. The scientists then use the methods of linear algebra to determine the dimensionless arguments (the closed vector loops) of the equation that must obtain if the equation is to be scale invariant.

In many situations, the scientists are guided by their own intuitions and experience as to which quantities and constants may arise in the equation for the phenomenon - perhaps they have a particular causal explanation in mind - or they use arguments based upon the similarity of physical systems to apply a set of equations of motion and associated constants to the phenomenon. Without such arguments and assumptions, dimensional analysis by itself will not yield new equations of physics.

The failure to appreciate this point, led to much misunderstanding of the use and abuse of dimensional analysis. Campbell (1924b and 1926), in particular was strident in his criticism of dimensional analysis, but a close reading of his and Bridgman's account, (1926 and 1931), which favoured the careful application of dimensional methods, show that their positions differ only in emphasis.

Changing dimensions by substitution

Returning to consider the first aspect of the conventionalist attack, we can now see how the dimensions of any quantity may be changed by rotating the basis vectors of the representation. We can also see how, if we straitjacket a constant into particular dimensions, the dimensional representation of one or more other constants or quantities must adjust so as to maintain the integrity of the dimensionless products which form the arguments of any equation relating to the quantities in the vector space (as described for α in Chapter 3). Quite clearly the dimensions, as defined by the structure of a vector space, of any quantity or constant is conventional, but the key point to emphasise is that the conventionality resides in the choice of representation, and defining equations, not in the structure of the laws describing the phenomena (this last remark will be made clearer in due course).

Beginning with Planck, certain representations have been put forward as more "natural" than others:

> In contrast with this it might be of interest to note that, with the aid of the two constants h and k which appear in the universal law of radiation, we have the means of establishing units of mass, time and temperature, which are independent of special bodies or substances, which necessarily retain their significance for all times and for all environments, terrestrial and human or otherwise, and which may, therefore, be described as "natural units". (Planck 1913 p. 175)

By adopting particular quantities as reference quantities, and by assigning particular values to them we may remove all artificial specificity in our choice of reference quantities and units. Campbell (1924, 1928) and others have pointed out the impracticality of such choices, but this has not deterred others from proposing more exotic systems of units, in which many traditional quantities have a secondary, derived status. For example, both Hartree and Ludovici have developed systems based on a subset of our most cherished fundamental constants. In the Hartree system, we have:

Table 4.1
The Hartree system

Fundamental Quantities	Definition	Value
mass	m_e	9.1×10^{-31} kg
action	$h/2\pi$	1.1×10^{-34} Js
charge	e	1.6×10^{-19} C
electric constant	ϵ_0	8.9×10^{-12} F/m
Derived Quantities		
velocity	$a_0 / \tau_0 = e^2 / 2\epsilon_0 h$	2.2×10^{6} m/s
length	$a_0 = \epsilon_0 h^2 / \pi m e^2$ Bohr orbit	5.3×10^{-11} m
time	$\tau_0 = 2\epsilon_0^2 h^3 / \pi m e^4$ Bohr orbit period	2.4×10^{-17} s
energy	$e^2 / 4\pi\epsilon_0 a_0$	4.9×10^{-18} J

While under the Ludovici alternative:

Table 4.2
The Ludovici system

Fundamental Quantities	**Dimensional Form** G	e	μ	ϵ	**Value**
gravitational constant	1	0	0	0	6.7×10^{-11} Nm²/kg²
electron charge	0	1	0	0	1.6×10^{-19} C
magnetic constant	0	0	1	0	1.3×10^{-6} H/m
electric constant	0	0	0	1	8.9×10^{-12} F/m
Derived Quantities					
length	½	1	1	½	4.9×10^{-36} m
mass	-½	1	0	-½	6.6×10^{-9} kg
time	½	1	3/2	1	1.6×10^{-44} s

In neither of these systems is the number of basis vectors reduced: instead we substitute vector identities. The values of each of the fundamental quantities could also be set to unity, (i.e. specific measures), and unit names could be given to the fundamental quantities.[19] *No elimination of reference quantities or constants is involved*, and one is not better than the other. As Palacios remarked:

> In physics more dimensionally independent constants are available than are necessary to form a complete basis. This results in the possibility of forming several universal bases, but there is no reason to believe that any one of them has any special merits over any other. (Palacios 1964 p. 71)

Others have thought differently and proposed various systems of "ultimate rational units". Lewis and Adams (1914) showed that with a particular choice of dimensions and by suppressing certain constants, certain "simple" relationships were derivable, for instance, the value of Stefan's constant ($\sigma = k^4/(4\pi\epsilon)^6$), expressed in a particular set of units was almost identical to unity when known experimental values for known constants were inserted. Lewis and Adams concluded that the true value of σ was indeed unity, and that the simplicity attached to this value (i.e.unity) was support for their particular choice of units. They believed that in their system of units other relationships involving primitive constants would also be simple. In fact, as Campbell (1924a) showed, the result they obtained was a coincidence that was derivable from any choice of representation which satisfied certain specific constraints, and hence not unique, even if we accept that we know what "simple" numbers are.

Returning to the discussion of alternative systems, we may also consider those suggested by Sedov (1959) which use specific measures throughout. If we replace in every equation each term x by x / x_s, where x_s is a specific measure of x, all quantities becomes dimensionless. Consider specific gravity, which relates the weight of one liquid to the weight of an equal volume of water. If we change the units in which we measure weight from ounces to grams, this has no effect on specific gravities because both numerator and denominator are subject to the same scale transformation. In terms of our vector representation, we could define the representation of the specific mass of an object as a scalar given by the dot product of the coincident vectors representing the quantity 'mass of the object' and the quantity 'mass of an electron'. (Note, however, that the lengths of these vectors is the same and does not represent the value of the specific mass in question).[20] Sedov concluded that in this way we could do away with dimensions if we so wished. The same result would be obtained if we used universal constants as specific measures for the reference quantities in our system: derived quantities would be dimensionless provided we rigidly stuck to a unique set of universal constants. Eddington reached the same endpoint when he proposed that the traditional list of seven universal constants be reduced to four dimensionless universal constants by eliminating the customary c.g.s. units used to represent these seven constants (Eddington 1936).

> Finally, we can consider all physical quantities to be nondimensional if we regard appropriate physical quantities as absolute nondimensional constants. In this case, the possibility of using different systems of measurement units is ruled out. The single system of measurement units obtained is based on the physical quantities selected (for example, on the gravitational constant, the velocity of light and the coefficient of viscosity of water) and the values of these are taken as absolute universal constants. (Sedov 1959 p. 7)

Whyte (1954) has suggested that ultimately all physics should be reducible to fundamental equations involving dimensionless quantities, (although he did not anticipate that this could be achieved in the mundane way we have described). He posited essentially some type of angle measure. This indeed might be the case, but as we have shown earlier, whether a particular quantity is dimensionless or not, is a matter of convention and is without significance.[21] We might choose a particular representation that has this feature, but that would not in itself be of interest and would, if others are to be believed, result in a lot of unnecessary complication. A redeeming feature of the conventionalist account of the representation of physical quantities, is that there is no cash value in being dimensionless.

Elimination of constants and dimensions

The mechanics of linear algebra which lie behind the Π theorem, also allow us to understand the circumstances in which constants and dimensions are created and destroyed. In his book on dimensional analysis, Palacios built upon the foundational work of Ehrenfest-Afanassjewa, and provided a comprehensive account not only of the use of homogeneous equations in physics, but also of the consequences of particular choices of reference basis. Before discussing the general results relating to constants and dimensions, let us review the astronomical system of mass, as described by Planck, Pankhurst, Ellis and others. As we have seen in Chapter 2, we may formulate the system in terms of two basic equations:[22]

$$f = k\,m\,a$$
$$f = G\,m^2/r^2$$

Customarily, we assign the value $k = 1$, and use M, L, and T as reference quantities, whereby k, called the dynamical constant, is dimensionless. We may, however, select L and T to be the reference quantities and G to be dimensionless and $G = 1$. This is known as the astronomical system of mass. Dimensional homogeneity is then satisfied if the dimensions of mass are given by the equation for two equal masses:

$$m = a\,r^2$$

i.e. mass as a derived quantity in this system has the dimensions $L^3\ T^{-2}$. By suppressing the constant G i.e. by making it dimensionless and equal to unity, we have obtained a derived scale of mass and reduced the number of dimensions by one.

This linking of constants and dimensions is not coincidental: it is generally the case that if we wish to reduce/increase the number of dimensioned derived constants in a chosen system of equations, we must reduce/increase the number of reference quantities used in dimensional formulae by the same number. To see why this happens, we must consider the matrix algebra that underlies the Π theorem.

Consider the following examples:

1 Let us try to express Newton's second law using first M, L, T, then M, L, T and F (force) as our reference quantities. Using standard matrix methods of dimensional analysis, we can express the dimensional aspects of this law as:

	f	=	m	a
M	1		1	0
L	1		0	1
T	-2		0	-2

Considered as three homogeneous equations, each corresponding to one of the reference quantities, involving three unknown variables (the quantities f, m, and a), we would not generally expect to find a solution. In this case however, the determinant of the matrix describing these equations is zero (-1x((1x-2)-(1x-2)), and the rank of the matrix is one less than the number of rows (i.e. one less than the number of reference quantities) and equal to two. The number of solutions is given by the number of unknown variables (3) minus the rank of the dimensional matrix (2), which in this instance equals one, Thus we are able to satisfy the requirements of dimensional homogeneity in this instance because of a degeneracy which gives rise to a zero determinant. This degeneracy is associated with the linear dependence of one reference quantity on another: mathematically, one row of the matrix can be expressed as a linear combination of one or more other rows. In this case the third row is equal to the second row times minus two. In other words, relative to the unknown variables, the reference quantities used to define them derivatively are not independent of each other. In the vector representation, the vectors representing length and time in the vector space share the same direction differing only in length. This linear dependency is a form of slackness in the dimensional description which can be eliminated without affecting the dimensional formulae attributed to the unknown variables.

2 Consider next the use of M, L, T and F as reference quantities.

	f	$=$	m	a
M	0		1	0
L	0		0	1
T	0		0	-2
F	1		0	0

It is not possible to assign dimensions to the quantities f, m , and a such as to confer dimensional homogeneity: we have three unknowns and three independent equations with a determinant of rank three. By inspection, we see that we cannot match the occurrence of 1 that appears in the F row on the left hand side by a combination of the entries in the other rows of the equation. In order to make the equation dimensionally homogeneous and scale invariant, we are obliged to introduce a dimensioned constant k .

	f	$=$	k	m	a
M	0		-1	1	0
L	0		-1	0	1
T	0		2	0	-2
F	1		1	0	0

The introduction of the new dimension, F, requires the introduction of a new dimensioned constant.

3 Consider Newton's law of gravitation without the occurrence of G:

	f	=	m^2	/	r^2
M	1		1		0
L	1		0		1
T	-2		0		0

The rank of the dimensional determinant is (3) and the number of variables is also (3), hence, there is no assignment of dimensions which will support dimensional homogeneity. If we reduce the number of dimensions to two, we may obtain a solution:

	f	=	m^2	/	r^2
M	2		1		0
L	2		0		1

Unfortunately, if we then assign [F] = [M²][L²], we encounter problems with our customary representation of Newton's second law.

	f	=	m	a
M	2		1	0
L	2		0	1
T	0		0	-2

The determinant is non-zero and of rank three, so no solution along these lines is possible. In order to remove G we are forced to introduce a new constant if we are to keep three dimensions.

4 If we insist upon the elimination of G, we must be prepared to sacrifice a dimension (as Planck (1916), Ellis (1966) and Pankhurst (1964) are prepared to do). If we make mass a derived quantity in this astonomical mass representation,[23] $[M] = [L^3][T^{-2}]$ and $[F] = [L^4][T^{-4}]$ and we have:

	f	=	m	a
L	4		3	1
T	-4		-2	-2

where the determinant rank is (2), the number of variables is (3) and hence there is a solution; and:

	f	=	m^2	/	r^2
L	4		3		1
T	-4		-2		1

Again the rank of the determinant is (2), which allows a solution. Elimination of G has only been possible by the reduction in the number of dimensions.

What of the general case? Consider first taut representations, where we do not have a surplus or lack of dimensions or of constants. It is possible to show straightforwardly, that in a dimensional representation that is taut, any change in the number of dimensioned constants must be mirrored by a change in the number of dimensions. This is because, the number of solutions equals the number n of quantities occurring in the equations under consideration less the number of reference quantities k, and this number, n-k, equals one for a taut representation. If we add an additional dimension, k increases by one, which requires an increase in n of one if a solution is to exist. The increase in n corresponds to the introduction of a new dimensioned constant. Similar results obtain if n is reduced: if we reduce the number of constants, the number of dimensions must reduce.

A dimensional representation may fail to be taut either because we have more reference quantities than we need, or unnecessary constants have been introduced. Fortunately a surplus of reference quantities shows up in a linear dependency in the matrix of dimensional coefficients, and surplus quantities may be eliminated without impact on the mathematical results. Unnecessary constants give rise to the need for extra variables (n increases), and may occur either because we have used a composite constant or because the constant is spurious. Composite constants may be replaced by their defining formula in terms of primitive constants. Spurious constants may occur if we do not adopt a consistent set of units whereby the numerical value of all derived units is determined by the numerical values assigned to the units of the reference quantities. In such circumstances, dimensionless scale factors of the type Campbell identified, and discusssed in Chapter 2, will occur associated with each derived quantity which is not consistently derived. Such spurious constants may also be eliminated without affecting the representation. They therefore need not be included among the quantity variables which arise in the equations under consideration. If the redundant reference quantities and constants are not removed the representation will be slack, or what Palacios calls a *superabundant basis*, and the removal of constants will not force a reduction in the number of dimensions, and an increase in the number of reference quantities may not require an additional constant. The rank of the matrix will be less than k

because of linear dependencies, so there will be more than one solution. If the number of unknowns declines, because of the removal of a constant, it is still possible for there to be solutions. Similarly, there will be solutions if the number of reference quantities increases but the number of constants does not.

Dimensional proliferation and reduction

Having established the general connection between dimensioned constants and dimensions, it is now easier to appreciate the extreme cases of representation discussed by Dingle: if we increase *k* as much as we can, we will be obliged to increase the dimensioned constants we use; if we reduce *k* as far as possible, we will be able to eliminate a number of dimensioned constants. Are there grounds, however, for selecting a particular value of *k* ?

Palacios examined this question closely, and he found that there were empirical consequences arising from the choice of different representations. He first rejected slack representations on the ground that they were isomorphic to the associated taut representations, and then examined the results of dimensional analysis in those circumstances where the number of reference quantities was reduced below the number used in the original representation by suppressing constants. He found that the application of the Π theorem gave rise to a greater number of dimensionless monomial arguments (π terms) in the permitted solutions to the equations governing a particular phenomenon.

For instance, let us consider again the case of a simple pendulum when we have suppressed the gravitational constant G, and obtained $[m] = L^3\, T^{-2}$ and $[f] = L^4\, T^{-4}$. The dimensional matrix is:

	t	l	m	w
L	0	1	3	4
T	1	0	-2	-4

We obtain after manipulation, the following two π terms:

$$\pi_1 = t\sqrt{(g/l)} \qquad \pi_2 = l\sqrt{(g/m)}$$

and the solution becomes:

$$t = t\sqrt{(l/g)}.f(l\sqrt{(g/m)}, \alpha).$$

The solution, suggesting in general that the period is affected by the mass of the pendulum, does not agree with the true result. It is also less precise, since the unknown function *f* now depends on two parameters instead of only one. Palacios observed:

> We have classified them as indispensable and superfluous constants, and it has been seen that if one of the former is suppressed the application of dimensional analysis can lead to false solutions, due to the appearance of spurious monomials, that is monomials which will have dimensions with regard to a complete basis but are dimensionless in an incomplete basis. (Palacios 1964 p. 67)

Where reduced bases are chosen, the additional Π terms are not observed empirically, and they reflect a lower degree of specificity, and a higher degree of degeneracy in the mathematical equations describing the phenomenon. The effect of suppressing constants, and reducing dimensions is to express a given set of equations in a subspace of the larger initial vector space. This results in certain quantities, which have different vector directions in the larger space, being represented by the same vector in the subspace, corresponding to the decline in the discrimination available in this more humble space, to describe phenomena. In particular, certain monomial vector combinations which correspond to a dimensionless Π term in the smaller space become dimensioned in the larger space i.e. are no longer a Π term. If we add a reference quantity to a dimensional basis, and we generate additional monomials, then the basis must initially have been incomplete; if we add a reference quantity to dimensional basis that is taut, no new monomials will be added because one of the dimensions will be a linear combination of the others, and hence will be redundant.

An example of a subspace is shown in Figure 6 with reference to thermodynamic quantities. The decision not to allow temperature θ to be a separate reference quantity and to enforce mechanical dimensions on thermodynamic quantities results in the projection of the higher order thermodynamic space onto a mechanical sub-space.

Figure 4.3
Thermodynamic and mechanical vector spaces

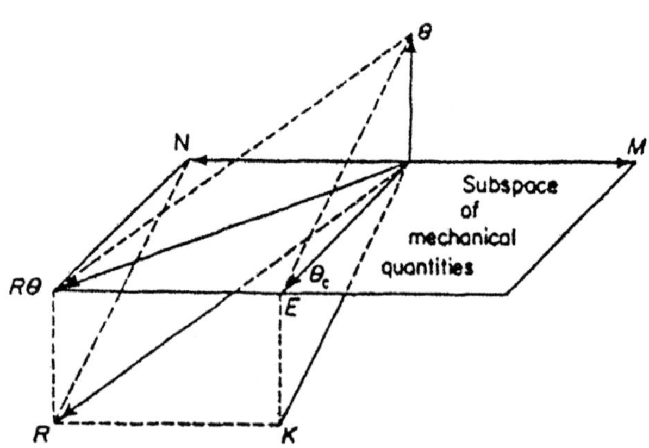

The consequences of dimensional reduction by the suppression of constants had been discussed in part previously by others. Rücker (1889), in particular, pointed out at an early date that the equations of electromagnetism can only be solved without the introduction of additional reference quantities by suppressing constants, since otherwise we have on occasion only one equation, but two electomagnetic unknowns (typically q and ϵ or μ). With the benefit of this insight, it is then easy to analyse the representations put forward by Burniston-Brown, Duncanson and the specific electromagnetic representation preferred by Dingle. In each instance, the authors replace the full vector space defined by the set of equations describing the phenomenon under investigation, by a vector sub-space in which one or more dimensions are eliminated. This occurs commonly in the case of quantities which are well understood, where laws relating two quantities via a constant are often used to eliminate the constant by assimilating the two quantities involved (consider, for instance, J, the mechanical equivalent of heat, which relates heat and work, and which has all but disappeared from textbooks).

> Now it should be clear that many such hidden universal constants lie at the core of the main statements of classical physics, at most in the oldest theories such as geometry or Newtonian mechanics, in which a long practice has led to the complete incorporation of their significance at an all-implicit level. The absence of universal constants in this part of physics is but an apparent privilege of old age. One might thus classify the universal constants (type C above) into three subclasses according to their historical status:
>
> i) the modern ones, such as h and c, the conceptual role of which is still dominant;
>
> ii) the classical ones, such as k or J, which today appear essentially as unit conversion factors, their conceptual role having become almost implicit;
>
> iii) the archaic ones, which have been so well assimilated and digested as to become totally invisible. (Levy-Leblond 1977 p. 198)

In some of these reduced representations, particular curious identities occur, to which the authors attach great significance. Palacios was at pains to show that these results were the consequences of choosing an impoverished representation, and were worthless. Each of the accounts also gives rise to mathematical terms which do not appear in the equations describing phenomena which we obtain in practice, and he considered this misleading and grounds for rejecting them as general representations. Palacios concluded (1964 p. 43):

> Many authors believe to have made an important discovery in forming dimensional systems with the aid of an insufficient basis. To think so is akin to maintaining that the details of a scene would be better appreciated from its shadow projected on a screen, rather than by looking at it directly. There is no inconvenience, beyond the unnecessary complication, in adopting a superabundant basis, but there is no advantage either. We shall see that if a defective basis is used, less information is in general obtained than with a complete basis.

The other general difficulty arising when the number of reference quantities is reduced relates to reference. The law describing the relations between the force impressed upon two objects, their masses and their separation is an empirical law about certain objects. When we measure mass by derived means, "mass" in this new system becomes a *defined* quantity in Campbell's terminology, and as we have seen in Chapter 2, it is not clear that this new term has the same referent as the old.

For instance, in the case of the Planckian analysis of Newton's second law and law of gravitation, where G is suppressed, what basis is there for choosing the dimensions [L][T^{-2}] for acceleration, thereby seeming to provide a plausible dimensional system that we recognise in terms of length and time? Why could we not use the conventionality of the representation to pick completely arbitrary reference quantities q and h such that [acceleration] = [q][h] and then we would have:

	f	=	m	a	f	=	m^2	$/r^2$
q	2		1	1	2		1	0
h	1		0	1	1		0	-½

These equations are dimensionally homogeneous, but how do we know m refers to mass as opposed to some other quantity? [24]

There are three possibilities: (i) there is some other law which allows mass, denoted by m, to be a derived, as opposed to a defined, quantity supporting the use of the dimensions of q and h, or (ii) the measurement of the quantity denoted by m by fundamental means involves only q, so in fact m is really q or (iii) this representation is artificial and we are not talking about mass at all. For Planck, Ellis and Pankhurst, there is no further simple law linking m directly to L and T, and hence to q and h, which rules out (i). The fundamental measurement of mass only involves M, thereby giving rise to its own dimension. If this dimension is q, then the Planckian reduction will have failed since we will have three reference quantities M, L, and T. On the other hand, if this dimension is not M, then m will not be mass. As a result, the artificiality of the representation is made clear.

In order to obtain the Planckian result, the f which appears in Newton's second law and the f which appears in Newton's gravitational law are equated. This assumes a common referent and that there are two independent derived laws of force. In our account, however, there is no absurdity in postulating a world where we discover a Newtonian gravitational law, but not Newton's second law, and a world where mass is fundamentally measured, and where we use [M][L][T] as our reference quantities. It is difficult to see how Planck would be able to carry out his dimensional reduction of mass (via the suppression of G) in this world, since the reduction depends critically upon the availability of Newton's second law.

This is a particular case of the general problem for operationalists of the incommensurability of quantities defined by different procedures. Dingle tried to overcome this difficulty by stating that it is an empirical finding that different procedures result in measurements of the same quantity, but this argument is only convincing if its tacit realist assumptions are made explicit.

Mass elimination of constants

The route is now well-signposted for those who would like to rid physics of the supposedly unnecessary evil of constants[25]: reduce the number of dimensions to one, and hope that thereby, the number of constants will be reduced to one. To show why this would not work, consider the following light based system.

The manufacture of aerospace frames requires very high degrees of precision, and has led to the development of many metrological devices and instruments, including thickness gauges which rely upon the time-delayed retransmission of ultrasonic signals. Similarly, laser interferometry has had a significant impact on surveying, theodolites giving way to laser instruments not only in the factory, but also on the building site. Given these developments, it is not hard to imagine that we might develop a scale of length based upon the uniform transmission of light or sound signals.[26] The primacy of c will probably incline us to the former, so let us imagine a scale of length based upon the propagation of light.

We might define length as a derived quantity on a ratio scale based upon the following equation:

$$x = k\,t$$

where k is a scale factor, which we might choose to set equal to unity. The single reference quantity in this maximally centralised scale system is time, t, defined by a fundamental process relying upon some periodic behaviour (such as the rotational period of a quasar, which may now be measured to an accuracy of one part in 10^{14}).

Based upon this fundamental time scale, we may wish to select some particular time interval as the basis of a standard of length in our derived scale, but it is not necessary that we do so. Instead, we might simply rely upon the correct application of the equation in any given instance of length measurement. We will assume a conventional principle of correlation for the scale (i.e. combination of time intervals is represented mathematically by addition).

Using the derived scale of length would pose no dimensional problems: the dimension of length, according to Campbell's definition of dimension, would be "one" in time; using Ellis' terminology, we would say that there is only one dimension in this maximally centred system of scales, namely that of *time*, in which all other quantities would be expressed. Area and volume would have the dimensions of $[T]^2$, and $[T]^3$ respectively.

Turning to mass, we might define this quantity derivatively by means of a complex law relating the angle by which light is bent by a massive object. According to Einstein in his Introduction to Relativity (1920), a simple approximation to this law is given by:

$$\alpha = 4\, Gm / r_0 c^2$$

where α is the angle of deflection, m the mass of the object and r_0 the distance of closest approach of the ray.

Hence, the application of this law to define a scale of mass, is not ludicrously far-fetched. Angle we might define derivatively from length, and in this way we might arrive at a scale of mass involving only the fundamental quantity time.

An alternative would be to specify mass in terms of the volume of some specified substance, which our science has revealed to be of constant density (though it is not a necessary condition that we should already know the density is constant). Both Ellis and Campbell recognise that standard objects may be set up by specification in this way, and both recognise the dependent nature of the scale so defined.

Our reason for not doing so here, is that the possibility of standard objects established by specification or definition for the derived scale of mass, muddies the water when it comes to questions of the need for standard objects. The deflection-of-light-rays approach, while less plausible, is neater in that it does not suggest the need for any standard object in order to make determinations of mass.

The fact that all quantities have dimensions of time does not create difficulties with established laws. If we allow, for the sake of the argument, the density approach to be taken with regard to a derived scale of mass, Newton's law of gravitation will apply if:

$[r] = [\mathrm{T}]$	$[m] = [\mathrm{T}]^3$	$[\text{acceleration}] = [\mathrm{T}]^{-1}$
$[\text{force}] = [\mathrm{T}]^2$	$G = [\mathrm{T}]^{-2}$	$c = [\mathrm{T}]^0$.

The same dimensions will satisfy Newton's second law: $f = ma$. Similarly, α is dimensionless in the law for light ray deflection.

This approach could be continued using the reference quantities, for which we can provide scales of measurement centred on time, traditionally chosen in classical physics for the expression of laws: mass, length and time.

We are not alone in suggesting a single-centred system of scales: similar systems have been proposed by others: Dingle (1942) and Wilson (1942) both used the single dimension of length. Eminent scientists such as Eddington were also prepared to use such systems: *For the sun the quantity m, called the gravitational mass, is only 1.47 kilometres; for the earth it is five millimetres.*[27]

Some conventionalists found this too big a pill to swallow. O'Rahilly (1938) reviewed the lengthy dimensional disputes concerning electromagnetism and ridiculed the scientific community for failing to recognise quickly the conventional aspects of the various representations. He could not accept, however, talk of time and length being one, and other similar uni-dimensional talk, which he regarded as instigated by the development of Special Theory of Relativity and encouraged by Minkowski's work. To defend his position, he looked closely at the suppression of the values of h, G and c, and concluded, *correctly*, that for a vector-space in which the number of dimensions is *not* reduced, it is not possible to express one reference quantity in terms of another, for instance specifying the dimensions of time in terms of length. Unfortunately, O'Rahilly failed to distinguish between a change of vector representation which involved the substitution of one set of reference quantities for another (a rotation of the reference quantity vectors), and one which involved the projection of the original vector space onto a sub-space. He attempted to have his cake and eat it: conventionalism does indeed make it legitimate to measure mass in seconds or inches.

Consequences

In spite of their simplicity, such representations do not result in the elimination of all primitive universal dimensioned constants, if only because we do not have a sufficient number of starting dimensions to eliminate them all. For instance, in the time-only representation, G is still a dimensioned quantity albeit in the dimensions of time alone.

> In the introduction to the present thesis it was indicated that there is a tendency to reduce the number of universal constants in use. The simplest thing would be to get rid of them all, but as there are not enough disposable units to do this, each author suppresses those which he likes least and a certain amount of published work exists in which, thanks to the suppression of such and such constants a certain esoteric sense is supposed to be given to the laws of physics so obtained. (Palacios 1964 p. 24)

Our conclusions concerning this more extreme situation are not qualitatively different from the case of limited suppression of constants. Certainly, it is possible to collapse the dimensional representation to a single quantity, but that does not eliminate all primitive derived constants, and provides a poorer palette with which to paint the complexities of physical interactions. The choice of an extreme basis is a matter of representation; it has no implications for the independent existence of the quantities concerned. It is, in fact neutral ontologically, and needs to be supported by some general operationalist principle, if it is to have teeth. We agree with Guggenheim:

> In other words, it would be possible to express the dimensions of any physical quantity whatever in terms of a single dimension. The conclusion is, perhaps not absurd, but, if it is accepted, there remains nothing of dimensional analysis, and we might as well give up altogether the concept of dimensions. (Guggenheim 1942 p. 495)

Substantive notions of dimensions

Palacios' account

In a further break with the conventionalists, Palacios was also able to provide a notion of dimension that was free of questionable metaphysics and of conventionality. He first drew a distinction between empirical laws relating quantities and dimensioned universal constants (system-independent parameters in my parlance), which we discover empirically, and laws by which we define certain quantities in terms of others (displacement in terms of electric field and absolute permittivity for instance): i.e. the distinction between derived and defined quantities. For a given set of phenomena, it is possible to specify the minimal set of empirical laws which govern the phenomena, and to represent these laws by equations. Typically this minimal sufficient set of laws comprise the core axioms in a set-theoretic approach to theories.

The dimensions of quantities are then unambiguously determined by the taut representation of the empirical equations governing the phenomena in question.

> In the present work, the author has tried to show that the dimensions of primary quantities are not to be derived from instrumental definitions (methods of measurement), but from the group of fundamental equations of each theory and from the criteria which determine the superfluous constants. (Palacios 1964 p. 207)

This approach is similar to that of Campbell who insisted that dimensions could only be assigned to quantities in respect of a particular equation or theory.

> Our final conclusion then is this. Dimensional analysis is useful and valid only when the assumptions concerning the magnitudes involved and their dimensions are based on the inspection of equations expressing fully the numerical laws or theories by which the process under discussion is determined. (Campbell 1924 p. 494)

In particle mechanics, for instance, Palacios gave three laws;[28] in the case of electromagnetism, there are five fundamental empirical laws governing the phenomena.

In each case the number of empirical laws fixes the number of reference quantities which are required to provide a solution to the underlying homogeneous equations that guarantee scale invariance: the number of reference quantities is equal to the dimensionality of the vector space used to represent the physical quantities that appear in the equations under consideration. To each quantity there corresponds a vector in this vector space, which may be decomposed into a combination of the orthogonal reference vectors which are chosen to define the space. While the choice of reference vectors is conventional, the structures of all vector spaces so generated are isomorphic to each other.

In the same way that vectors exist in physics independently of the system of axes chosen, so to all physical quantities there corresponds a dimension independent of the basis adopted. The dimensional exponents play the role of components of the dimension, as they behave like the components of a vector when a change of basis is made. (Palacios 1964 p. 40)

The dimensionality of different physical quantities is captured by their relative spatial orientation, which is independent of the choice of reference basis. By this means, Palacios provided an account of dimensions embedded in the structure of the equations governing the phenomena.

A pre-representation account of dimensions

While pointing the way forward, Palacios' account may not satisfy the most ardent conventionalist. It may be argued that the key factor discriminating against alternative, suppressed representations, is the presence of additional dimensionless monomial terms which are permissible in the suppressed vector sub-spaces. The conventionalist may accommodate this further largesse either by saying that it is just so happens that no dependency on this mathematically permitted Π-term occurs, though it might in principle, or by saying that we, via a choice of co-ordinative definition, conventionally ignore these alternative solutions, knowing them to be a kind of mathematical poltergeist. Certainly, it cannot be denied that Palacios' argument relies centrally on certain features of the mathematical representation of phenomena and on our systems of measurement. For a realist like Putnam[29] the existence of good methodological criteria, such as the avoidance of superfluous solutions, is sufficient reason to reject conventionalism, but such reasoning requires nonetheless independent support.

To address these concerns, we propose to formulate a notion of dimension that is logically prior to the mathematical representation of the measurement of physical quantities and which supports the approach of Palacios based upon the existence of certain sets of empirical laws and not others. The distinction between physical systems and their representation is extremely important. It is our contention that much of the confusion concerning dimensions, and the conventionalist platform have their origin in a failure to take full account of this distinction (which, as we have seen, amounts often to conflating the derived-defined, and the primary-secondary distinctions introduced by Campbell).

There are *two* legitimate notions of the dimensions of physical quantities. One is firmly embedded in the representation of physical relations by isomorphic mathematical structures: dimensions allow us to determine the orientation of different quantities in the vector space which represents the physical quantities interrelated by equation. In more traditional analyses, the vectors of the reference quantities in the vector space are described as units, and the customary square-bracketed dimensional formula of derived quantities contain the reference unit combinations which serve as the units for derived quantities. Applying a dimensional formula, allows us to anticipate the impact of changes in the numerical values assigned to the reference units.

In the limit, as Sedov observed, we can do away entirely with the need for this concept of dimension, which describes the way the values of derived quantities change when we choose alternative reference units, by using constants as universal units in a system of equations that use specific measures. For then, we would have no need to effect unit transformations, and the Maxwellian concept of dimension would be redundant.[30]

> The introduction of a single system of units of measurement excluding all other systems [of the type previously described using universal constants], is equivalent to abandoning the dimensions concept completely. The numerical values of all the variables in a single universal system of units of measurement determine their physical magnitude uniquely. (Sedov 1959 p. 8)

The unit transformationalists need not worry, however, for while there would be advantages in standardizing measurement methods in this way, these are more than outweighed by other practical and procedural considerations.

The second concept of dimensions is grounded in the empirical laws which govern empirical systems. Newton's law is an inverse square law in distance, and is a square law in mass: this is not a matter of convention and is not affected by whatever representation we choose for the equation describing this law. Using the combination operations and procedures characteristic of extensive systems it is possible to give a representation-free account of dimensions. For example, let us consider Newton's law of gravitation, using the axioms of extensive measurement and notation developed in Chapter 2.

Let there be a standard set A of small positionable masses $\{a, a', a'', a''', \ldots a_2, a_2', a_2'', a_2''', \ldots, a_3, a_3'', a_3''', \ldots a_n, \ldots\}$ such that

$$a =_m a' =_m a'' =_m a''' \ldots.$$
$$a_2 =_m a \oplus_m a' \qquad a_n =_m a \oplus_m a_{n-1}$$

Let there also be a standard set R of thin measuring rods of negligible mass $\{ r, r', r'', r''', \ldots r_2, r_2', r_2'', r_2''', \ldots, r_3, r_3'', r_3''', \ldots r_n, \ldots\}$ such that:

$$r =_l r' =_l r'' =_l r''' \ldots.$$
$$r_2 =_l r \oplus_l r' \qquad r_n =_l r \oplus_l r_{n-1}$$

We also need to define an operation $\odot$ by which we measure the separation between two objects b and c, members of A. In simple terms $\odot$ involves selecting rods from R until we find a rod whose ends are in contact with b and c when inserted between them. Since the extensive axioms for length generate a standard set, we know that for some r in R:[31]

$$b \odot c =_l r$$

Then let us consider an operation $\square$ which involves the placing of masses *b* and *c*, members of A, at a separation equal in length to rod *r*, and then determining by some appropriate means the attractive force between the masses.[32] We may define this operation as:

$$b, c \,\square r$$

Our empirical investigations will reveal that the gravitational force is doubled when we replace *b* by *a* and *c* by an object twice as massive as *a* . This finding may be written symbolically:

$$a_2, a \,\square r \quad =_f \quad a', a \,\square r \quad \oplus_f \quad a'', a''' \,\square r'$$

where $\oplus_f$ represents the combinative operation characteristic of an extensive measurement system for force[33] that combines the gravitational forces arising from the interaction of members of A under the operation $\square$.

Now, let us imagine that we discover that if the separation between two equal masses is doubled, the gravitational force is quadrupled. In our notation:

$$a'', a''' \,\square r_2 \quad =_f \quad a_2, a \,\square r \quad \oplus_f \quad a_2', a' \,\square r'$$

Let us denote the lefthand side by $\square^2[2, a, r]$, then we may define:

$$\square^2[\text{n}, a, r] \quad \equiv \quad a_n, a \,\square r \quad \oplus_f^{n-1} \quad a_n', a' \,\square r'$$

where $\oplus_f^{n-1}$ is given recursively:

$$x \oplus_f^n x' \quad \equiv \quad x \oplus_f (x' \oplus_f^{n-1} x'')$$
$$x \oplus_f^2 x' \quad \equiv \quad x \oplus_f (x' \oplus_f x'')$$

where x is a product of the operation $\square$.

Then the more general result that if we multiply the separation by n the force increases by n squared, is given by:

$$\forall n \{ \square^2[\text{n}, a, r] \quad =_f \quad a', a'' \,\square r_n \}$$

This empirical result expresses the fact that under the gravitational law, force increases with the square of distance. No mathematical representation, involving a numerical system isomorphic to the empirical system of masses, rods and operations, has been established.

Higher level laws may be expressed similarly: for instance a cube law is given by:

$$\forall n \{ \square^3[n, a, r] \quad =_f \quad a', a'' \square r_n \}$$

where we define:

$$\square^3[n, a, r] \quad \equiv \quad \square^2[n, a, r] \quad \oplus_f^{n-1} \quad \square^2[n, a', r']$$

and similarly:

$$\square^4[n, a, r] \quad \equiv \quad \square^3[n, a, r] \quad \oplus_f^{n-1} \quad \square^3[n, a', r']$$

Thus for a dependency to the α th power, we would discover the following result:

$$\forall n \{ \square^\alpha[n, a, r] \quad =_f \quad a', a'' \square r_n \}$$

Inverse laws may be catered for in a similar fashion:

$$\forall n \{ \square^\beta[n, a, r] \quad =_f \quad a', a'' \square r/n \}$$

where r/n is a member of the standard set R such that:

$$r \quad =_1 \quad r/n \quad \oplus_1^{n-1} \quad r'/n$$

and the power of inverse dependency is β.

By using the combination operation repeatedly for the fundamental quantities involved, it is possible to provide a rigorous definition of the dependency of one of the quantities upon the other. The dimension of each quantity in the law is given by the exponent α or β. With further development, this approach could accommodate fractional exponents.

Because our laws are scale invariant, we know that we will always be able to represent them in standard form, and hence that this approach to empirical dimensions may be generally extended to derived quantities. It may seem, however, that this conclusion is parasitical upon the mathematical representations used to formulate the equations used in derived measurement, which equations we have been at pains to avoid. Luce has shown, however, that the constancy of relative magnitudes which gives rise to scale invariance is entirely a result of *similarities* between the relational structures that describe the objects of the empirical systems which give rise to the laws. These similarities may be represented as *automorphisms* defined upon the relational structure of the empirical systems. It is then possible to show the formal equivalence between the automorphic structure of the empirical systems and the dimensional structure of the mathematical representations used to describe law-like properties of the empirical systems as equations. In other words, the physical similarity of empirical systems, which is insensitive to absolute magnitudes, gives rise to linear homogeneous equations which support the Maxwellian concept of dimensions.[34] The similarities of the empirical systems will also then require that the homogeneous equations have standard form (see Luce 1978), and hence that they can be represented in the way described. Thus the generality of this account of empirical dimensions arises from the similarity structures embedded in the empirical systems in question, rather than as a consequence of our use of representations.[35] The important conclusion is that we have been able to provide an account of the dimensionality of a law in terms of objects, relations and operations, without recourse to an isomorphic numerical system.

Empirical dimensions

We now have a set of empirical operations which allow us to explain what, for instance, an inverse square law in distance is. If we describe the dimensions of each of the fundamental quantities occurring in the law, we may be held to have given an account of the dimensionality of the law. This empirical notion of dimension, embedded in the structure of the empirical system of objects, ordering relations and operations, thus allows us to formulate a notion of the dimensionality of laws involving quantities which are fundamentally measurable. At this point some may prefer to consider the dimensionality of the quantities which occur in the law, to be a property of the law itself. Others may be prepared to go further and regard the dimensionality of the law to be a property of the empirical systems to which it relates, in the same way that mass or length relates to these empirical systems.

With regard to the dimensions of the fundamental quantities themselves, we may say either that each quantity, such as mass, may be considered in isolation, (in which case its dimension, if this has a meaning, is to be equated with its kind), or considered as a characteristic property of the complexes of objects and operations defined by the law in question, in which case a dimensional formula based upon α, β, γ etc. (as defined empirically above), could be provided to explain the interdependencies of one of the fundamental quantities upon the others that is captured by the law. As Campbell maintained, if a quantity is involved in more than one extensive law, then it could have more than one set of empirical dimensions as a matter of fact.

Furthermore, the interaction of the fundamental quantities described by the law in question is a characteristic similarity feature of the empirical systems to which the law relates, and the dimensional characteristics of the law expressed in terms of the fundamental quantities allows us to predict certain empirical relations between different rod-object combinations (*complexes*, we may say) which obey the gravity law. These complexes are members of a set S which we can define as

$$S \equiv \quad \{x, y : x \in A, y \in R \Rightarrow \forall n \{ \square^2[n, x , y] \quad =f \quad x', x'' \square y/n \}\}$$

For example, if we know the mass of two objects in terms of the standard object for mass, and their separation in terms of the standard object for length, the force exerted between the two objects in terms of the standard object for force, will be determined without resort to the operation $\square$. The interaction or coupling of the fundamental quantities for each complex has the same structure of dependency on the quantities mass and length. This invariant structural feature of the interaction is a system-independent feature, which scientists identify with a universal constant. In the case of energy and period, both fundamental quantities, the constant is h; in the case of distance and time, it is c; for force, mass and distance, we have G; for charge, force and distance we have ϵ; for entropy and probability it is k. The situation may be likened to the shared similarity of Euclidean circles relating their circumference to their diameter, which we represent mathematically as π.

Campbell held that equations for derived quantities mirrored a physical relation of uniform association between extensive properties such as mass and volume, in the case of density. This uniform association he described by saying the extensive properties were properties of the same system.

This notion of uniform association has been elaborated by Levy-Leblond:

> Coming back to Planck's constant, the relationship $E = \hbar\omega$, according to this point of view, is not to be interpreted as linking two classical concepts, but rather as transcending them through their synthesis, to establish a new single concept with a broader scope. The quantum energy indeed is a new concept, since it associates to any physical state a whole spectrum of numerical values and is to be represented by a Hermitian operator, as opposed to the numerical function which represents energy in classical mechanics. Here again a new name should have been given to stress the emergence of this concept, as an intrinsic one. Energy and pulsation then appear as two particular facets of a more general notion, each of which being the only visible one from either one of two quite specific points of view. The role played here of the Planck constant in bringing together these two facets is characteristic of universal constants. (Levy-Leblond 1977 p. 193)

Palacios independently developed a similar position. In eliminating composite constants from equations as a preliminary to developing a taut vector representation, he was obliged to identify a list of primitive constants. The list developed is similar in many respects to the one given in Chapter 3. To justify his selection, Palacios noted that the fundamental quantities which appeared in the defining equations for these constants were inseparable:

> The other equations of group (a) have a common characteristic; they relate *inseparable quantities* that is two quantities such that the presence of one of them in a body involves the presence of the other in the same body, so that equal amounts of the first correspond to equal amount of the second. Thus: ....
>
> 4. With each particle possessing unit kinetic energy is associated a periodic phenomenon whose frequency is equal to the inverse of Planck's constant.

5. Each unit of energy carries with it an inertial mass equal to the inverse of the square of the velocity of light ... (Palacios 1964 p. 25)

The Second Postulate: Indispensable universal constants are those which occur in relations between two inseparable quantities; all others are superfluous. (Palacios 1964 p. 26)

Not only can we now make sense of the substantive aspects of these primitive coupling constants, which cannot be measured themselves by fundamental means, but we can also make sense of the dimensionality of these constants. The dimensional formula of these constants denotes the specific structural interdependency of the fundamental quantities of the empirical complexes which are governed by the same physical law. For instance, if we attribute dimensions of $[energy][period]^{-1}$ to h, we will thereby recognise the linear dependency on energy and the inverse dependency on period which characterises the structure of the interaction between the energy and period of individual complexes. In other words *the dimensions of the constant provide information about the structural similarities that characterise the empirical relations, discoverable by defined operations, amongst the objects which make up the empirical systems which are under study*.

Furthermore, we can provide a specific referent for each of the primitive derived constants under consideration: the complexes formed from the interaction of the standard objects relating to each fundamental quantity that occurs in the law in question. In the case of G, this would be the complexes formed by the standard objects for force, mass and length under the operation of the law of gravitation.

It is important to recognise, however, that the same derived constant may be grounded by more than one set of empirical complexes. For instance, if we investigate the systems which exemplify Kepler's Third Law ($GM = 4\pi^2r^3T^{-2}$), we may embed a notion of G which involves different extensive, fundamentally measured quantities from those involved in Newton's gravitational law. The possibility emerges of alternative empirical systems to ground primitive derived constants, giving rise to an interesting case of underdetermination, because any attempt to show the notational equivalence of the derived constants concerned presupposes a particular numerical representation or an isomorphism of the empirical systems. Neither presupposition is warranted. There may be more than one empirical system grounding a particular primitive derived constant, and we may not be able to choose between them.

At this point, we may note, perhaps with some surprise, that Dingle placed a heavy emphasis upon the experimental origins of dimensioned constants, when we might have expected him to argue that dimensioned constants have merely a conventional existence as Ellis later did. This latent inconsistency in Dingle's approach leads to problems. For Dingle, while recognizing the experimental footing of dimensioned constants (as opposed to the definitional origins of the dimensionless scale factors introduced by the equations that define a derived quantity), was not able to provide an account of what the specific dimensions were of a given dimensional constant in a given law e.g. h in Planck's law. In order to do this, he would either have (i) to consider the constant in question as being entirely defined by the equation (i.e. $h \equiv E / \nu$) - in which case his experimental / defined distinction is unsound, or (ii) to accept the only other choice available to him, that the constant was a fundamental quantity, possessing its own dimension - in which case Dingle would have been forced to abandon his assertion of the dimensional homogeneity of physics (which, then, would not necessarily hold for $E = h\nu$). We are not faced by this difficulty, whereby h has its own dimension, because we can ground our account of the dimensions of h in the structure of the empirical systems that characterise Planck's law. Dingle put himself in this unhappy position by insisting that dimensions *"are not characteristic of physical quantities themselves"* and to overcome it, simply asserted (1942a p. 330) that the experimental constants have the appropriate dimensions and satisfy homogeneity.[36]

The case of derived quantities in general, i.e. system-dependent parameters and not just universal constants, is similar. If we can discover an empirical law relating the derived quantity uniquely to fundamental quantities, we can develop an empirical account of the dimensions of the derived quantity. The ability to do so provides a clear means of distinguishing between *derived* and *defined* quantities: we will not be able to identify the necessary physical systems, operations and relations to provide an empirical account of dimensions for the latter. The structure of the interrelationships captured by the analysis of empirical dimensions for derived quantities warrants further investigation. The author believes it should be possible to establish a representation theorem which shows that the empirical structure conveyed by the relations defining empirical dimensions (for instance □) is isomorphic to the derived scale $\langle \Xi, \mathcal{L}, g \rangle$, considered by Suppes.[37]

In the case of G, we note that the empirical dimensions of $[\text{force}][\text{length}]^2[\text{mass}]^{-2}$ are not those traditionally assigned if we use mass, length and time as reference quantities. The use of a smaller number of quantities, and therefore representation dimensions, is a convenience, of which we avail ourselves. (See note 28). From an empirical point of view, it is clear that G refers to the complex interaction between the mass, separation and force between objects. We differ in our specification of reference quantities from Palacios, who settled the size of reference quantity basis by reference to his own set of equations governing related phenomena. This does not in fact produce the most adequate, efficient representation of those laws in vector space. In our empirical approach, the number of reference quantities to be considered in the case of a particular law is fixed by the number of fundamental quantities involved, which is four in the case of G.[38]

The bounds of conventionality

By providing a grounding in the structure of empirical systems of objects bound by empirical laws, we have curbed the conventionalist threat to our substantive notions of primitive derived constants, much as we overcame the criticisms launched on the back of the supposed failure of the fundamental/derived distinction in Chapter 3 against the status of primitive fundamental constants. It remains, however, to explain what aspects of conventionality are legitimate.

With regard to the representation of quantities, and the laws which relate them, there is no logical constraint on the representations we may choose: Dingle's first paper (1942a), fairly captures the limits of what is possible, and provides sensible practical reasons for using the types of representation that we customarily do. Palacios' views give us further ground for preferring certain representations to others - the preferred representations are based upon the sets of empirical laws that collectively characterise a particular theoretical domain - but the ardent conventionalist, while fairly attacked all round, may yet avoid surrender by clinging on to the the scraps of logic that his position retains.

While the selection of certain fundamental quantities, and not others, to characterise the structure and interrelationships of empirical systems, may also represent a conventional choice to suit practical considerations, the fact that we make such choices does not diminish the ontological significance of those quantities that we choose not to use, nor of the constants which convey the structure of the interrelationships, described by laws, which exist between these fundamental quantities. There are some empirical aspects of the world which we have chosen either to ignore or to know little about. A lack of knowledge does not, however, alter the empirical situation regarding actual and possible relationships between the fundamental properties of empirical systems which are captured by derived constants.

Realism reasserted

The approach presented offers the prospect of a realist account of dimensions and quantities based upon empirical considerations, which is distinct from a conventionalist account of their representation. Such an account would not only allow us to explain why different measurement methods relate to the same quantities, and the repeated occurence of the same quantities in laws and theories, but also the success of our methods in predicting the future behaviour of physical systems.

The operationalist, on the other hand, does not enjoy this favourable position, and is not able to address a number of these issues satisfactorily. In particular, it is hard to see how Dingle and his colleagues can escape from the logical incompatibility and incommensurability that arises from measurements made by different individuals, let alone by different methods. Having overcome the customary conventionalist ploys which are used to disguise this problem, Ellis owes us a new account.

This account of fundamental and derived constants also embodies a number of interesting features, in particular aspects of underdetermination and conventionality, which will need to be accommodated by the general philosophical tradition in which we seek to embed the account. We might use this work as a foil with which to investigate current modest realist accounts, seeking to test their philosophical robustness. Given the shift in recent years away from convergent scientific realism, we will be particularly interested to apply the notions of constants developed in the context of the debate surrounding the Natural Ontological Attitude (NOA).

In the next chapter, we will review the emergence of NOA and consider NOA's strengths and weaknesses relative to traditional forms of realism, instrumentalism and constructive empiricism. Given NOA's strong commitment to the existence of theoretical entities and belief in the supremacy of the empirical methods employed by science, a NOAer will have no choice but to accept the substantive nature of the constants of physics. While at first sight this seems no more problematic than accepting the existence of entities such as molecules or atoms, this account of constants does pose some interesting challenges to a NOAer.

Key to the debate surrounding realism, is the question of what entities really exist. We have proposed that both primitive fundamental and derived constants exist. Primitive fundamental constants are properties of elementary particles which may function as the standard objects in a formal fundamental measurement system; primitive derived constants are properties of complexes of particles which may function as the standard objects in a formal derived measurement system, as described in this chapter. The role of constants as standard objects is a case of a coordinative definition linking entities to theories of physics. Such definitions give rise to aspects of conventionality as we have seen, but the conventionalist critique may be diffused by recognising that the possibility of different choices of representation does not undermine the firm empirical underpinnings which these notions of constant enjoy. To support the existence of primitive constants as real entities does, however, expose us to two sceptical attacks.

First, we must be prepared to answer critics, like van Fraassen, who deny the reality of scientific entities which we cannot observe - a general underdeterminative threat arising for both fundamental and derived constants. Second, we must explain how our underlying philosophical tradition can tolerate the existence of alternative empirical systems which underpin each of the primitive derived constants - this is an interesting, specific case of underdetermination. In Chapter 6, we will explore the challenge posed generally and specifically to NOA by underdetermination, and will argue that NOA can tolerate a notion of limited relativity similar to the ecumenical line described by Quine to deal with the specific underdetermination posed by primitive derived constants. Faced by general underdetermination, NOA fares no worse than other non-traditional realists accounts, and can be defended by appeal to Common Sense Realism.

Summary

We have examined in detail the threat posed to our account of the status of primitive derived constants in this chapter. The origins and development of the conventionalist case have been described, and the philosophical implications of this doctrine, drawn out.

Careful examination of the methods of dimensional analysis shows that while a notion of purely conventional dimensions may be maintained, such a notion belongs entirely to the mathematical representations we choose for physics. Manipulation of this representation may transform and remove derived constants, but only at the price of distorting the adequacy of the representation.

An alternative notion of dimension has been provided, firmly grounded in the empirical realm of objects, relations and operations. Using this notion of dimensions, we can anchor our account of the substantive nature of primitive derived constants to the world, and to the empirically discovered laws of physics.

Notes

1 As an aside, we may note that to say the choice of fundamental quantities is conventional does not imply that choices are to be made on the grounds of simplicity alone. Davies (1981) has argued, for instance, that any concept of length involves a certain commitment to geometry in order for us to have concepts of lines, points etc. Assumptions about geometry may be required for us to have a concept of space, and place constraints upon acceptable conventions.

2 In Bridgman's terminology *primary* corresponds to Campbell's *fundamental*.

3 See remarks pp. 53-4.

4 Tolman, by way of contrast stipulated that any quantity that was regarded as a primary dimension, should be capable of being measured by fundamental means.

5 Similar remarks may be found in Focken (1953) pp. 22-3.

6 The same point is made by Palacios (1964) in his footnote to p. 12.

7 In making this criticism, we consider with Campbell that 'fundamental' is synonymous with 'extensive'. Dingle clearly did not make this identification. He defined fundamental quantities as those whose measures were unaffected by changes in the measurement or units of other quantities (specific measurements would meet this criterion). Nonetheless, Dingle would have been required to provide an account of representation and uniqueness for his fundamental quantities, which would have exposed the vulnerabilities of his operationalist approach.

8 Campbell spoke of the number of *basic* fundamental quantities in a dimensional system (1920 p. 378).

9 In our terminology, we may say that equations relate measures, i.e. values x units, not simply values.

10 By *designation symbol* understand dimensional formula, and by *concept* understand quantity.

11 Dalzell's succinct summary is worth quoting: *The dependence of the magnitudes of the derived units upon those of the fundamental units is called dimensionality (Dalzell 1945 p. 487)* C.f. Campbell (1920 p. 371): *The relation between the units of the derived and of the fundamental magnitudes is expressed by the conceptions of "dimensions".*

12 There are instances where more than two quantities share dimensional formulae: elastic modulus, energy density, pressure, resilience and stress all have dimensions $M\ L^{-1}\ T^{-2}$.

13 As discussed, the choice is, more correctly, of the number of reference quantities, not fundamental quantities.

14 Also called a form factor.

15 As a consequence of scale invariance the equation will have standard form i.e. be a monomial.

16 The tone of Campbell (1926) and Bridgman (1926) is surprisingly condescending and dismissive.

17 The converse is not strictly true, as Bridgman showed by artificial construction of equations which are dimensionally homogeneous but not scale-invariant, e.g. $v + s = at + \frac{1}{2} at^2$.

18 The components of the unit mass vector in the FLT basis are 1, -1, 2 corresponding to the dimensional formula F T^2 L^{-1}.

19 We again note that, more correctly, we should speak of reference rather than fundamental quantities.

20 The use of specific measures described here is not the same as, but is consistent with, that described on page 53. Here, we modify the equation that defines a derived quantity by introduction of specific variables for reference quantities, thereby rendering the equation dimensionless (we replace in every equation each term x by x / x_s, where x_s is a specific measure of x). On page 53, we introduced specific measures for derived quantities in order to increase the number of dimensions used in the defining equation, which was not modified (we measured ***h*** in units of ***h***, just as we customarily measure mass in units of mass). Both results support Sedov's assertion that dimensionality of representation is a matter of convention. In the earlier case the use of specific measures allowed all quantities to be represented as though fundamentally measured, and allowed each quantity to be considered to be a reference quantity. Here most quantities are defined by derived means using a small number of reference quantities, but only the reference quantities (and none of the the terms in the equation incorporating specific measures of the reference quantities) have dimensions. In the earlier situation, we have maximised the number of dimensions for derived quantities, here we have minimized them.

21 As a practical matter the use of dimensionless numbers to make the display of experimental results efficient and scale invariant is well established prompting Douglas (1969) and Massey (1971) to list known dimensionless parameters.

22 We ignore the form factor implicit in the second equation.

23 We could have eliminated either of the other dimensions. See Pankhurst (1964) p. 37.

24 Clearly when we suppress a dimension, derived quantities that are defined in equations involving the suppressed reference dimension, are strictly redefined in the reduced basis. This for an operationalist should mean they are new, different quantities from the old.

25 For instance, Duncanson (1941 p. 433) remarked: *it is possible, and manyways desirable, that as our knowledge increases the integration of physics will become more complete and a smaller number of indefinables will suffice, and it may be hoped that ultimately only one such indefinable will be necessary.*

26 See 'A Plea for Chronometry' by Prof J. L. Synge in The New Scientist 19 February 1959, where the author argued that a broad science of chronometry should precede geometry.

27 Space Time and Gravitation 1920 p. 98.

28 In fact Palacios is here guilty of choosing a reduced basis. More correctly in his account of mechanical quantities, he should consider that he has the following unknowns f, m, r, a, G, k (the suppressed dynamical constant in Newton's second law) and two equations: Newton's law of gravity and second law. This requires four reference quantities, which are usually force, mass, length and time (see earlier). Palacios suppresses force. His situation is not helped by the distinction he introduces between gravitational and inertial mass, since this introduces an extra equation but also an extra variable (gravitational mass). The fact that force is suppressed in the most adequate representation is relevant to our concluding remarks concerning G.

29 See Putnam's 1975 paper on conventionalism.

30 A system of specific measures, which representationally treats all quantities as though they were fundamental, would still support a notion of dimension to accommodate the choice of initial specific unit. Sedov avoids this need for dimensions by making a once and for all choice of specific units: certain universal constants. See p. 53 and notes 16 and 20. Campbell overlooked the assignment of values to the chosen standard object and was mistaken when he asserted: *Again it must be remembered that fundamental magnitudes have no dimensions; there is nothing to force us to change the unit of one fundamental magnitude when we change the unit of another (1920 p. 377).*

31 Choosing r involves no loss of generality.

32 Campbell and others provided descriptions of how force may be measured fundamentally. What precise arrangements would be required in practice would need to be settled by trial and error, and are beyond the experimental skills of the author.

33 We may recall Campbell's remark (1920 p. 392): *as a matter of fact, I deny totally that force is properly regarded as a derived magnitude at all; it is fundamental, just as volume is fundamental.*

34 The equivalence of the automorphic and the mathematical structures, does not preclude further mathematical manipulation of the representation, as is for instance represented by eliminating dimensions. The empirical consequences of

such moves are to distort the relational structure of the empirical systems under consideration.

35 The author surmises, but has not proved, that similarities and dimensions will also be key features of systems of measurement that use alternative principles of correlation, and hence have different absolute values for relative magnitudes compared to our customary measuring systems, provided they meet the constraints for acceptable representations given in Chapter 3. The merit of our customary systems is that they make scale factor changes easy to handle.

36 In a later paper (1943), Dingle himself discussed aspects of the problem: *Thus, an arbitrary standard mass having been chosen, the mass of any other body could have been measured by the force which the standard exerted on it at a fixed distance. This would have needed an independent definition of force, which might have been provided by the reading of a specified type of spring balance. If this had been done, force would have been a fundamental magnitude, and the result embodied in* [Newton's second law including a constant] *would have had to be determined by experiment. N would then have been a dimensional constant,* [rather than dimensionless] *for the dimensional equation would have been* $[F] = [N\,MLT^{-2}]$ *which would not have been homogeneous unless N had the dimensions* $[FM^{-1}L^{-1}T^{2}]$. This difficulty is part of the general problem whereby Dingle fails to distinguish between derived and defined quantities.

37 Suppes himself provides what is a representation theorem for *defined* quantities, and does not concern himself with the structure of empirical relationships which characterise derived quantities. Having established a representation theorem for each fundamental quantity, he simply defines the numerical assignment of a derived measurement as a mathematical function of the numerical assignments of the fundamental quantities.

38 Sedov (1959) discussed whether f=ma is to be considered to be a definitional or an experimental equation. Given its origins in the work of Kepler et al. Sedov argued that it made sense to consider the equation to be experimental, thus supporting the view proposed. Dingle recognised the legitimacy of the approach we have suggested, but when Benham (1942)argued for there to be a constant in Newton's second law on the grounds that this was an experimental relationship, Dingle (1942a) objected that Benham had failed to provide a definition of force. We can do so using the axioms for extensive measurement of force, an approach Dingle himself followed in a later paper (1943).

5 Constants and reality

Introduction

In the two previous chapters, we have addressed the challenge posed to our account of constants by conventionalism: we concluded that primitive fundamental constants are properties of individual elementary particles, and that primitive derived constants relate the different particle properties that are involved in the systematic interaction of elementary particles.

In this chapter, we will review the realist-instrumentalist-empiricist debate, focussing on the emergence of more moderate accounts of the scientific enterprise typified by the Natural Ontological Attitude (NOA). Our purpose will be to understand the strengths and weaknesses of such accounts in order to establish the context in which we can use the account of constants developed in earlier chapters to subject them to scrutiny.

Synopsis of chapter

While sophisticated instrumentalists such as Laudan, through his commitment to research traditions,[1] may accept that particles exist, are highly explanatory and useful predictors, such views mask a very divergent perspective as to what these claims import when compared with the commitments of a realist.[2] This divergence of perspective will be examined and a number of the principal difficulties associated with the traditions of realism, instrumentalism and constructive empiricism will be highlighted and reviewed. The intention is not to be exhaustive, but illustrative, given the primary focus of the present work is not to defend NOA or other, realist accounts against all possible counter arguments. We seek, more modestly, to explore the compatibility of such accounts with a non-conventional view of physical constants.

Even when expressed in their most sophisticated forms, each of these positions faces intractable difficulties, especially compared with a more moderate emergent series of positions taken by philosophers recently such as Fine.

After reviewing the principal advantages of Fine's Natural Ontological Attitude, we turn to consider its potential weaknesses. These include its parasitical dependence on everyday or Common Sense realism (CSR), and NOA's vulnerability in the face of underdetermination. The former difficulty is shared with constructive empiricism, and while weakening the supremacy of NOA, is not considered to be overwhelming. The second objection is considered in greater detail in Chapter 6.

The emergence of NOA

The failure of positivist philosophies of science, typified by that of Carnap, to provide an adequate formalism for the implementation of verificationist theories of meaning,[3] and the emergence of radical constructivist accounts of science (most importantly, the accounts of Kuhn and Feyerabend), led to a resurgence of interest in realism. In the late 1970's sophisticated metatheoretical arguments were formulated by Putnam, Boyd, Newton-Smith and others in an attempt to substantiate further the realist case.[4] While initially these arguments, drawing upon the instrumental reliability and systematic convergence of mature scientific theory, seemed plausible, pressure was subsequently directed to the realist edifice as a result of the emergence of more sophisticated counter positions, such as the epistemic instrumentalism of Laudan, and the constructive empiricism of Van Fraassen.[5] Not only did these revised accounts highlight some of the traditional failings of realism, but they also helped to discredit the higher-level arguments advanced, particularly by Boyd, that had appeared to provide the icing on the realist cake.

In turn, the novel aspects of the new instrumentalist and constructive empiricist traditions were subject to scrutiny, and found not to deliver the adequate, unproblematic philosophical platform claimed by their pioneers. Fine exposed these failings of the anti-realists as well as those of the traditional realist in his seminal article "The Natural Ontological Attitude" (NOA). (Fine himself called NOA non-realist in outlook, contrasting its minimal commitments to those of full-blown, traditional realism. It has been argued, however (Newton-Smith 1988, Musgrave 1989, Psillos 1996) that much of what NOA involves is shared with a modest form of realism, and NOA will, for the purposes of this chapter, be held to be "non-realist" only in contrast to traditional, as opposed to scientific, realism. These distinctions are elucidated in due course). Similar conclusions to those of NOA were also reached independently by Horwich (1982).

In response to these searching criticisms, we may observe a shift towards a less bold realism, which endorses a weaker[6] version of the correspondence theory of truth, accepting realism about everyday objects at the outset: Putnam, Ellis (1985), Newton-Smith, Levin, Fine, Horwich and Miller have all developed weak-realist / non-realist accounts to address the failings of traditional, or what has been called (Newton-Smith 1988) "faded", realism. There remain a number of committed realists who have refused to abandon a realist account that involves a strong version of correspondence, such as Boyd, and Leplin, but their recent efforts either involve more sophisticated inferences to best explanation that may always solicit an instrumentalist riposte, or introduce other intractable difficulties (for instance, correspondence difficulties in the case of Giere).

Other philosophers, such as Hacking, Ellis (1979) and Cartwright have restricted their realism to entity realism, which involves a straightforward commitment to the existence of theoretical entities, but does not involve an ontological or epistemic commitment to the availability of true theories describing the behaviour of such entities. Such accounts are deemed by their proponents to have the merit of meshing well with the experimental activities of practising scientists.[7]

The response of the instrumentalists and constructive empiricists to Fine et al. has been muted, largely consisting of the reiteration and clarification of their respective positions.

Difficulties with realism

Following Newton-Smith and Boyd, for the rest of the chapter we will hold realism to comprise the following key elements: ontological (theories are true or false in virtue of the way the world is); epistemological (the application of scientific methodology enables us to arrive at theories which are approximately true); causal (unobservable theoretical entities exist independently of us and are causally responsible for phenomena); convergent (successor theories are closer to the truth than their predecessors).[8]

The traditional Achilles heal of realism, as contrasted with idealism, has been its failure to justify adequately the existence of an independent externalised world to which our beliefs and theories ideally correspond: what some have called 'a transcendent reality'.[9] This element of realism was dubbed *metaphysical realism* by Putnam, and he, building upon the earlier work of Quine[10] on the indeterminacy of reference, has shown just how problematic the notion of external access is. In his paper "A Problem about Reference" (Putnam 1981), he showed that even everyday sentences suffer indeterminacy of reference: 'A cat sat on the mat' can be reinterpreted as 'A cat* sat on a mat*', where this sentence has the same truth values as the original in all possible worlds but the intensions (i.e. assignment functions for extensions) of cat / cat* and mat / mat* are different. In the actual world cat* refers to cherries and mat* refers to trees.[11] The truth conditions for whole sentences underdetermine reference. He concluded:

> To me, believing that some correspondence intrinsically just is reference (not as a result of our operational and theoretical constraints, or our intentions, but as an *ultimate* metaphysical fact) amounts to a magical theory of reference. Reference itself becomes what Locke called a 'substantial form' (an entity which *intrinsically* belongs with a certain name) on such a view. Even if one is willing to contemplate such unexplicable metaphysical facts, the epistemological problems that accompany such a metaphysical view seem insuperable. For, assuming a world of mind-independent, discourse-independent entities (this is the presupposition of the view we are discussing), there are, as we have seen, many different 'correspondences' which represent possible or candidate reference relations (infinitely many, in fact, if there are infinitely many things in the universe). (Putnam 1981 p. 47)

Elsewhere[12] Putnam argued not only was metaphysical realism untenable, it was also incoherent.[13] In his attack, he claimed that any notion of realism which supported the convergence of rational enquiry, and yet made it possible for our beliefs in the epistemic limit to be false, was irrational and therefore incoherent:

> The most important consequence of metaphysical realism is that *truth* is supposed to be *radically non-epistemic* - we might be 'brains in a vat' and so the theory that is 'ideal' from the point of view of operational utility, inner beauty and elegance, 'plausibility', simplicity, 'conservatism', etc., *might be false*...The supposition that even an 'ideal' theory (from a pragmatic point of view) might really be false appears to collapse into *unintelligibility*. (Putnam 1978 pp. 125-6)

Faced by these challenges, realists have generally adopted one of two tactics. One category of realist has collapsed the ontological ingredient in their notion of truth into an epistemic criterion, adopting a position labelled *internal realism* by Putnam (following Carnap 1956). For instance, difficulties concerning external access prompted Putnam to advocate a concept of truth that was thoroughly epistemic, echoing Peirce in the adoption of the "idealization of rational acceptance" as the determinant of truth.[14] One advantage of this approach is that it deals with both the problem of metaphysical skepticism and the status of theoretical entities relative to the status of everyday objects in a single account: if truth is obtained at the idealized limit of rational enquiry, skepticism may be excluded, for it makes no sense to suppose that at such a limit, our beliefs might be false given that the criterion of truth guarantees that they will be true. Theoretical entities will be ontologically well-grounded, like everyday objects, provided they are supported by our beliefs. In this account, at the idealised limit, there will be no distinction to be drawn between what we believe exists and what exists.

The other response has been to bracket Putnam's concerns with other varieties of skepticism and to set this question aside, accepting the reality of everyday macroscopic objects as a philosophical starting point. The key issue for *scientific realism*, as contrasted with instrumentalism or constructive empiricism, then becomes whether theoretical entities are to be treated differently from everyday objects with regard to claims about belief, truth and existence. Hacking has clearly explicated these distinctions:

> The internal realist acts, in practical affairs, as if the entities occurring in his working theories did in fact exist. However, the direction of Putnam's metaphysical antirealism is no longer scientific. It is not peculiarly about natural science. It is about chairs and livers too...There might be two kinds of internal realist, the instrumentalist about science and the scientific realist. The former is, in practical affairs where he uses his present scheme of concepts, a realist about livers and chairs but thinks that electrons are only mental constructs. The latter thinks that livers, chairs, and electrons are probably all in the same boat, that is, real at least within the present system of classification. I take Putnam to be an internal scientific realist rather than an internal instrumentalist. The fact that either doctrine is compatible with transcendental nominalism and internal realism shows that our question of scientific realism is almost independent of Putnam's internal realism. (Hacking 1984 p.159)

Fine argued, however, that there was more to be said about an externalised reality. He observed that while realists and anti-realists might be able to agree a common shared starting position that embraced the truth of scientific claims on the same footing as claims about the everyday world, realists wanted to add to this core an explicative justification of truth in terms of an externalised (metaphysical) correspondence (anti-realists likewise added to the core position their own interpretation of truth). The fact that both realists and anti-realists could accept talk of livers, chairs and electrons unproblematically, disguised the very different perspectives on truth held by these philosophical traditions. It is clear that Fine thought NOA was different from (traditional) realism in its attitude to truth.

> So far I have managed to avoid what, for the realist, is the essential point: what of the "external world"? How can I talk of reference and existence claims unless I am talking about referring to things right out there in the world? ... For the problem of the external world (so-called) is how to satisfy the realist's demand that we justify the existence claims sanctioned by science (and, therefore, by NOA) as claims to the existence of entities "out there" ... If I am right, then the realist is chasing a phantom, and we cannot actually do more, with regard to existence claims, than follow scientific practice, just as NOA suggests. (Fine 1986a p. 132)

Subsequently, Newton-Smith (1988) has argued that Fine was mistaken in supposing that scientific realists endorsed a strong notion of external correspondence in their account of truth: the scientific realist holds much the same account of truth as a NOAer.[15] If Newton-Smith is correct, it would seem that Fine has attacked a straw man. An examination of the writings of other realist philosophers suggests otherwise. Leplin, for instance, wrote:

> That is because the concept of truth itself is unavoidably metaphysical, as I have argued in attempting to discredit surrogates for it. Truth as ordinarily conceived is a condition that could remain concealed despite our best efforts to elicit it. There is no inconsistency in

> supposing that at the level of deep structure, of the entities and processes ultimately responsible for our experience, the world is other than our best supported theories represent it. Perhaps our evolutionary history, in equipping us to flourish in an environment of middle sized objects, has selected against the sort of attributes we would require to read microstructure or superstructure correctly. Perhaps we are systematically misled in out efforts at theorizing, and are unequipped to correct the error. Perhaps it is impossible for us to acquire evidence against certain false beliefs, because those beliefs do not differ from true ones at an experientially accessible level. According to the natural conception of truth as representation of a theory-independent world, such possibilities are always entertainable. (Leplin forthcoming pp. 54-5)

In the remainder of this chapter, we shall assume for the purposes of mainstream discussion of realism that the question of an externalised reality has either been (1) accepted as an important but problematic metaphysical element in the notion of truth employed by *traditional realists*,[16] such as Leplin, or (2) addressed through a restructured notion of truth in the case of *internal realists* (such as Putnam and Ellis), or (3) has been set aside by *scientific realists* (such as Newton-Smith and Miller) who have adopted a concept of truth, without additional metaphysical or epistemic overhead, that simply uses a Tarski / Davidson account to explicate how correspondence may be understood in terms of the satisfaction relations between predicates and objects.[17] This interpretation of Tarski is entirely semantic in outlook, and is shared by NOA. Before turning to other challenges facing realists, one other realist approach warrants comment: that of Giere.

Putnam's (and Quine's) arguments also pose problems for the constructive realist account recently developed by Giere. In his account, Giere proposed a naturalistic theory of science, which draws upon recent developments in the field of cognitive science. He abandoned the need to provide a categorical notion of rationality based upon epistemological precepts in favour of a naturalistic notion of rationality that relates to the successful pursuit and attainment of goals through learning processes such as satisficing. In keeping with his naturalist approach to epistemological questions, Giere adopted a thoroughly model-theoretic approach to scientific enquiry: scientists develop theoretical models which are true interpretations of the various possible linguistic formulations of axiomatic theories; the models are conjoined with a theoretical hypothesis which relates the models to the world, describing in what respects and to what degree the models are similar to the world.

> The relationship between some (suitably interpreted) equations and their corresponding model may be described as one of characterization, or even definition. We may even appropriately speak here of "truth". The interpreted equations are *true* of the corresponding model. But truth here has no *epistemological* significance. The equations truly describe the model because the model is defined as something that exactly satisfies the equations ...
> Unlike a model, a theoretical hypothesis is, in my account, a *linguistic* entity, namely a statement asserting some sort of relationship between a model and a designated real system

(or class of real systems) ...
The appropriate relationship, I suggest, is *similarity* ... The general form of a theoretical hypothesis is thus: Such-and-such identifiable real system is similar to a designated model in indicated respects and degrees. (Giere 1988 pp. 79-81)

In this way Giere believed he had avoided the correspondence difficulties associated with traditional realist accounts of truth.

> Most theories of science, whether old or new, assume that any representational relationship between theory and reality would have to be understood as a "correspondence" between scientific statements and the world ... The interpretation I have offered above undercuts these arguments by denying the common assumption. There is on this account, no direct relationship between sets of statements and the real world. The relationship is indirect through the intermediary of a theoretical model ... Of course, assertions about the existence of similarity relationships between models and real systems do require theoretical hypotheses, which are indeed linguistic entities ... And there is a truth relationship of the correspondence type between statements characterizing an abstract model and the model itself. But this correspondence, which reduces to definition, is not a problem. The relationship that does the heavy representational work is not one of truth between a linguistic entity and a real object, but of similarity between two objects, one abstract and one real. From this point of view the difficulties with the standard view arise because it tries to forge a direct semantic link between the statements characterizing the model and the world - thus eliminating the role of models altogether. (Giere 1988 p. 82)

Unfortunately, the notion of similarity employed cannot sustain the weight placed upon it.[18] By *defining* his theoretical models in terms of the theories for which they are models, Giere has doubled the ontology of science: not only do we encounter electrons, but we also are presented with model-theoretic entities which obey the theory of quantum electro-dynamics, which for want of better terminology, we might call "gierelectrons". Giere's thesis is that gierelectrons are similar to electrons. But how can we tell, and why do we need gierelectrons as well as electrons? If, following Ockham, we believe ontological parsimony is a virtue, Giere's account may be criticised for duplicating entities. In the case of observable entities, we might be able to support an innate cognitive faculty that allowed us to make successful judgements of similarity between the observable entities and their counterparts defined by theory, but with more abstruse entities this seems less likely, particularly given the difficulties encountered historically (Putnam 1981 pp. 56-9) by accounts of reference which relied on a notion of similitude between concepts and their referents. (The analogy here is the problematic similitude between theory-defined gierelectrons and electrons). Giere's account seems to create more problems than it solves as far as correspondence is concerned.

A second major difficulty for realism results from what has been called "the negative induction": our former theories were all false, and hence the hypothesis that our current and future theories will turn out to be false, is inductively well supported. To address this problem, realists explored the notions of approximate truth and convergence, accepting that while science might literally be false we were getting closer to a true description of the world (what Laudan called Convergent Epistemological Realism, CER). It was held that this view provided the best explanation of the spectacular success of science, in particular the instrumental reliability of our theories which was entailed by the CER account. Based on the merits of its explanatory success, abductive reasoning supported the case that the realist account was true.[19] Furthermore, since the CER account was held to provide a causally explanatory account of instrumental reliability, the basic claims of CER were taken to be subject to empirical investigation.

Unfortunately, a close historical examination of individual cases by Laudan (1981) seriously called into question the supposed links between instrumental reliability, approximate truth, and reference:

> There are, however, potential hazards as well as advantages associated with the "scientizing" of epistemology. Specifically, once one concedes that epistemic doctrines are to be tested in the court of experience, it is possible that one's favorite epistemic theories may be refuted rather than confirmed. It is the thesis of this paper that precisely such a fate afflicts a form of realism advocated by those who have been in the vanguard of the move to show that realism is supported by an empirical study of the development of science. Specifically, I will show that epistemic realism, at least in certain of its extant forms, is neither supported by, nor has it made sense of, much of the available historical evidence. (Laudan 1981 p. 19)

In reply one might first contend like Leplin that Laudan missed the point:

> Putnam does not infer the truth of realism from the predictive success of science. Rather, he infers the truth of realism from its alleged, unique ability to explain the predictive success of science. Once again, the telling criticism seems to be one that attacks realism directly on the basis of a skeptical reading of history, and then concludes indirectly either that realism fails to explain predictive success because it is false, or that the explanation it provides is unacceptable. The explanatory problem Putnam has raised remains outstanding. (Leplin 1984 p. 204)

Even if we concede that Laudan's criticisms do not attack the abductive arguments of faded realism in the most direct manner, they nonetheless damage the foundations of the realist's platform: much of the explanatory content of the realist explanation of the success of science derives from the pivotal role played by approximative truth in the convergence of mature science. Leplin's counter does not deflect Laudan's criticisms of the inadequacy of current accounts of approximative truth in terms of the links between approximative truth, success and reference.

Hardin and Rosenberg (1982), by contrast, have contested Laudan's historical analysis of cases: they have claimed for example that the term 'ether' does have a referent, namely the electromagnetic field, and that they have suggested that theories of the past may be held to be approximately true even though certain key terms do not refer (for example, the term 'gene' in Mendel's theory of inheritable properties). They have also, for the purposes of their argument, distinguished periods before and after the "take-off point" of particular scientific disciplines. The difficulty with their reply is that, even if they can sustain Laudan's criticism that their approach involves a Whiggish interpretation of history, they have failed to provide what is lacking: a convincing and comprehensive account of approximate truth and its relation to reference and scientific enquiry. While counter-examples to Laudan's particular claims of approximate truth, reference or success relative to individual theories may be challenged, the connection between the realist's notions of truth and the explanation of success in science remain murky at best.

A more telling objection to Laudan's criticism, however, is to question the notion of "success" employed, looking forward rather than back. The epistemological significance of the claims of CER do not relate to the failings of scientists in the past: what is of greater interest is the warranted confidence we place in our theories looking forward. In other words, what justifies our expectations of future success? The methodology of science, which is thoroughly theory dependent, has allowed us to develop theories which work: the methodology is reliable.

> Call a theory instrumentally reliable if it makes approximately true predictions about observable phenomena. Call a methodology instrumentally reliable if it is a reliable guide to the acceptance of theories which are themselves instrumentally reliable. (Boyd 1985 p. 4)

How can this be explained? The realist is in a better position, Boyd argued, to account for the instrumental reliability of methodology (as opposed to individual theories), particularly theory-driven inductive judgements of projectibility, than his counterparts.[20]

Whether convergent realists can provide, however, a convincing, closely structured argument from realist assumptions about approximate truth and reference to the instrumental reliability of theories or methodology, no longer matters. Laudan's criticisms were reinforced by Fine's attack on abductive arguments, constructed by realists to support their position, which were based on the instrumental success of scientific theories or scientific method. Fine observed that a putative instrumentalist, who had concern about the abductive arguments used at the level of individual theories to justify the existence claims for the theoretical entities involved,[21] would not be reassured by arguments that (1) made use of the same type of abductive reasoning, used at a high level, to derive the truth of realism from its success in explaining the instrumental reliability of scientific methodology, and that (2) then used the truth of realism to justify the abductive arguments used at the level of individual theories. The instrumentalist would claim the realist had begged the question.[22]

> Thus, both at the ground level and at the level of methodology, no support accrues to realism by showing that realism is a good hypothesis for explaining scientific practice. If we are

open-minded about realism to begin with, then such a demonstration (even if successful) merely begs the question that we have left open ("need we take good explanatory hypotheses as true?"). (Fine 1986a p. 115)

Boyd (1983) has countered that the rejection of abductive inferences - inferences to the truth of underlying theory, given these theories best explain observed regularities - poses a serious problem for empiricists. Boyd claimed that without abduction the inductive judgements which scientists make from observables to observables are unjustified, and that, viewed side by side, the realist philosophical offering is more attractive than the empiricist philosophical offering. He has not, however, directly compared his realist account with NOA. Newton-Smith, also formerly in the forefront of convergence realists, similarly conceded the circularity of the transfer of abductive, inference-to-the-best-explanation (IBE) methods from the practice of science itself, to the defence of CER. The stumbling block to such arguments is that instrumentalists can provide an alternative explanation[23] to that of the convergence-realist for any methodological principle that is successfully advocated by the scientific community.[24] Newton-Smith summarised the situation as follows:

Let F be any feature of scientific praxis which the realist purports to explain or justify. The realist has to show that F is a feature operative in the history of science which has brought empirical success (even if we do achieve something more than empirical success in science, it remains the only sign we have of the something). But the instrumentalist can simply assert that the history of science provides inductive support for continuing to use F. Thus there is a justification, a justification which involves less contentious assumptions than the realist one for the continued deployment of F. Scientific praxis underdetermines the choice between realism and instrumentalism. (Newton-Smith 1988 p. 180)

In spite of the perceived difficulties of mounting abductive arguments for realism, Leplin has recently advocated a defence for convergent realism based upon a carefully elucidated account of the novelty that characterises the development of successful theory.[25] Unfortunately, the arguments from realism, as the best explanation of novel prediction, to the truth of realism are not different in kind from those rejected by Newton-Smith. Instrumentalists can mount an equally strong inductive case to support the adoption of more fertile, creative theories which make novel predictions over less adventurous alternatives even within the framework of conditions for novelty drawn up by Leplin. Instrumentalists may prefer to conclude that where a theory explains a novel fact, the theory is to be considered useful rather than true. It might be the case that not only do we find that a theory works well in one domain, but it brings the added advantage of working in an additional area where it was not anticipated that it would work.[26] Based upon induction on past instances, an instrumentalist might have good grounds for saying that the most useful theories provide novel results.

In an attempt to strengthen and to differentiate his account, Leplin has carefully formulated conditions which he considers sufficient to establish (1) that a particular observed effect is independent of a given theory yet can be uniquely explained by that theory, and (2) that as a consequence the effect may be considered novel for the theory. In order to rule out the use of auxiliary hypotheses with alternative theories, which may give rise to the same observed effect, Leplin is obliged to insist, however, that the alternative theories provide acceptable mechanisms and structure in their explanatory account of the effect, in addition to prediction. If these alternative theories do not provide the explanatory infrastructure Leplin demands, they are ruled out of contention as alternative accounts of the novel effect: the realist assumptions that lie behind these constraints clearly beg the question.[27] Even his showpiece example of light deflection, a novel observable effect relative to general relativity, turns out to be problematic because it can also be predicted by a Newtonian account.[28] To deal with this difficulty, Leplin outlaws the Newtonian alternative:

> Although it is natural and satisfactory in many contexts to suppose that the ability to predict reflects the explanatory resources of a theory, the expression "explain and predict" is not redundant. And I have been careful in formulating my analysis to require not merely that T for which O is novel predict O and that O not be predicted by an alternative to T, but also that T alone provide a viable reason for expecting the effect which O instantiates. Thus light deflection satisfies the analysis [of novelty for general relativity] even though Newtonian theory could be used to predict it. (Leplin forthcoming p. 133)

We may contrast the difficulties of Leplin's realist account with Laudan's epistemic instrumentalism which can accommodate novel solutions to problems, and the impact of anomalies quite straightforwardly.

In addition to these difficulties, Leplin's account of novelty, as he himself recognises, is potentially vulnerable to underdetermination: if it were possible to show that, in a particular experimental setting, that a novel prediction might be equally well obtainable from another empirically equivalent theory, novelty will not confer truth.

> The uniqueness of the theory's explanation [of a novel fact] prevents a competitor from preempting this claim to truth. If a competing theory also explains the result, especially if it does so with similar independence of development, then chance becomes the better verdict. (Leplin forthcoming p. 107)

The carefully constructed arguments he provides against underdetermination, which rely on the impossibility of establishing empirical equivalence, are not telling. Leplin argues first that if we do not circumscribe the choice of auxiliary hypotheses to be used in the determination of the observational consequences of a pair of supposedly empirically equivalent theories, equivalence is trivial, since all observational consequences are permitted. Yet if we are to attempt to impose some constraint on the choice of auxiliary, this supposes we can make epistemic judgements concerning the choice of auxiliary, but such judgements are undermined by underdetermination (other more neutral selection criteria, such as conformity with observation, simply push the problem back in light of the Duhem-Quine thesis, which permits all specific theories in the extreme to be conformable with observation).

As a second line of defence, Leplin argues that if, instead, we show that we can offer two alternative theoretical accounts for a *given* body of observational data, this seems to beg the question of empirical equivalence of the two theories: on what grounds can we justify the selection of the observational data without seeming to beg the question?

> In effect, a dilemma has been created: either the choice of auxiliaries is unconstrained, different choices yielding different observational consequence classes for theories, or the status of permissible auxiliary [theories] is relativized to the specification of observational consequences, which must proceed independently of the theory whose consequences they are to be. Both horns vitiate the presumption that theories possess empirically equivalent rivals. All of this is inevitable if, with UD, we deny recourse to a standard of epistemic warrant for auxiliaries. (Leplin forthcoming p. 256)

It still remains possible, however, to establish empirical equivalence and to employ alternative theories. We may find a pair of alternative theories which produce the same set of equations to interface with common sets of auxiliary theories in order to derive observations; alternatively we may establish the empirical equivalence by induction over large numbers of specified sets of data, thereby avoiding the accusation of begging the question and without the need to proscribe the choice of auxiliary.[29] We might also posit empirical adequacy as an epistemic selection standard: underdetermination imposes limits on the epistemic warrants for theories, but does not imply there is no epistemic warrant at all. For van Fraassen, in particular, the warrant of empirical adequacy is held to be sufficient for the purposes of science.

Leplin himself accepts that there are current examples of underdetermination, but claims these are in principle defeasible. This is a poor argument for a realist, because against non-realists and selective skeptics, Leplin himself is at pains to point out that the possibility of error is not a good reason in and of itself to refuse epistemic warrant for successful theories. Overall, one is inclined to think that, for Leplin, it is a case of "back to the drawing board".[30]

Leplin's account highlights the third major difficulty for traditional realism presented by the underdetermination of theory by empirical evidence. A genuine case of underdetermination, as opposed to a contrived example, would pose challenges for all three categories of realist that we have touched upon (metaphysical, internal and scientific). The traditional realist is perhaps best placed, since she can claim that our epistemic limitations in deciding between empirically equivalent theories do not impugn the ontological status of an externalised reality which our methods of rational enquiry are intended to capture. Turning to an internal realist, the truth of two competing theories will only be decideable in the epistemic limit, at which point mankind will possess a single unified account of all knowledge. The internal realist may then argue that it will be highly unlikely that two competing theories, which differ significantly and interestingly from each other, will both be compatible with the unified theory of knowledge at our disposal. It may be objected, however, that two competing theories might give rise to two competing unified accounts of knowledge, but the internal realist will accuse us of trying to foist metaphysical realism on him and will dust off his old lecture notes from Putnam. The scientific realist has, in general, contemplated two possible responses, according to whether she believes there is or is not a fact of the matter at stake, in the choice between rival theories that are genuinely empirically equivalent. We will examine closely these responses when we consider how NOA may respond to underdetermination.

Attempts, other than those attributed to Leplin alone, have also recently been made to show that underdetermination cannot arise. Laudan and Leplin (1991), who adopt opposing basic philosophies of science, are curiously united in claiming that (local)[31] underdetermination cannot occur generally because any claim of empirical equivalence depends on a shifting observable / non-observable distinction, and the use of various auxiliary hypotheses which may themselves be unstable.

These arguments are not telling since the authors accept that they have not ruled out the possibility of instances of local underdetermination, and Hoefer and Rosenberg have argued that these arguments for defeasibility of claims of empirical equivalence are not valid for global underdetermination. Amongst examples of putative underdetermination, Hoefer and Rosenberg included the (surrogate) total theories of Newtonian mechanics, with or without absolute velocity, embraced by van Fraassen, and certain hidden-variable accounts in quantum mechanics. They concluded:

> Another, more recent example of theories whose joint content allows a proof of their empirical equivalence is nonrelativistic quantum mechanics and Bohm-type hidden variable theories. Because these theories, like TN (0) and TN (**v**), entail (given reasonable background assumptions) that their differences cannot be observed, Laudan and Leplin appear to have no room to argue that the judgement of their equivalence is defeasible. (Hoefer and Rosenberg 1994 p. 599)

Underdetermination remains a possibility and, as we shall see later, there are other examples in mechanics and quantum mechanics which add to the plausibility that underdetermination can occur.

Difficulties with instrumentalism

According to traditional realists, even the most sophisticated accounts of instrumentalism suffer from the classical problems of inadequacy of explanation, and failure to ground satisfactorily the instrumental reliability of theories:

> We have learned to control experiments so that a hypothesis will not be confirmed by results that could equally well be taken to confirm a rival hypothesis ... These checks may explain how we come to identify useful and reliable theories, but they do not explain why the theories we identify as useful and reliable have these virtues. It is at most the success of science as a human activity that evolutionary hurdles explain; they explain why we develop successful theories. But why are successful theories developed at all? (Leplin forthcoming p. 15)

In addition, the semantic instrumentalist who denies that it makes sense to talk of the truth or falsity of theories, is compelled to adopt in general either an empiricist or idealist outlook, both of which lead to well known philosophical difficulties. If instrumentalism is to be compatible with CSR, workable distinctions between theoretical / non-theoretical and observable / non-observable entities are also needed; in light of the critiques of these distinctions by Grover Maxwell and others, a robust distinction will be hard, if not impossible, to provide. (See later).

As Leplin has observed, wily (i.e. epistemic rather than semantic) instrumentalists have responded to this situation by donning a realist fleece to disguise their fur:

> Contemporary instrumentalism allows that theories are not merely conceptual devices in the service of pragmatic ends, but correct or incorrect representations of unobservable entities and processes. It allows theoretical pronouncements to be read literally, largely out of despair at finding an acceptable alternative way to read them. But it denies that the representativeness of theories, the correctness of their representations, is assessable on the basis of the evidence in principle available to us. Theories must still be judged by instrumentalist standards, even if they are not themselves to be interpreted as instruments. Thus the question of truth, although in principle applicable to theories, is held to be irrelevant to the ends of theorizing and to the evaluation of theories. (Leplin forthcoming p. 176)

There are perhaps two explanations for such tactics. The first is motivated by underdetermination (for instance in the case of van Fraassen). If it were possible to show conclusively that once we leave the realm of what is observable by humans, we inevitably confront an underdetermined choice of theory, one could justify commitment to and acceptance of a realist phenomenology of science, while withholding belief in the truth of our theories, in just the way van Fraassen advocated. We will look more closely in due course at arguments in favour of ubiquitous underdetermination.

The second explanation for these tactics is as a response to the felt need to address the explanatory weakness of a rudimentary, minimalist instrumentalist account. As an example of this type of instrumentalism, consider the *quasi-realism* extended by Fine to science from earlier work by Blackburn.

> As a form of instrumentalism, quasi-realism ... would seek to explain how we come to employ the highly theoretical language of science in just the way that we do employ it. If successful, this explanation would justify our commitment to theory, and in a non-reductive way. Thus quasi-realism is set up to conform to the first two ideals of instrumentalism; it is a non-reductive, pro-attitude towards science. When it comes to the issue of truth, quasi-realism is, in typical instrumentalist style, prepared to settle for something less. For the justification of scientific practice that it would provide only extends to treating theories as if they were true, and their entities as if they were real. Again, this is no trivial kind of fictionalism, but precisely the robust version embodied in the third ideal of instrumentalism. [The third ideal relates to the employment of a notion of truth] : Thus, we might say that instrumentalism treats scientific stories as though they were true, just in so far as it relies on them, and their postulated entities, as useful guides for whatever practical and theoretical jobs may arise. To make the connection with pragmatism that I have exploited in the preceding section, we can say that instrumentalism treats scientific theories as true in the pragmatic sense, and admits truths concerning the existence of theoretical entities in that same sense as well. (Fine 1986b pp. 160,157) [32]

To see how quasi-realism works, imagine we ask the instrumentalist to justify the inductive predictions of a particular theory, and the instrumentalist produces a purely inductive justification for the predictions. We may feel his account is less satisfactory than a realist explanation that makes use of mechanisms, theoretical entities and so forth.[33] The justification for the legitimacy of the demand for explanatory power, is that these explanatory features are customarily available in our everyday account of observable phenomena. We may, then, expect the instrumentalist to struggle to explain why he endorsed that particular theory, rather than any other which made the same predictions.

The instrumentalist could, of course, simply ignore this question if he wished to be obdurate. He might argue, like van Fraassen, that there really is a telling epistemic divide between the world of theoretical entities and the everyday world. This type of hard-nosed instrumentalism has already been alluded to as a way of explaining methodological practice and success in science. Given that the maintenance of this epistemic divide may be considered problematic in turn (see later) let us imagine, in order to highlight a weakness (or what we might choose to call, instead, a disadvantage) in his account, that the instrumentalist has some sensitivity to the explanatory needs of scientists, as nurtured by our explanatory practices with regard to the everyday world.

The explanatory parsimony of his initial position may incline the instrumentalist to borrow the theoretical explanation proffered by his realist opponent, on the grounds that such explanations work.

Let us then suppose the instrumentalist is asked to justify the adoption of this theoretical explanation. The instrumentalist offers induction on past uses of this theoretical explanation (a smaller number of instances than in the case of the predictions). Imagine that we next insistently ask what explains why this theoretical explanation works. When his realist opponent provides a cogent explanation of realist methodology that supports the use of the theoretical explanation in question (involving truthful explanatory theories, approximative truth, convergence etc.), the account of the instrumentalist may be held to be lacking. (Again, an obdurate instrumentalist may insist that he has provided an adequate account of the standing of the theory by citing its inductive success). The instrumentalist will not be able to explain why this particular theoretical explanation works when incompatible alternatives may exist i.e. there may be alternative explanations (for instance sociological or institutional explanations) of the reliability of aspects of scientific methodology such as the use of well-grounded theoretical explanations. This may incline the instrumentalist to adopt the methodogical explanation proffered by the realist on the grounds that it works. The instumentalist will rely on induction over a yet smaller number of instances to justify his position. As this game continues and we ascend to higher and higher levels of instrumental justification, while converging all the while on the behaviour and actions of realists, albeit modest ones, the strength of the instrumentalist case ebbs away. (Note, we are not saying it is impossible to maintain an instrumental position, but that it is, perhaps, uncomfortable).[34]

On the grounds of consistency, if we, as realists, find the lower level induction suspect, must we not immediately reject the induction at a higher level? Boyd (1983, part 8) argued that an instrumentalist cannot strengthen his case by an appeal to theory, for the use of theory is illegitimate:

> The inductive justification for theory-dependent inductions about observables cannot be invoked by the empiricist, because the generalization we are discussing is a premise for that inductive justification. (Boyd 1985 p. 32)

Ascending to higher levels of inductive justification (from the specific entities used to support an induction about observables, to an inductively justified theory about those entities, to an inductively justified pseudo-realism about that theory) may allow an instrumentalist to salvage his account, but there is sufficient weakness in this account for the realist to turn the tables on the instrumentalist. The realist has been roundly criticised for using the sort of abductive inferences to defend realism that an instrumentalist finds problematic even in the case of low-level instances. Yet the defence of an instrumentalist stance relies on an inductive base that requires ampliative inferences in order to defend its commitment to the projectibility of predicates: *tu quoque*.[35] Leplin has recently spelt this out clearly:

> A consistent skepticism that disavows all ampliative inference may be an option. A selective skepticism that proclaims the reliability of our theories, but disallows any possible grounds for accepting them, is not. Reliability can be projected only to the extent that it can be explained. Instrumentalism, by itself, contains no explanatory resources. Positioning the theoretical mechanisms used to predict observations beyond all possible epistemic access, it offers no understanding of why they should happen to work. Without such understanding,

> we have no grounds to project their continuing to work. Instrumentalism gives us no more than a record of past successes. (Leplin forthcoming p. 193)[36,37]

A further difficulty, highlighted by Putnam, is that the instrumentalist attributes of good theories do not support the process of logic:

> But from the fact that T_1 leads to successful predictions and the fact that T_2 leads to successful predictions it does not follow at all that the conjunction T_1 & T_2 leads to successful predictions. The difficulty, in a nutshell, is that the predicate which plays the role of truth - the predicate "leads to successful predictions" - does not have the *properties* of truth ... Nor does it help to bring in "simplicity". It is not obvious that the conjunction of simple theories is simple; and even if simplicity is preserved by conjunction, the conjunction of simple theories which separately lead to no false predictions may even be *inconsistent* (examples are easy to construct). (Putnam 1992 p. 211)

The instrumentalist has difficulty in explaining this "principle of the unity of science" (Boyd), which may be extended to include not only deductive consequences of theories, but their inductive consequences, where theoretical terms are shared. Van Fraassen (1980) accepted the legitimacy of the need for a philosophy of science to explain the principle of unity, and thought he had a solution. He claimed that even in the best circumstances unification is more a process of correction of the component theories rather than their conjunction. While it is clear the application of freshly unified theories to a new domain of application is never a foregone conclusion, the unification argument can, however, be mounted within the confines of recognised, legitimate applications. We can contemplate the observation of two types of well-defined phenomena simultaneously, where one phenomenon is held uncontroversially to be accurately described by theory A, and the other by theory B. The realist can combine A and B, without risk of incompatibility (other than that permitted by holding the theories to be approximately true rather than true) and derive accurate predictions about both phenomena. The evidence in favour of theory A as true also counts in favour of theory A+B. The instrumentalist cannot straightforwardly make the same move: on the basis of a pragmatic notion of truth, or on the basis of empirical adequacy, it is possible that theories A and B will be incompatible. As Boyd pointed out (Boyd 1985 p. 22), the evidence for either theory A or theory B does not count *at all* for theory A+B. Van Fraassen (and Fine (1986) p. 121) assumed that this crucial question of incompatibility was resolved at the outset:

> This hypothesis is significant only, of course, if it is at least logically possible, that is, if T and T' have models in common - a theoretical question which should surely be taken seriously before any joint application is attempted. (Van Fraassen 1980 p. 85)

Why is the instrumentalist justified in making this assumption? Imagine that the instrumentalist has developed two very successful theories which are incompatible.

Why should the instrumentalist not be content to have incompatible models and theories? While this aspect of scientific praxis (i.e. compatible models for the theories) could, as Newton-Smith (1988) has pointed out, be justified by induction, it remains to be seen whether a careful scrutiny of the history of science in fact supports such an argument. To correct or modify the theories so as to be compatible would seem to play into the hands of the realist, yet not to do so may conflict with the actual history of science.

Difficulties with constructive empiricism

Constructive empiricism incorporates a correspondence notion of truth for those beliefs that relate to observables, but advocates a lower epistemic standard of empirical adequacy for beliefs which involve unobservable theoretical entities. In order to maintain a positive stance towards scientific endeavour, constructive empiricism is strongly instrumentalist in outlook. As a result, constructive empiricism shares a number of the weaknesses of its instrumentalist cousin, in particular, an unsatisfactory account of explanation and the projectibility problem. The separation of truth from explanation, where explanation is taken to be entirely a function of the needs of the explainer,[38] and the strain of "accepting" theories, as opposed to "believing" them, seem problematic.[39,40]

Many realists have objected that the empirical adequacy of a theory is no explanation of the observational consequences of the theory: only the theory itself can provide an adequate explanation for the ampliative aspects of the derivation of the observational consequences of the theory. Implicit in an assessment of empirical adequacy is an implicit assumption of the justified projectibility of predicates which can only be provided by the truth of the theory, and which cannot be warranted by simple induction given Hume's skepticism. The constructive empiricist deflects this criticism by accepting induction about observables as an epistemic principle at the outset, and hence does not provide a direct response to the realist.

Where empiricists describe physicists as making choices about which theoretical model to use in the course of an experiment (thereby implying mere acceptance of the model rather than belief in it), such discourse is typically between physicists at the cutting edge of science. By contrast, if we consider the behaviour and talk of materials scientists looking at diffraction studies of crystals, or chemists discussing the properties of sodium chloride, it is very hard to square their activities and dialogue with the view that they merely accept and use, but do not believe, the well-established theories and explanations in their respective fields. Van Fraassen himself recognised this was the case:

> While the only belief involved in acceptance, as I see it, is the belief that the theory is empirically adequate, more than belief is involved. To accept a theory is to make a commitment, a commitment to the further confrontation of new phenomena within the

framework of that theory, a commitment to a research programme, and a wager that all relevant phenomena can be accounted for without giving up that theory. (Van Fraassen 1980 p. 88)

Nonetheless van Fraassen contended that the use of scientific language, and scientific behaviour patterns did not require an epistemic commitment to the ontology of current theories. Not only may it be objected that such a guarded view of commitment involves a rational reconstruction of the beliefs of scientists, but it provides only an instrumental account of the way theory impinges upon the practicalities of experimental design. Leplin cites a recent case of interest concerning the use of quarks to describe the internal structure of hadrons:

> The experimenters were attempting to determine the scattering pattern of electrons bombarding protons. They wanted to know whether the proton acted as an indivisible unit in deflecting electrons with its positive charge, or whether the deflecting force of the proton was localized within it. The question to be answered was whether the proton possesses internal structure. Just to pose this question requires stipulating the existence of the proton itself. The question of the existence of distinguishable constituents of the proton makes sense only against a background of belief in the existence of protons. How is the experiment to be interpreted, how is its rationale to be reconstructed, if, with Constructive Empiricism, the existence of the proton is not to be regarded as a proper object of credence? Researchers cannot sensibly be represented as attempting to determine whether or not entities that they do not believe in have constituents that they also do not believe in. Contrary to Constructive Empiricism, researchers must be credited with theoretical beliefs as a condition of understanding their practice. (Leplin forthcoming p. 274)

The mechanisms and structures available to realists to explain experimental success in the case of unobservables are contiguous with those van Fraassen is prepared to accept in order to justify everyday empirical conclusions that strictly go beyond the observable evidence. It seems, consequently, that Van Fraassen did not provide a satisfactory account of why his epistemologically minimal approach is to be preferred to that of the realist in the context of experiment: he merely showed that it was logically possible to formulate such a position. Giere came to similar conclusions:

> There is one final rejoinder that an empiricist like van Fraassen would make. He would grant that my descriptions of activities in the laboratory are the "appropriate" descriptions ... Nevertheless, we should understand scientists as operating under a "supposition" that this is what the world is like ... Except for the desire to save an empiricist account of science, there is no reason in the world to think that the activities in the laboratory are part of a grand supposition. If that were true, then, indeed, all the world is a stage. All our lives are nothing but complex sets of suppositions. That is a strange conclusion from someone who would "deliver us from metaphysics". (Giere 1988 p. 130)

If the implausibility of this account of the behaviour of scientists is not a concern, then we may turn to the epistemic role of theory in scientific method.

Boyd has methodically argued how the epistemological principle, that empirically equivalent theories are evidentially indistinguishable, undersells theory and overvalues experience. Given the reliance upon auxiliary hypotheses to obtain observational consequences from a theory, the central testing procedures for science are inevitably theory dependent. Similarly, measurement and detection methods are profoundly theory dependent. These aspects of scientific methodology led to the abandonment of the search for an empirical criterion of meaningfulness for sentences or theories in isolation in the 1950's. Since then empiricists have struggled to reconcile the fact that in general the methods of science are theory dependent with their assertion that knowledge of unobservable theoretical entities is impossible.

As an example of the failure of constructive empiricism to explain specific aspects of theory-soaked scientific methodology, Boyd (1983) cited the failure of empiricism to explain the instrumentally reliable aspects of theory-driven methodology which support judgements of the invariance of meaning, univocality, across theory change, and judgements of the projectibility of predicates. (Projectibility is key to establishing the empirical adequacy of theories, which is the critical first step in the constructive empiricist's argument to show that empirically adequate theories, as opposed to true theories, are instrumentally reliable).

> Thus, the empiricist can explain the epistemic adequacy of only those theory-dependent features of scientific methodology whose dictates are preserved under the substitution, for the actual body of accepted theories, of any other empirically equivalent one. But, as we have just seen, none of the central methodological principles which govern the evaluation of scientific evidence have this property! The consistent empiricist cannot explain the instrumental reliability of the methodology which scientists actually employ. (Boyd 1985 p. 14)

Realism, on the other hand, is able to explain the role played by theory: if our theories are approximately true, they will provide evidential support for the methodological standards we apply to assessments of projectibility and confirmation, and together with a causal theory of meaning, they will support our judgements of the univocality of theoretical terms.[41] In other words, according to Boyd, while the theories of science may be underdetermined, the methodology of science is not.

By denying the evidential role played by theory, constructive empiricists may be accused of distorting the core tenet of empiricism - that factual knowledge must be grounded in experience, which is not the same as saying that we can only have knowledge of what we experience i.e. no knowledge of theoretical things. The conclusion to be drawn from knowledge empiricism is not that theories which have the same empirical consequences are necessarily evidentially equivalent, but that all knowledge, including theoretical knowledge, is not immune to revision in the light of experience. This latter notion of the fallibility of all knowledge is consistent with the empirical, naturalistic view of realist methodology which Boyd endorsed.[42]

A second major difficulty that plagues constructive empiricism is that it establishes an arbitrary epistemological principle: observational privilege is defined by human biology.[43] Against the criticisms of Churchland and others, van Fraassen has failed to provide an adequate justification for the epistemic divide he advocates.[44] For him, this is supposedly an empirical matter:

> If there are limits to observation, these are empirical, and must be described by empirical science. The classification marked by "observable" must be of entities in the world of science. And science, in giving content to the distinction, will reveal how much we believe when we accept it as empirically adequate. (Van Fraassen 1991 p. 191)

If this is so, it is hard to understand why the epistemic boundary is not defined by the cutting edge of current theory, but van Fraassen has denied that the empirical domain extends so far. Van Fraassen, when challenged (1985 pp. 254, 258), relied on the fact that theoretical entities, such as electrons, are strange and unimaginable when compared with everyday objects. As McMullin (1984) pointed out, the fact that classical and microworld concepts are different does not mean that the latter do not exist, but simply reflects a somewhat parochial view of science:

> The realist claim is that the scientist is discovering the structures of the world; it is not required in addition that these structures be imaginable in the categories of the macroworld. (McMullin 1984 p. 14)

Boyd has argued (Boyd 1983 p. 49), however, that the fact, that no clear distinction can be drawn in practice between observables and unobservables,[45] is not a telling argument against the empiricist, because the inapplicability of the distinction is founded upon scientific practices that traditionally involve realist assumptions.[46] The same conclusion might, however, be drawn from an instrumentalist perspective with regard to the methodology of science: it is useful *methodological* practice, which produces the best calculations and predictions, not to attempt to discriminate as a matter of kind between observables and unobservables. Scientists do not distinguish between those entities which are observable to humans and those which are not (they consider, in general, that what is detectable is observable):

> More important than these philosophical arguments is the fact that the required distinction is simply not found in the practice of science. Textbooks on mechanics, for example, do not distinguish the observability of forces as opposed to positions. Nor are any difficulties of principle raised about measuring forces as opposed to positions. Occasionally, one finds discussion of the typically philosophical issue whether forces can be defined in terms of other quantities, like mass and acceleration. But this is an entirely different issue from the question of observability. (Giere 1988 p. 95)

Shapere believes that scientists do indeed observe phenomena with their instruments and has proposed a pair of conditions which he considered sufficient to give rise to an observation:

> x is directly observed (observable) if:
> (1) information is received (can be received) by an appropriate receptor; and
> (2) that information is (can be) transmitted directly, i.e., without interference, to the receptor from the entity x (which is the source of the information).(Shapere 1982 p. 492)

Using these conditions, and separating the observation into source, transmission and receptor elements, Shapere was able to explicate in what sense physicists could be said to observe solar neutrinos and the interior of the sun. It is important to note that the conditions of observability he proposed may be construed on a basis acceptable to an empiricist. Shapere concluded:

> Thus we may say that what we have learned about the way things are has led to an extension, through a natural generalization, of what it is to make an observation, and furthermore that various relevant aspects of that knowledge are applied in making specific observations. It would therefore be a mistake to say that there is no connection between the astrophysicist's use of the term 'observation' with reference to this experiment and uses (at least certain ones) of that term which associate it with sense-perception; nor can the relation between the two sorts of use be dismissed by saying that the astrophysicist speaks of observation only by "analogy" or "metaphorically". Rather, the relation lies in the fact that the astrophysicist's use is a generalization of (certain) uses having to do with sense-perception, and in the fact that whatever reasoning has led to our current understanding of the electromagnetic spectrum, the fundamental interactions (forces) of nature, and the means of receiving information conveyed by the entities and processes we have found to exist, functions also as reasoning leading to the generalization. The generalization, that is, is not made capriciously, arbitrarily, but rests on reasons. (Shapere 1982 p. 507)

If we strip Shapere's remarks of their realist overtones, we may contemplate a version of his argument along instrumental lines: we seek to justify the generalization of observation he has carefully explicated on the grounds that the methods employed to support the generalization have been shown inductively to be useful and reliable.

It may be argued that we cannot settle whether this assessment of the instrumental value of abandoning the observable/unobservable distinction is correct. But van Fraassen was helpful here: he insisted the determination of such questions was a matter for science - *If there are limits to observation, these are a subject for empirical science, and not for philosophical analysis* (1980 p. 57) - and it would appear that science, as currently practised, finds it useful not to make the type of epistemic distinction van Fraassen required, but supports the generalization of observation as described by Shapere.

We may also reflect upon observational difficulties that occur at the macroscopic level: the inside of iron bars, the bottom of the ocean, objects on a very dark night, sunlight, dinosaurs are not observable in practice. To allow the extension to observability *in principle* involves problematic reasoning: examples can be given (for example, the contrasting cases of the moons of Jupiter and bacteria inside the human body, where the former, according to van Fraassen's reasoning is observable in principle,[47] while the latter is not) where the use of theory and induction would justify equal epistemic status for a pair of phenomena which are not observed, but where van Fraassen's distinction, based upon the biology of our own epistemic community, sanctions a difference in status. Fine (1986 p. 145) has also pointed out that a rigorous definition of observability for an empiricist either leads to regress, or to illicit assumptions about theories that support observability that are suspiciously realist in tone.

Furthermore, starting from van Fraassen's acceptance of CSR, we may use inductive principles related to the reliability of instruments and procedures (involving for instance observable theoretical items such as theodolites, cameras, electronic clocks) to enlarge systematically by mediation the epistemic circle to bring various objects strictly *unobserved* by humans into the category of 'observ*able* by humans' (as described in Boyd 1983 part 3). As an example of this type of mediation, consider photographs brought back by a robot of the fine structure of the rings of Saturn, which was not observed by astronomers on earth, but which is observable by them in principle without the mediation of instruments. It seems inconsistent not to allow the same methods and procedures to warrant belief in entities which remain unobserved and unobservable in principle by *unaided* humans: for example, the tectonic structure of the ocean floor as shown by remote cameras over very long observation periods, which could not be observed by humans unaided, since the changes occur too slowly. But if we accept mediation here, why would mediation not be acceptable in the case of a molecule or a particle?

> If the existence of atoms or of the moons of Jupiter were a legal issue, I think almost any jury would find the case proven by the ordinary rules of evidence. (Ellis 1985 p. 58)

At the same time, there is also the converse problem of the unreliability of the evidence of our senses: given they often deceive us and are subject to correction by theory, why should the content of our sense experiences have a privileged status? What is observable is a problematic notion.

We might ask why van Fraassen ended by drawing a line in the wrong place. In responses to his critics, he made the uncontroversial empiricist claim that all knowledge is grounded in experience ("experience is the legitimate and the only legitimate source for our factual opinions"), but then explicated the limits of experience: "experience can give us information only about what is both observable and actual" (1985 p. 253). His explication is not well-founded. As Shapere pointed out, constructive empiricists have conflated the perceptual and epistemic aspects of observation:[48]

> The philosopher's use of the term 'observation' has traditionally had a double aspect, and has played a double role. On the one hand, there is the *perceptual* aspect: "observation", as a multitude of philosophical analyses insist, is simply a special kind of perception, usually interpreted as consisting in the addition to the latter of an extra ingredient of focussed attention. "The problem of observation" is thus seen as a special case of "the problem of perception", to be approached only in the light of an understanding of the latter. On the other hand, there is the *epistemic* aspect of the philosopher's use of 'observation': the *evidential* role that observation is supposed to play in leading to knowledge or well-grounded belief or in supporting beliefs already attained. For the empiricist tradition in epistemology proposed that all knowledge (or well-grounded belief) "rests on experience", where "experience" was interpreted as sense-perception. In that tradition, as indeed in most other philosophy, these two roles have been identified: the question of observational support for beliefs or knowledge was interpreted as the question of how *perception* could give rise to knowledge or support beliefs.
>
> In sophisticated areas of science, however, these two aspects have come to be separated, *and for good reason*. Science is, after all, concerned with the role of observation as evidence, whereas sense-perception is notoriously untrustworthy ... Hence, with the recognition that information can be received which is not directly accessible to the senses, *science has come more and more to exclude sense-perception as much as possible from playing a role in the acquisition of observational evidence*; that is, it relies more and more on other appropriate, but dependable, receptors. It has broken, or at least severely attenuated, the connection between the perceptual and epistemic aspects of "observation". (Shapere 1982 pp. 507-8)

While it may be reasonably accurate to assert that *an* experience always involves stimulation, which we may loosely call an 'observation', it does not follow that *experience* gives us information only about what is observable, unless we can show that higher level concepts which are illuminated by experience are reducible to the ground-level experiential components of basic statements. The failure of the efforts of positivists such as Carnap to effect such a reduction suggest it is unlikely that a constructive empiricist will be able to do so. Without reduction, it is clear that experience can give us knowledge of items which are not observable: consider a concept such as "deception", (or "war" or "entropy" or "mutation") which itself is not observable, and which is given to us in our experience. The concept "deception" no doubt involves some observational component, but some type of mental overhead is required to derive this concept from a set of observations. The same conclusion holds for psychological states, of which we have knowledge, but which are not observable. Reduction of a complex concept to observational elements is no more possible then the reduction of a software icon to a set of software or hardware instructions. Van Fraassen's wish to restrict knowledge to what is given in experience does not mean we should only be concerned with what is observable. As in his handling of theory, van Fraassen's account of observation distorted the core claim of empiricism.

Part of van Fraassen's motivation for the establishment of an observational perimeter arose from concerns about the weaker epistemic footing of theories (relative to facts about the observed world). When we see that theory, involving unobservable theoretical entities, plays a major role in the implementation of the observable / non-observable distinction, particularly in the application of "observable in principle", we may ask why unobservable theoretical entities do not warrant belief. The answer, that such entities are epistemically suspect, seems to beg the question given the role played by such entities in underpinning the distinction between observables and non-observables, which itself is supposed to give content to the epistemic distinction sought by empiricists. Part of this bias against unobservables may stem from the fact that they are, logically speaking, the product of inferences from theory, and, as a result, less well-grounded than observations. But, as Shapere has discussed, to call such entities theoretical is to settle on a sense of "theoretical" which is unnecessarily disparaging: because theory is not certain (in the sense that it might be mistaken, or subject to a range of error), it does not follow that it is uncertain (in the sense of arbitrary or shaky). We have good reasons for the theories we currently possess, and to object to theories because theories involve inferences is to adopt an outlook that is overly steeped in logic and set theory: from an epistemic point of view, judgements of whether a theory is inferential relate to whether we have sufficient reasons to believe the theory or have specific reasons to doubt the theory (in which, latter, case the theory is held to be an inference based on background assumptions and other theories). The fact that a theory is a theory is not, of itself, a sufficient reason to doubt it. Consequently, many theoretical conclusions should not be regarded as inferential in an epistemic sense, given that we have good reasons to support the theory in question. Supporters of van Fraassen might offer underdetermination as a specific reason to doubt any given theory, but this requires them to show that underdetermination is always possible. Ellis (1985) and Laudan and Leplin (1991) have argued convincingly that while the empirical consequences of a pair of (locally) empirically equivalent theories may be well defined, the set of possible empirical discoveries relevant to the truth or falsity of the theories is open, and hence we can not establish a general thesis of underdetermination; we are restricted to citing particular, plausible instances of underdetermination (see later).

If we are to draw an epistemic line which distinguishes between what we believe to be true and what we simply accept as useful for the time being, it should be drawn between those things which are well substantiated and those which are not; there is no convincing reason to believe this coincides with *any* notion of what is or is not observable:[49]

> The *epistemically* important line between the inferential and the non-inferential is drawn in terms of the distinction between that which we have specific reason to doubt (but which we are nevertheless still able to use to a certain extent and for certain epistemic purposes) and that upon which we can build confidently. And this is just where one would expect the line to be drawn if we are trying to further our knowledge on the basis of what we have learned. (Of course, as I have said repeatedly, that on which we build confidently can always become subject to actual specific and compelling doubt; our confidence *can* always turn out to have

been misplaced). (Shapere 1982 p. 517)

In the absence of a firm foundation for the priority of everyday observation statements, constructive empiricism seems to be a means of hedging one's bets in a weak-hearted way against the likely modification of current theories, while believing in all the practical everyday benefits that the application of these theories confer. Van Fraassen's account endorses everyday or common-sense realism (CSR), including a correspondence notion of truth (Fine 1986 p. 143, Ellis 1985 p. 62) but refuses to extend its application beyond a contingent epistemic perimeter defined by our own biology. This is rather like a person who borrows someone's car without authorisation and refuses to give a disabled friend a ride.

Epistemic complementarity

In response to the strengths and weaknesses of epistemic realism, epistemic instrumentalism and constructive empiricism, we may sketch, in a speculative fashion, the rudiments of a thesis of *epistemic complementarity* which may help to explain the recent manoeuvres of proponents of these various positions. The complementarity thesis may be taken to assert that realism and instrumentalism are both well-founded, persistent and complementary components of rational scientific enquiry, and any account of epistemology in science needs to accommodate, support and define their complementarity.

The seeds of this thesis are to be found in van Fraassen's own selective skepticism: the worlds of everyday objects and theoretical unobservables are epistemically distinct. What is problematic about constructive empiricism is the criterion used to demarcate the two epistemic territories of realism and instrumentalism: it is determined by observation - the boundary of human observation. Instead, the epistemic boundary between what warrants belief and what warrants acceptance, should depend upon the evidence, observational and non-observational, theoretical and non-theoretical, which is available. The decision whether a realist or instrumentalist epistemic posture is appropriate will depend upon the evidential context (again contextuality is a lesson we take from van Fraassen), which is decided by the practice of experts: in science, scientists. Miller (1987) has described how this occurs in science. As an example of where instrumentalism might be appropriate, because perhaps our own constitution and perceptual machinery forever rule out any other epistemic posture, we may suggest general relativity:

> In particular, following his conversion, Einstein wanted to claim genuine reality for the central theoretical entities of the general theory, the four-dimensional space-time manifold and associated tensor fields. This is a serious business, for if we grant his claim, then not only do space and time cease to be real but so do virtually all of the usual dynamical quantities. Thus motion as we understand it, itself ceases to be real. The current generation of

> philosophers of space and time (led by Howard Stein and John Earman) have followed Einstein's lead here. But, interestingly, not only do these ideas boggle the mind of the average man in the street (like you and me), they boggle most contemporary scientific minds as well. That is, I believe the majority opinion among working, knowledgeable scientists is that general relativity provides a magnificent organizing tool for treating certain gravitational problems in astrophysics and cosmology. But few, I believe, give credence to the type of realist existence and non-existence claims that I have been mentioning. For relativistic physics, then, it appears that a nonrealist attitude was important in its development, that the founder nevertheless espoused a realist attitude to the finished product, but that most who actually use it think of the theory as a powerful instrument, rather than as expressing a "big truth". (Fine 1986a p. 123)

It may turn out to be possible to define epistemic contexts in a way reminiscent of the 'discovery' and 'justification' distinction of Reichenbach, or the 'pursuit' and 'acceptance' distinction of Laudan. Instrumentalism may be epistemically justified more frequently in the contexts of 'discovery' or 'pursuit'; realism may be more appropriate in contexts of 'justification' or 'acceptance'. Given that evidential considerations will distinguish between these contexts, if they are in fact distinct, the epistemological account proposed will be naturalistic in setting the epistemic boundary, and will treat the claims of science in the same fashion as knowledge claims in other areas (we may think of many day to day situations where we make use of instrumental or realist reasoning depending upon the evidence available to us).

We would also expect the boundary to shift: typically in science, a new entity might initially be postulated for instrumental reasons, experiments might then be developed which produced the results anticipated; further experiments might then lead to the postulation of further entities, which would be subject to yet further investigation. The postulation of the second set of entities will ground the original set (as in Leplin's example of quarks and protons), not making it impossible for them to be shown to be non-referential by some further experiment, but making them less vulnerable to refutation. This procedure of inquiry may lead without discontinuity from everyday objects to unobserved (but detected) theoretical entities. While everyday objects are prey to an extreme skepticism, this is not a genuine concern for the current protagonists in the debate between competing philosophies of science. Our slogan: "Conjecture and affirmation".

It is important to state clearly, though, that the thesis of complementarity is *not* to be considered to be an historical thesis about the pattern of development of theoretical knowledge, subject to comparison with the accounts of Kuhn, Lakatos, Laudan and the like. Philosophers of science are aware that in many cases, such as that of the molecular hypothesis carefully described by Miller (1987 pp 470-482), a period of caution, termed "agnosticism" by Miller, may be rational, before the scientific community is convinced of the reality of a particular theory. In other situations, however, *persistent*, intrinsic instrumentalism may be appropriate (for instance, some would argue this is the case for quantum mechanics), or conversely, a direct route to realism may be warranted. Certain domains of scientific enquiry are held to be best supported epistemically by legitimate instrumentalist interpretation of theory; other domains are supported by realism. The boundary between domains marks an epistemic frontier which van Fraassen wished to capture by empirical adequacy, but which was was not well captured by observability by humans. According to the thesis of complemetarity the attempt to establish the hegemony of either realism or instrumentalism is misguided. What we require is more insight into the epistemic characterisation of the boundary between these two warranted epistemic postures, and a careful characterisation of the epistemic territory on either side.

Furthermore, in light of the foregoing comments, the thesis of complementarity is not to be identified with a "special situations" account of scientific method, where instrumentalism is held to be an unsatisfactory fall back position which is advocated in certain specialist domains (for example, singularity cosmology). Certainly some advanced corners of the scientific endeavour will support an instrumentalist approach, but it would be wrong to think that instrumentalism is not epistemically warranted in more mundane situations (as we have mentioned, even everyday life). It is possible that certain complex, but mundane, non-linear systems might support instrumentalist accounts given the inherent intractibility of their domains: meteorology, hydrodynamics etc. are obvious candidates. In these areas, the type of instrumental findings we obtain need not always be very technical or detailed. In many areas phenomenological laws exist which are useful, and lack explanation, for instance Bode's laws regarding the efficient design of boat hulls. In these domains of inquiry, we are not facing a situation characterised by a plurality of alternative models - we are faced, instead, by the prospect, perhaps in principle, of never having any models at all. This might occur because of the chaotic, systemic or acausal underpinnings of the domain. We do our best, in Duhemian fashion, relying on whatever snippets of knowledge we can get to work - our judgements and principles of selection are grounded in instrumentalist methodology.

Another way of thinking about complementarity is in the context of different possible worldviews. Contrast, for instance, two world views offered by Allport (1993):

> In terms of this world view, an exhaustive set of accurate phenomenological laws provides the goal for the scientific enterprise. Covering laws are either totally superfluous or at most they can prove valuable for remembering and classifying the true (i.e. useful) practical laws.
>
> The contrary tradition, which I will dub 'monotheorism', makes the finding of an absolute minimum of empirically adequate principles the hallmark of 'great' science. According to this tradition, the discovery of a few abstract laws of great generality (and the protagonists of theoretical science would also say of great beauty), which are sufficient in principle to account for all known 'fundamental' phenomena, provides the surest route to a thorough understanding of the workings of the universe. (Allport 1993 p. 248)

The argument between realists and anti-realists is often perceived as being about which of these two worldviews is correct. The two worldviews are seen as incompatible and in conflict, consequently, philosophers have been inclined to see the choice as that between realism or instrumentalism. But let us contemplate a murkier, more confused world, which is in part open to customary realist methods, but part of which is intractable. The sort of world in question is similar to that attributed to Duhem by Cartwright:

> Duhem believes that phenomena in nature fall roughly into natural kinds. The realist looks for something that unifies the members of the natural kind, something they all have in common; but Duhem denies that there is anything. There is nothing more than the rough facts of nature that sometimes some things behave like others, and what happens to one is a clue to what the others will do. Explanations provide a scheme that allows us to make use of the clues. (Cartwright 1983 p. 95)

The key difference between the world that supports complementarity and the complex Duhemian version of Cartwright, is that laws and theories do work in some contexts (but not in others). Their failure to work elsewhere, however, is not a consequence of our own human limitations, but reflects an intrinsic ontological intractability about the world which cannot be processed by the machinery of realism: at least in parts, the world really is a mess.

The significance of the thesis of complementarity as an epistemic thesis is that it asserts that in certain epistemic circumstances instrumentalism is legitimate, rational and to be encouraged. Unlike Miller, we do not regard instrumentalism as a temporary, unfortunate staging-post in a view of science where realism dominates and is epistemologically higher up the pecking order than instrumentalism; we do not hedge our views by talking of agnosticism. Instead we recognise a permanent and important role for instrumentalism in scientific enquiry: in certain contexts atheism is rational and appropriate. Not only is it possible that certain domains of scientific interest may only be susceptible to an instrumentalist approach, but it also likely that around a core of realist belief in a developing domain, a periphery of inquiry which warrants instrumentalist methods will be sustained. As realist knowledge increases in the domain, new areas of research are likely to emerge which will favour an instrumentalist response. In this way, we may envisage a permanent instrumental element of scientific inquiry: perhaps some domains of instrumental application may shift over time, but perhaps some will be permanent. Strong support for the creative impetus to be gained from advocating a proper role for instrumentalism are to be found in the writings of Feyerabend (1975), Laudan (1977), and Fine (1986).

This "presents for all" account also unlocks some of the persistent difficulties observed in the accounts of realists, instrumentalists and constructive empiricists. According to the complementarity thesis, realists are not required to vouch for the truth of theories at the cutting edge of science, yet the notion of the embedding of entities allows for the development of a notion of the accumulation of knowledge and progress which is more than simply the accumulation of observable phenomena. If they do not posit an externalised reality for ever beyond our ken, realists need not endorse a view of convergence; instead a naturalist/evolutionary account of the development of knowledge may be endorsed along the lines of Boyd, Giere and Churchland. Instrumentalists need not strain to provide weak explanatory accounts that deny the truth of theories in areas of science which are well established, and their wish to behave like realists can be made intelligible. Constructive empiricists preserve a selective skepticism that is no longer biologically defined, and achieve a consistency of epistemic method (for instance in the application of induction and abduction) that fits with scientific practice.

The thesis of complementarity might be said to be obvious or to dodge the genuine epistemic challenge of when instrumentalism is warranted or when realism is warranted, but I believe the insight it offers is that the established positions of realism and instrumentalism are both oversold in the sense that they are both intended to cover the entirety of scientific inquiry. (Miller rightly criticised the tendency of philosophers of science to search always for principles of great generalization, and focussed his account of the methods of science on topic-specific principles, which are consistent with local realism and local instrumentalism of the type advocated.) Van Fraassen placed bounds on the epistemic reach in science of these underlying epistemic postures, but did so from a decidedly skeptical viewpoint. No one, I believe, has stated in an explicit, neutral fashion that both realism and instrumentalism are philosophical components of epistemology: all the discussion has focused on whether to adopt one or the other position. Complementarity suggests the focus of philosophical inquiry should shift from the supposed global battle between realism and instrumentalism, to the investigation of the evidential local circumstances and criteria that define the epistemic boundary.[50]

The attractions of NOA

The principle tenets of NOA, according to Fine, are (1) that we are justified in applying the same methods of rational inquiry to the realm of science that we use in the world of everyday physical objects, (2) that science embodies the most stringent methods of rational inquiry, and (3) that we should consequently accept the truths and objects of scientific theory with the same standards and scrutiny as we accept the truths and objects of our everyday world. As Fine put it:

> One can summarize this homely and compelling line as follows: it is possible to accept the evidence of one's senses and to accept, in the same way, the confirmed results of science only for a realist; hence, I should be one (and so should you!).

> What is it to accept the evidence of one's senses and, in the same way, to accept confirmed scientific theories? It is to take them into one's life as true, with all that implies concerning adjusting one's behavior, practical and theoretical, to accommodate these truths ... When the homely line asks us, then, to accept the scientific results "in the same way" in which we accept the evidence of our senses, I take it that we are to accept them both as true. I take it that we are being asked not to distinguish between kinds of truth or modes of existence or the like, but only among truths themselves in terms of centrality, degrees of belief, or such. (Fine 1986a p. 127)

In believing in the reality of theoretical entities, we are not required to commit to an externalised metaphysical reality, The Real World,[51,52] a transcendental noumenon for ever beyond our epistemic reach, but instead may adopt a neutral correspondence notion of truth, which satisfies Tarski / Davidson semantics, without feeling the need, as a traditional realist or anti-realist might, to add a further interpretative element to our account of truth:

> It will be apparent by now that a distinctive feature of NOA, one that separates it from similar views currently in the air, is NOA's stubborn refusal to amplify the concept of truth by providing a theory or analysis (or even a metaphorical picture). Rather, NOA recognizes in "truth" a concept already in use and agrees to abide by the standard rules of usage. These rules involve a Davidsonian-Tarskian referential semantics, and they support a thoroughly classical logic of inference. (Fine 1986a pp. 129-30)

NOA enjoys a number of obvious advantages relative to its competitors. It does not suffer from the correspondence difficulties of the traditional (metaphysical) realist;[53] it does not involve a commitment to convergence. As Fine said:

> There is no possibility for justifying the kind of externality that realism requires, yet it may well be that, in fact, we cannot help yearning for just such a comforting grip on reality. If I am right, then the realist is chasing a phantom, and we cannot actually do more, with regard to existence claims, than follow scientific practice, just as NOA suggests. (Fine 1986a p132)

NOA imposes the same epistemic standards in a neutral and even-handed fashion to the macro- and the microworld; NOA also fits the experimentalists' view of what they are doing when they carry out experiments, which would satisfy entity realists such as Hacking, Giere, Cartwright and Leplin. In this way, we expect NOA straightforwardly to accommodate constants on the same basis as is seen in the accounts of practising scientists such as Pedley, Saunders, and Levy Leblond.[54]

Relative to instrumentalists and constructive empiricists, NOA can offer a rich account of explanation, and of the value of the pragmatic virtues. By taking its lead from the activities of scientists, NOA has no need to proscribe or rationalize the activities and developments of science and offers a middle position from which to assess the goals and activities of science that is liberal and neutral, sitting comfortably between the extremes of the positivists and the unorthodoxies of

Feyerabend. NOA may appeal to scientists for the single reason that it cautions philosophers from meddling in their affairs.

With interpretation and perhaps some minor modification, NOA can also develop a less isolationist stance towards philosophy of science, thereby accommodating the thesis of epistemic complementarity. Science would settle cases of epistemic warrant, deciding where evidence supported a realist or an instrumentalist posture, but the framework for these decisions would be provided by rigorous philosophical accounts of the preconditions and character of evidence that justify epistemic instrumentalism or epistemic realism.

Potential failings of NOA

Relative to other positions, NOA is new, and consequently less eroded and tarnished by the seas of philosophical debate. Even at this stage though, we may perceive certain potential failings which in due course will need to be addressed.

NOA is parasitical on Common Sense Realism, which some philosophers may hold to be doing all the work. It thereby ducks rather than resolves the problem of skepticism. In response, we may observe that this is not a unique failing: it is shared by constructive empiricism, by scientific realism and by instrumentalists. Traditional realism, on the other hand, genuinely strives to rid us of skeptical demons, but only at the expense of an untenable metaphysical superstructure. To reinforce NOA's justification for assuming CSR, a higher level transcendental justification, focussing on the invariances that might be supposed to exist between the experiences of all putative sentient entities, might be constructed. This line of reasoning lies outside the scope of the current work.

Even if we put this parasitism aside, it may still be objected that NOA is problematical because it allows theories which are simply 'adequate' (as opposed to 'empirically adequate'): somehow we succeed in developing theories of the world that never let us down, but which are not correct. Leplin clearly had such a criticism in mind when he labelled NOA as "Surrealism" (surrogate realism in full). It may be argued that in advocating adequate theories, NOA is really instrumentalist in outlook. McMullin observed:

> Second, we might distinguish between *strong antirealism*, which denies any kind of ontological status to all (or part) of the theoretical entities of science, and *weak antirealism* which allows theoretical entities existence of an everyday "chairs and goldfish" kind, but insists that there is some further sense of "really really there", which realists purportedly have in mind, that is to be rejected ...These (weak antirealist) critics are often, as I have shown, hard to place. They reject any attempt to justify scientific realism as involving dubious metaphysics, but appear to accept a weak (realist) claim of the "everyday" kind without any form of supporting argument ... Fine's essay in this volume appears to fall into this category ... the final section proposes, as the consequence of a "natural ontological attitude", that "there really are molecules and atoms" and rejects the instrumentalist assertion that they are just

fictions. But some argument is needed for this, beyond calling this attitude "natural". (McMullin 1984 p. 25 and footnote 42)[55]

Fine might reply that a NOAer and a sophisticated instrumentalist share a common core ("That is, they must both accept the certified results of science as on a par with more homely and familiarly supported claims" (Fine 1986 p128)), but that the instrumentalist then adds a pragmatic account of truth which is unsatisfactory relative to a minimal disquotational account. This argument might tempt instrumentalist rejoinders which assert that NOAers and *sophisticated* instrumentalists behave in the same way, and a NOAer may be forced to fall back on CSR to defend his or her position, which suggests there is some merit in McMullin's criticism. But one way to interpret this line of criticism is as a hankering for the table-thumping traditional realism that Fine has attacked. The response is to say that in spite of our feeling that we should obtain something more, a kind of warm feeling in the tummy, NOA is all we are going to get in terms of truth.

Another way to think of this concern about adequacy and truth, is that NOA is vulnerable to underdetermination. Without the anchor of an externalised Real World, NOA would in principle have difficulty in accommodating alternative empirically equivalent theories. It might be thought that NOA's minimalist notion of truth would be sufficient to allow Fine to avoid this thorny question, but as Newton-Smith (1988) has pointed out, ontological choices in the face of underdetermination are genuine issues for a NOAer. We will address this concern about relativity in detail in the next chapter, but before doing so it remains to observe that NOA's liberalism may be held to be unsatisfactory in some respects.

By not allowing philosophers (or scientists) to conduct the score, NOA does not seem to set a convincing rationale for science. Boyd's arguments that realism (a realism which advocates the search for true explanatory theories while dropping the metaphysical component) provides a good explanation of inductive inferences based on theory, is accepted by a NOAer, but the problem is that an ardent instrumentalist / empiricist cannot be converted to this point of view. Newton-Smith (1988) has highlighted NOA's failure to incorporate some notion of progress into its account of science, and his brand of modest realism, MOR, is consequently less minimalist. NOA should ideally provide an account of the role of theory, and the development of science that is as credible as Boyd's, and not one which uncritically accepts all aspects of the scientific enterprise. Fine's exhortation "Try to take science on its own terms, and try not to read things into science" (Fine 1986 p. 149) is not sufficiently reflective nor discriminating.[56]

Summary

In this chapter we have considered a number of difficulties associated with traditional realism, instrumentalism and constructive empiricism, which have contributed to the emergence of a series of more moderate realist positions, among which NOA is a leading candidate. A thesis of epistemic complementarity has been sketched, which recognises the inherent strengths and weaknesses of different epistemic attitudes and which does not seek a normative, preferential choice of posture for scientific enquiry. If we accept that modest realism at times seems warranted then we may concur in NOA's acceptance of current scientific beliefs, in which case the constants of physics merit a realist construal. How such a construal may be reconciled with the existence of alternative empirical systems that anchor derived constants is the subject of the next chapter.

Notes

1 Laudan wrote: *a successful research tradition is one which leads, via its component theories, to the adequate solution of an increasing range of empirical and conceptual problems* (1977 p. 82)*; These few examples should make it clear that research traditions can play a decisive role in specifying the sorts of things that are to count as potentially solvable empirical problems for their constituent theories* (1977 p. 88)*; A research tradition, we have said, is a set of assumptions: assumptions about the basic kinds of entities in the world, assumptions about how those entities interact, assumptions about the proper methods to use for constructing and testing theories about those entities* (1977 p. 97)*; Determinations of truth and falsity are* irrelevant *to the acceptability or the pursuitability of theories and research traditions* (1977 p. 120). Furthermore, Laudan rejected purely empiricist accounts of science: *Empiricist philosophies of science (including those of Popper, Carnap and Reichenbach) and even less strident empiricist methodologies (including those of Lakatos, Collingwood and Feyerabend) - all of which imagine that theory choice in science should be governed exclusively by empirical considerations - simply fail to come to terms with the role of conceptual problems in science, and accordingly find themselves too impoverished to explain or reconstruct much of the actual course of science* (1977 p. 47).

2 Witness Boyd (1991 p. 19): *From the perspective that thus emerged from Tarski's work [on truth], a new option became available for anti-realist philosophy of science: the antirealist might accept, for example, that we know that there are electrons, that electrons are unobservable entities to which the term "electron" refers, and that electrons are not merely social constructions, while denying that the truth claims she thus accepts about them should be understood with respect to a realist correspondence conception of truth.* For instance, Ellis' brand of internal realism, with its pragmatic account of truth, is

significantly different in outlook to Boyd's account.

3 Hempel (1965 p. 116) summarised the situation: *The history of scientific endeavour shows that if we wish to arrive at precise, comprehensive, and well-confirmed general laws, we have to rise above the level of direct observation. The phenomena directly accessible to our experience are not connected by general laws of great scope and rigor. Theoretical constructs are needed for the formulation of such higher-level laws ... we have to recognise further that cognitive significance in a system is a matter of degree: significant systems range from those whose entire extralogical vocabulary consists of observation terms, through theories whose formulation relies heavily on theoretical constructs, on to systems with hardly any bearing on potential empirical findings.*

4 Boyd concluded: *What I have argued in the works cited above is that this [realist] conception of the enterprise of science provides the only scientifically plausible explanation for the instrumental reliability of the scientific method. In particular, I argue that the reliability of theory-dependent judgements of projectibility and degrees of confirmation can only be satisfactorily explained on the assumption that the theoretical claims embodied in the background theories which determine those judgements are relevantly approximately true, and that scientific methodology acts dialectically so as to produce in the long run an increasingly accurate theoretical picture of the world. Since logical empiricists accept the instrumental reliability of actual scientific methodology, this defense of realism represents a cogent challenge to logical empiricist antirealism.* (Boyd 1983 p. 65) Fine (1991) has dubbed Boyd's argument the *explanationist defense of realism*.

5 The constructivist account of scientific methodology, developed by Kuhn and others, is not considered given the radical meaning variance it endorsed. Rather than providing a viable alternative to realism and empiricism, constructivism exposed the inadequacies of traditional positivist accounts of meaning. Kuhn himself has backed away from the views expressed in *The Structure of Scientific Revolutions*, and few philosophers of science continue to support the constructivist programme. For a recent critical appraisal of many of the key issues see Sankey (1994): *Where, finally, does this leave the notion of incommensurability? Since so few of the radical claims associated with the incommensurability thesis are warranted by the phenomenon of conceptual change in science, it is not clear that there is anything left for the word 'incommensurability' to stand for. If we like, the word may be retained as a loose name for a cluster of related problems having to do with conceptual change. But there seems little point in saying that theories are*

incommensurable. (Sankey 1994 p. 221)

6 We explicate strong and weak theories of correspondence as follows: traditional realists have endorsed a correspondence between the true statements of theory and an externalised independent metaphysical reality, a noumenon, which may be epistemically beyond our reach - this is strong correspondence. Progress in science may be understood, in the strong account, as convergence towards this metaphysical reality. Weak correspondence asserts that the correspondence between theoretical statements and the world is entirely captured by Tarski's (and Davidson's) schema, which explains correspondence in terms of the satisfaction of predicates by objects in the world. Weak correspondence does not involve a commitment to a transcendental reality beyond our reach: epistemology is not divorced from ontology. A similar explication is provided by Horwich (1982 p. 195) building on the work of Dummett in relation to notions of truth to be used in truth-conditional theories of meaning.

7 Fine (1991) has attacked both entity realism, and Miller's context specific account, which Fine calls *contextual realism*, but while drawing our attention to certain weaknesses in causal arguments, Fine's position sits uncomfortably with NOA's acceptance of the beliefs of scientists and its dependence upon Common Sense Realism. In the limit alternative instrumentalist accounts of science may be given, but McMullin (1991) is persuasive when we contemplate the implausibility of such accounts in geology and astronomy against a background of a shared everyday macroscopic reality.

8 The various strands of realism discussed can be accommodated by their distinct interpretations of the notion of truth employed: either a strong external correspondence (traditional realism), or a weak correspondence (scientific realism), or an epistemic notion of truth (internal realism).

9 For instance Schlick (1979 p. 276)

10 For example, in 'Ontological Relativity', Quine wrote: *It is meaningless to ask whether, in general, our terms "rabbit", "rabbit part", "number", etc., really refer respectively to rabbits, rabbit parts, numbers, etc., rather than to some ingeniously permuted denotations. It is meaningless to ask this absolutely; we can meaningfully ask it only relative to some background language. When we ask, "Does 'rabbit' really refer to rabbits?" someone can counter with the question: "Refer to rabbits in what sense of 'rabbits'?" thus launching a regress; and we need the background language to regress into. The background language gives the query sense, if only relative sense; sense*

relative in turn to it, this background language. Querying reference in any more absolute way would be like asking absolute position, or absolute velocity, rather than position or velocity relative to a given frame of reference. Also it may be very much like asking whether our neighbor may not systematically see everything upside down, or in complementary color, forever undetectably. (Quine 1969 pp. 48-9)

11 The inaccessibility of reference, which is an attack on the "words are labels / meanings are exhibits in the museum of language" account of meaning (see Quine 1969 p. 27), does not conflict with Putnam's causal account of the reference of theoretical terms: *a theory of how reference is* specified *is n't a theory of what reference is; in fact, it* presupposes *the notion of reference.* (Putnam 1978 p. 115)

12 Realism and Reason in Meaning and the Moral Sciences (1978 p. 123): Metaphysical *realism, on the other hand, is less an empirical theory than a model - in the 'colliding billiard balls' sense of 'model'. It is, or purports to be, a model of the relation of* any *correct theory to all or part of THE WORLD. I have come to the conclusion that this model is incoherent. This is what I want to share with you.*

13 Putnam has extended his criticism of metaphysical realism beyond the problem of reference, and has developed critiques of causal and essentialist approaches which are supposed to provide examples of the structure of a ready-made, externalised metaphysical world, that settle the problem of multiple indeterminacy in reference - these structural features are supposed to secure the *intended* reference for terms in a language. (Putnam 1982)

14 Fine has argued that Putnam's account of truth, like that of Rorty, adds an interpretative element to NOA that is not justified. In reaching this conclusion, Fine has discussed the difficulties (Fine 1986a pp. 138-42) associated with defining truth as acceptance, (*I will try to give this picture a canonical representation so that we can identify the features that these particular anti-realisms have in common. So represented, it portrays the truth of a statement P as amounting to the fact that a certain class of subjects would accept P under a certain set of circumstances*), but it is not clear that this is what Putnam had in mind when he talked of truth as the limit of rational enquiry. Putnam clearly recognised the contextual elements in acceptance (Putnam 1981 p. 55) and spoke of truth as an idealization of rational acceptance. Neither idealization nor a limit presupposes a criterion or definition for truth, and there is no reason not to think of Putnam's limit as simply the end result of continuous NOAesque activity. Cf. Ellis (1985 p. 68): *It is important to be*

clear that the internal realist does not *equate truth with* warranted assertibility *or* reasonable belief ... *No, for the internal realist, truth is a kind of limit notion of reasonable belief ... Truth, for the internal realist, is the supposed perfection of this process. It is what we should believe, if our knowledge were perfected, if it were based on total evidence, was internally coherent and was theoretically integrated in the best possible way.*

15 Similar conclusions are to be found in Musgrave (1989) and Psillos (1996).

16 The term 'traditional' has been chosen over the slightly pejorative term 'metaphysical'.

17 Horwich (1982) distinguished the same broad categories of realists as (1) metaphysical realists, (2) verificationists, (3) semantic realists.

18 Quine in Natural Kinds (1969 p.135) stated what might be required for such a definition, but also cast doubt on whether such a definition would ever be forthcoming: *A man's judgements of similarity do and should depend on his theory, on his beliefs; but similarity itself, what the man's judgements purport to be judgements of, purports to be an objective relation in the world. It belongs in the subject matter not of our theory of theorizing about the world, but of our theory of the world itself. Such would be the acceptable and reputable sort of similarity concept, if it could be defined.*

19 Van Fraassen in his critique of realism (1980 Chapter2) showed that this argument was unsound: the choice of theory is underdetermined by success. It is possible to offer an empirically adequate alternative to any theory held to be true by a realist (on the basis of IBE with regard to the theory's success).

20 Miller has argued (1987 pp. 453-61) that Boyd's arguments for realism (based upon the contribution to the development of instrumentally successful theories that is attributed to theoretical concerns, which can only be explained by realism according to Boyd) are not convincing, because examination of the historical contribution of theoretical concerns to the development of successful theories is a mixed record of success and failure i.e. there is no record of successful theoretical contribution that needs to be explained. Miller's analysis, however, misconstrues Boyd's argument. The theoretical contribution Boyd had in mind related to the projectibility of predicates, availability of methods of confirmation, experimental design in science i.e. methodological success. (See note 4) Whether the content of one particular theory contributed to the content of another is a different concern, and yet is the focus of Miller's arguments. Anti-realists can provide responses to Boyd (realism is not the only explanation

of the contribution of theory to scientific methodology) but the historical account proposed by Miller should not properly figure in them.

21 An obvious line of counter-attack for the realist, pursued by Boyd, is to object to the acceptance of abductive reason with regard to the everyday world but its rejection at the level of scientific theory. Psillos (1996) similarly develops plausibility arguments to defend abduction, but concedes that such arguments will not work on someone who is "abduction-blind", which is Fine's point.

22 Fine regarded the failed abductive argument for realism as a case of a more general failure of reasoning: he stated as a general principle that *Metatheoretic arguments must satisfy more stringent requirements than those placed on the arguments used by the theory in question, for otherwise the significance of reasoning about the theory is simply moot* (1986a p. 114), and the higher level abductive argument put forward by realists to defend specific cases of abductive reasoning does not satisfy this principle. He used the same approach to argue against a coherentist defence of realism (1986 p. 116 footnote), on the grounds that coherence arguments were used in science. Rather than defeating the realist, this line of argument looks suspect: if any type of reasoning used in science is not available to mount the realist case, it is hard to think of any argument a realist could ever make. Surely the principle requires to be amended to say that metatheoretic arguments must not be less stringent than (i.e. they can be *as* stringent as) ground-level arguments? The obvious strategy for the realist is to agree with his empiricist opponents as to what are acceptable types of reasoning. Similar thoughts may be found in McMullin (1991 p. 105) and Psillos.(1996 pp. 11-14)

23 Laudan would argue that his account of scientific method, which focuses on the ability of theories to solve empirical and conceptual problems, provides generally a better account of scientific progress than rival accounts. Fine (1986) summarised the situation: *Similarly, if it is the instrumental success of science that we think wants explaining then it seems that we require nothing more than the instrumental reliability of science in order to carry the explanation off. Indeed, anything more than that would be doing no explanatory work. Thus, the explanationist strategy for defending realism does not seem to pull all the way to realism itself. What it does pull to, ironically again, is another of the enemies of realism; namely, instrumentalism.*(Fine 1986b p. 153)

24 Even Leplin has conceded this point: *A further inconclusiveness results from the inability of a transcendental argument to establish its conclusion uniquely. I have sought to forestall this objection by offering an analysis of certain forms of scientific progress that requires the imputation of truth to hypotheses*

effecting such progress. Inasmuch as alternative analyses are possible, it may be said that the impossibility of a non-realist explanation of scientific progress has not been established.(Leplin 1984 p. 213)

25 Leplin's focus on novelty shares much with McMullin's work on the fertility of theories.

26 Leplin himself concedes: *A theory of any depth is bound to have novel consequences. It may seem unlikely that these will universally fail, whether there is any truth to the theory or not. Individual novel successes, even dramatic ones, are small inducement to abduction* (Forthcoming p. 197). Leplin is restricted to a weak emotive appeal: *But in the face of a sustained record of novel success uncompromised by failure, and the continuing absence despite prolonged effort of rival explanations of novel results, one becomes impatient with such reticence. It is an option, to be sure, but what recommends it over the hypothesis that our theory has identified, with some accuracy, the entities or processes responsible for what we experience? It is difficult to specify with complete generality when abduction is warranted, but surely abduction is warranted under* these *circumstances.*

27 Leplin's endorsement of the virtue of novelty is vulnerable to a metatheorem of Fine (*If the phenomena to be explained are not realist-laden, then to every good realist explanation there corresponds a better instrumentalist one* (Fine 1986b p. 154)) in just the same way that McMullin's fertile and resilient, progressive structures were argued to be by Fine (1986b p. 155). To remove the vulnerability requires question-begging realist assumptions.

28 It is interesting to note that Kuhn used a number of the same novel experimental results that Leplin cites as paradigms (in the sense of exemplars) as evidence of scientific revolutions in an account that is thoroughly anti-realist.

29 We may also draw attention to the fact, recognised by Putnam (1975), Newton-Smith (1978) and others, that empirical equivalence need not include counterfactual observation: it might relate only to what has and, perhaps, what will be observed. This type of equivalence was called *weak* empirical equivalence by Hoefer and Rosenberg. A *strong* type of empirical equivalence would require alternative theories to make the same predictions in all circumstances i.e. in conditions not found on earth.

30 In his forthcoming book Leplin demonstrates the yearning of traditional realists for an explanation of why a particular theory supports the observations it does: constructive empiricism and NOA are deemed to leave exploratory lacunae.

Besides stating his feelings of disatisfaction with these accounts, Leplin offers no new argument for traditional realism and the truth of explanatory hypotheses. He is forced to conclude in the face of the guarded epistemic commitments of Fine and van Fraassen: *I suggest, analogously, that explanation requires truth whether or not truth is knowable, and that it is at least as evident that explanation requires truth as it is difficult to establish what is true.*(forthcoming p. 35)

31 Hoefer and Rosenberg (1994) emphasised the distinction to be drawn between global, total theories which are compatible with all past and future observational evidence, and local theories, relevant to a narrow domain, for which an empirically equivalent alternative may exist.

32 Relative to constructive empiricism, quasi-realism is not obliged, through adoption of the "literal" truth of theories, to create the problematic distinction between acceptance and belief, but only at the price of a problematic account of truth.

33 An ardent instrumentalist might maintain that his inductive justification of the instrumental reliability of a particular theory is sufficient, but if that is the case, it is hard to see why instrumentalists do not content themselves with simply phenomenological laws, which are often the most predictively accurate laws, rather than endorsing grandiose theory. Miller came to the same conclusion: *The application of principles that are, on the whole, not believed, to see whether observables behave as if governed by certain causes, not claimed to exist, would be reasonable, if at all, as a means of arriving at formally simple summaries of observations, or some other familiar positivist goal. But if that goal is pursued, then the choices endorsed in premises 1 and 2 [acceptance of current laws and best theory] should not be made. Rival options, more superficial, formally simpler, less burdened with anomaly, and so forth, are more reasonable. The tolerance of anomaly, the preference for causal depth, the reliance on causal rather than formal simplicity, the weightings of failures against successes and many other aspects of arguments as paradigmatic as Newton's, Darwin's and any shrewd curve-fitter's are not reasonable ways of pursuing the goals that a fictionalist might reasonably pursue. (1987 p. 383)*

34 The weakness of instrumentalist explanations of the instrumental success of science is well described by Psillos (1996 p. 18).

35 Goodman's work on confirmation clearly put instrumentalists on the spot: *Any account of the methodology of science must account for judgements of*

"projectibility" of predicates or, to put the issue more broadly, it must provide an account of the standards by which scientists determine which general conclusions are even real candidates for acceptance given an (always finite) body of available data. (Boyd 1983 p. 62) Projectibility is not a problem for the realist as Boyd pointed out: *The realist's claim, then, is that the success of projectibility judgements is to be explained by the hypothesis that the background theories upon which they depend are approximately true of unobservable (as well as observable) entities.* (Boyd 1991 p. 15)

36 Instrumentalists have made two general responses to such a challenge: they have either appealed to the instrumental reliability of scientific methodology to defend induction (but then they leave themselves open to Boyd's criticism (1992) that the reliability of scientific method cannot be established inductively - this then may lead to a higher level reliability claim concerning meta-methodology, and so on), or they put the question of induction to the side as a question for philosophy in general (Laudan 1984) and focus on relative questions concerning reliability e.g. why our scientific methods are better than those of the ancients.

37 Clearly Leplin leaves himself open to the second thrust of Hume's critique of induction: the general principles (here explanatory causal mechanisms) used to support individual causal claims are only inductively warranted.

38 Leplin (forthcoming) has argued, for instance, in favour of a context-independent notion of explanation.

39 One is reminded of similar tensions seen in Popper's insistence that highly corroborated theories are highly valued, yet we have no grounds for accepting the theory as true, or even as probably approximately true.

40 Miller wrote (1987 p. 375 fn. 26): *As a matter of philosophical (and practical) psychology, distinctions between acceptance and belief can also become farfetched. A constructive empiricist working in statistical mechanics makes guesses about observables, designs experiments, chooses her research projects and guesses how the molecular model may have to be revised - by asking what would be the case if the molecular theory were basically true. The claim that she does not believe in the basic truth of the theory sounds like certain examples of farfetched casuistry about intentions, for instance, "The Joint Chiefs of Staff will never really intend the death of civilians in case of nuclear war, because they are only interested in Moscow and other Russian cities as military targets".*

41 One might be tempted to posit an evolutionary response from the empiricist to explain the nature of scientific methodology, but even if this could be provided, it is not an option available to van Fraassen: *But the "pure case" of evolutionary epistemology apparently runs like this: We need methods of forecasting if we are to plan and hence to survive at all. The methods we have been following are the methods of the most successful organisms on earth, namely, us. So they clearly have survival value. It remains to show how, specifically, each feature of that methodology (as described by some account X, say, a list that includes inference to the best explanation) contributes to our fitness for survival. As Popper apparently first said, that is epistemology for dinosaurs* (1985 p. 260). We also note that van Fraassen's position appears inconsistent with the evolutionary riposte he gave to Putnam's arguments from the success of realist explanations of the success of individual theories to the truth of realism: van Fraassen claimed (1980 p. 40) that competition between theories was sufficient to ensure that those we now possess are successful. Perhaps, we can take van Fraassen's views at face value, given one argument related to the instrumental reliability of methodology and the other to the instrumental reliability of theories.

42 We will also see that, in a similar way, van Fraassen confused the epistemic and perceptual aspects of observation in trying to establish an epistemic boundary for empirical adequacy.

43 *It is these limitations to which the 'able' in 'observable' refers - our limitations,* qua *human beings.* (Van Fraassen 1980 p. 17)

44 Interestingly certain ardent positivists such as Schlick were more generous epistemologically than van Fraassen, being prepared to accept inferences to the existence of unobservables: *But it is not necessary that the object or event itself should have to be perceived. We can imagine, for example, that the existence of a trans-Neptunian planet might be inferred by observation of perturbations with just as much certainty as by direct perception of a speck of light in the telescope. The reality of the atom provides another example, as does the back side of the moon* (1979 p. 273). What seems to have been a more important concern from the point of view of verification, was the logical impossibility of empirical evidence for or against a statement i.e. the epistemic divide was founded logically not empirically.

45 Boyd in fact talks of the observational/theoretical dichotomy, but we overlook the fact that theory and observation are not true opposites.

46 We may note that Boyd himself was forced to make recourse to the

observation/theory dichotomy in order to critique the empiricist's circumscribed use of abductive reasoning in her defence of everyday induction (restricting such reasoning to observables) in his defence of realism against Fine.(Boyd 1983 pp. 74-5)

47 *The principle is: X is observable if there are circumstances which are such that if X is present to us under those circumstances, then we observe it.* (Van Fraassen 1980 p. 16)

48 As an example of slight of hand, consider van Fraassen's defence of the dependence of belief upon the epistemic community: *Hence the anti-realist would, on my proposal, have to accept conditions of the form: If the epistemic community changes in fashion Y, then my beliefs about the world will change in manner Z. To see this as an objection to anti-realism is to voice the requirement that our epistemic policies should give the same results independent of our beliefs about the range of evidence accessible to us. That requirement seems to me in no way rationally compelling* (Van Fraassen 1980 p. 18). The argument is not that our beliefs should not change as a function of our epistemic profile, but that our beliefs should not change as a function of <u>what we can observe as humans</u>. Van Fraassen could defend his position only by making the false identification of 'evidence accessible to us' with 'human observation'. Observation by humans has some epistemic import, but is but one element in a satisfactory account of evidence.

49 Fine (1986) argued for similar conclusions and rejected constructive empiricism on the grounds that, without a justification for its a priori assumption that the move from the observable to the unobservable represents a genuine epistemic rift, constructive empiricism unnecessarily inflated epistemology with the distinction to be drawn between acceptance and belief.

50 Fine's NOA is consistent with epistemic complementarity, in so far as he advocated that scientists should simply be left to get on with science, and that we should believe what they believe. He did not, however, explicitly recognise an epistemic boundary, where on one side we are warranted in using realist methodologies, and on the other instrumentalism is to be preferred. *Both realism and instrumentalism are basically pro attitudes toward science. They tend to regard what science accepts as reasonable. They differ as to the character of that acceptance. Like science they favour principled judgement. But if we are persuaded that principles do not determine the character of the judgement, might we not draw the conclusion (or at least consider it?) that we may have been mistaken in thinking that a more determinate character is required. The point is that we build models and theories ("frame hypotheses"),*

and act on them without necessarily settling or even addressing the interpretative questions that realism or instrumentalism raises. The reason we cannot seem to find any principled resolution to these questions, even contextually, is that the usual criteria for theory choice, and the techniques and rules of evidence seem to reach only to the fact of acceptance, and not to its character ... NOA is a pro science attitude as well. It too is inclined to find what science accepts reasonable. In this regard it may be said to assent to what realism and instrumentalism hold in common about acceptance in science. But it differs from realism and instrumentalism in not pushing the issue of the specific character of ordinary scientific acceptance farther than the reach of ordinary scientific procedures and common reflective thought allow. So NOA suggests that in general we can get along without regard to the question of what accepting the theory amounts to, unless that question is scientifically relevant. (Fine 1991 pp. 93-4)

51 As Schlick put it: *In other words, the electron, and all physical realities likewise, are* not *unknowable things-in-themselves, and do not belong to a transcendent, metaphysical reality, if this is characterized by the fact that it embraces the unknowable.*(1979 p. 279)

52 For example, Miller (1987 p. 364) used the term the "One True Inventory"

53 NOA curiously is similar to positivism in a number of respects. Positivists believed in the unproblematic reality of everyday objects and scientific entities (Schlick 1979 p. 278: *But now how about science? When it speaks of the external world, does it, unlike daily life, mean something other than things such as houses and trees? It seems to me this is by no means the case. For atoms and electric fields, or whatever else the physicist may speak of, are precisely what houses and trees consist of, according to his teaching; the one must therefore be real in the same sense as the other ... We have long since convinced ourselves, in fact, that the existence of even the most subtle of the 'invisible' things postulated by the scientist is verified, in principle, in exactly the same way as the reality of a tree or a star.*), and found the commitments of both traditional realists and idealists to either an externalised or internalised reality to be problematic. (*Logical positivism and [non-metaphysical] realism are therefore not opposed ... There is opposition only between consistent empiricism and the metaphysician, and it is directed as much against the [traditional] realist as the idealist* (Schlick 1979 p. 283)). Both NOA and positivism are minimalist: what scientific method says about the world is all there is to say, hence no metaphysics, no transcendent reality. The key difference is that NOA does not endorse a verificationist theory of meaning, and embraces the role of theory and theoretical entities in empirical testing.

54 Surprisingly Fine argues (1991) against entity realism, which would indicate some change in his position.

55 This line of argument has been forcefully developed by Musgrave (1989), who maintained that while a disquotational account of truth is necessary for a philosophy of science, it is not sufficient to settle questions of what exists. Given that NOA "stubbornly" refuses to say anything further, Musgrave held that NOA is not committed to the existence of any entities, and NOA is *a complete philosophical know-nothing-ism* (p. 391). This argument may be countered by letting the methods of science dictate which entities are deemed to exist, and by drawing upon the epistemic methods we use to settle questions of existence for CSR, again relying upon the continuity between the world of science and that of everyday objects.

56 Psillos (1996) has similarly argued for a general epistemological warrant for NOA beyond the simple acceptance of the beliefs of the scientific community.

6 Constants and underdetermination

Introduction

Although the reader might be prepared to advocate NOA in general terms as an adequate philosophy of science, the potential vulnerability of NOA to cases of underdetermination may make it impossible to marry NOA to the account of constants developed in earlier chapters. In this chapter, the argument will be examined closely and the implications for NOA will be drawn out. Certain modifications will be required in NOA to accommodate the existence of alternative empirical systems for constants, but the consequences are not held to be destructive for NOA.

Synopsis of chapter

First, a non-scientific example of underdetermination taken from Putnam is discussed. Next, a more plausible scientific example of underdetermination, involving Newtonian and Hamiltonian mechanics, is examined. Various traditional responses for realists and anti-realists are considered. A number of manoeuvres available to realists, instrumentalists and constructive empiricists, to deal with underdetermination, are not available to a NOAer. Given that underdetermination cannot be formally ruled out, it is argued that as a result, NOA might most comfortably accommodate underdetermination if we accept a degree of relativity in its conception of truth.

This suggestion of relativity has been seen in the accounts of Quine and Putnam, and it is Putnam who most unambiguously showed how this account might work using an example taken from set theory.

While at first sight relativity of truth seems a severe blow for NOA, the circumstances where such underdetermination might occur are heavily conditioned.

Such limited relativity as might or does occur, appears to fit language usage in a number of scientific domains such as quantum theory. Relativity on a limited basis might be considered a positive, pragmatic feature of NOA. In the case of constants, this relativity, occasioned by circumstances of underdetermination, is called into play.

Underdetermination

In a footnote to his paper 'The Refutation of Conventionalism', Putnam gave a hypothetical example of a situation that might give rise to underdetermination: he described the possible endorsement of an alternative physics-cum-geometry by a character called Oscar:

> Coming to the geometry case: suppose Oscar accepts just the same atomic statements about 'distance' that we accept about $f(x, y, z, t, x', y', z', t')$, where x, y, z, t and x', y', z', t' are the coordinates of the points, and f satisfies the axioms for a metric. Suppose also that Oscar accepts $f = ma$, that he postulates strange forces acting on measuring rods in order to preserve the statement that 'distance = $f(x, y, z, t, x', y', z', t')$', etc. Finally, suppose that Oscar is 'bilingual' relative to us, and that he *tells* us that when he says 'distance' he means distance, that his theory is *right* and that ours is *wrong*, etc. In this case we will decide that Charity begins at home, and choose homophonic translation. We will say that Oscar's word 'distance' refers to distance in *our* sense, and that Oscar's theory is just false.
>
> If asked, 'How do you know it's false?' (given that Oscar's theory doesn't imply any false predictions), we will point to the fact that Oscar's theory assumes *improbably* complicated mechanisms. In short, speaking from the perspective of our theory, we will say that Oscar is wrong and that our theory is *truer*, not just *descriptively simpler* - i.e. there is a 'fact of the matter', and simplicity is here one indicator of *truth*.
>
> On the other hand, if Oscar himself regards the difference between us as 'semantic', if he doesn't postulate any strange forces - if he just talks as we would if our present language were changed in the one respect that 'distance' *meant* '$f(x, y, z, t, x', y', z', t')$' - then we will obey the Principle of Charity, and translate Oscar's word 'distance' as '$f(x, y, z, t, x', y', z', t')$'. In this case, we will say that the difference between Oscar's theory and ours is one of descriptive simplicity. (It is also an instance of Trivial Semantic Conventionality).(Putnam 1975 p.166)

Putnam also considered the possibility that the relative merits of our and Oscar's theory were reversed:

> Suppose, for example, we modify the example in the previous note by letting Oscar's theory be methodologically preferable to ours, rather than methodologically inferior, Then, instead of translating 'distance' by '$f(x, y, z, t, x', y', z', t')$', we would do better to use homophonic translation, and, in addition, *to adopt Oscar's theory*. In this case we will say that (1) the magnitude Oscar calls 'distance' is the one we did and do call 'distance'; and that (2) Oscar has *discovered* the fundamental physical law that distance = $f(x, y, z, t, x', y', z', t')$, and our

> theory was in some respects mistaken. On this account, the reference of 'distance' has not changed; only our *beliefs* about it have changed. (Putnam 1975 p. 167)

On the basis of these two examples, it is not incoherent to suppose that Oscar might advocate a theory which is, according to appropriate methodological canons, *just as good as* our theory. In these circumstances, we might feel justified in making a preliminary claim of underdetermination.

Critics of the thesis that philosophically significant underdetermination may arise in science, may counter that if Oscar's theory is just as good as our theory, then it must be equivalent to our theory, and what we have detected is a case of Trivial Semantic Conventionality (TSC).

> In one respect, it is a triviality that language is conventional. It is a triviality that we might have meant something other than we do by the noises that we use. The noise 'pot' could have meant what is in fact meant by the word 'dog', and the word 'dog' could have meant what is in fact meant by the word 'fish'. Let us call this kind of conventionality TSC (Trivial Semantic Conventionality). (Putnam 1975 p. 164)

Similarly, the truth of statements supported by one theory, and not the other, will be cases of what Newton-Smith has analogously called Trivial Semantic Relativism.[1] Underlying judgements of TSC, however, is an assumption of isomorphic language structures between the two theories, which is open to challenge. Putnam, in his paper, described how the notion of isomorphism was central to Quine's indeterminacy of translation arguments, if meaning preservation under translation was to be explained behaviourally without reliance upon the notion of a proposition, but there is no reason to assume that empirical underdetermination in science requires isomorphic theories. To assert this is so is to beg the question against underdetermination.[2]

Opponents of underdetermination may fall back on the slightly weaker, but non-trivial, claim that the terms of the two rival theories do not in fact, contrary to our initial impressions, have the same referents, and hence they are theories about different things, which share a common observable content, rather than alternative theories about the same thing. If we can establish that this is the case, it may be held that we are not in a position to assert that we do genuinely have alternative theories: are we in fact talking about the same features of the world? We can easily imagine, for instance, that a realist might accept that a common body of observation can be satisfactorily supported by more than one theory if we assume, on the principle of a common cause, that the alternative theories might ultimately both be entailed by some deeper, but as yet unavailable account. Fortunately, we may put Putnam's causal account of the reference[3] of theoretical terms to work, making explicit the philosophical underpinnings of why there is continuity of reference between the two theories, similar to that which occurred in the second Oscar example (where Oscar had a better theory). We can imagine that we and Oscar are linked to the same introducing events that provide a causal account of reference for the principal terms involved in the two rival theories. Note that the causal descriptions used for all principal terms might be shared between the two alternative theories ensuring a common set of referents: the alternative theories might then differ in what they say about the referents. To suppose that the causal descriptions for the principal terms might be different does not rule out the possibility that they might in fact be the same, and the assertion that the references are different leads us towards radical meaning variance and incommensurability of theories, which most philosophers would probably wish to avoid.

It is not then unreasonable to suppose that, on occasion, we can formulate different physical accounts, that make incompatible claims, where the proponents of both positions are confident that they understand how the same terms are employed by their counterparts. As Bergström has argued, substantive disputes can occur:

> We may also reason as follows. When people seem to disagree, their disagreement is often merely verbal: different individuals use the same words with different meanings. But there is also genuine disagreement. In particular, the history of science is usually taken to show that people can be in genuine disagreement over theoretical sentences. Such theoretical disagreements can sometimes be resolved by empirical investigations. But we cannot take it for granted that this is always possible. Hence, for all we know, there may be genuine theoretical disagreement among empirically equivalent systems of the world. (Bergström 1993 p. 350)

It also remains possible that the alternative theories may make different, but not incompatible claims.

Let us suppose, then, that the opponent of underdetermination concedes that there may be occasions when scientists are able to explain a significant number of phenomena in more than one way, using a common language of science for which the meaning of theoretical terms is not, in general, problematic: TSC does not occur and the continuity of reference of key terms is assumed.

It may then be objected that any underdetermination is only temporary pending further development of theory or additional experiments. A supporter of underdetermination may be tempted, in these circumstances, to draw upon the Duhem-Quine thesis of holism, relating to the indefeasibility of any particular set of theoretical claims, to support his case:

> Holism ... is the thesis that single hypotheses cannot be tested in isolation from the auxiliary hypotheses required to draw out their empirical consequences. Accordingly, the single hypothesis is not the unit of empirical test, and any single hypothesis may be retained in the face of adverse observations by withdrawing at least one of the other hypotheses which accompanied it in the false prediction. (Hoefer and Rosenberg 1994 p. 593)

Hoefer and Rosenberg have pointed out, however, that holism and underdetermination are not to be confused, and that underdetermination amounts to a more interesting claim than the straightforward observation that alternative theories may always be maintained, even if it becomes increasingly unreasonable to do so:

> The notion of theoretical holism must be sharply distinguished from the concept of empirical underdetermination ... [Holism] leads to an obvious underdetermination problem: The empirical data at hand do not logically preclude a theoretical framework including the individual hypothesis at hand, or one including its denial. Such underdetermination of theory choice is ubiquitous and unavoidable in actual science. However, as the portion of science that we are inclined to hold constant and unrevised increases, holism becomes increasingly unreasonable ... By contrast, the thesis of underdetermination of theory by evidence is about empirically adequate total science; it is a thesis about what Quine calls "systems of the world" - theories that comprehensively account for all observations - past, present and future. It is a thesis about theories that entail all and only the true observational conditionals, all the empirical regularities already confirmed by observation and experiment. (Hoefer and Rosenberg 1994 p. 594)

To deal with Hoefer and Rosenberg's concerns, let us examine an example of underdetermination that amounts to more than holism.

It is well known to applied mathematicians that an alternative Hamiltonian formulation may be given for mechanics instead of relying on the laws of mechanics described by Newton. Under the Hamiltonian formulation, the motion of a body may be derived from a series of differential equations relating the potential and kinetic energies associated *with* the body; in Newtonian mechanics the emphasis is on the action of an agent *on* the body (the applied force). Hamiltonian mechanics enjoy certain advantages: occasionally it is not possible to determine the forces which are acting (for instance in certain quantum mechanical situations), but it is possible to define energy functions. The Hamiltonian formulation is scalar and invariant under co-ordinate transformations, hence many problems can be advantageously described by scalar Lagrangian equations of motion in configuration space. It may be argued that these two formulations are "merely" notational variants, but such a view ignores many substantive questions of philosophical interest (such as whether forces are responsible for the motion of bodies), and is contrary to the view of experts in the field:

> The differential statement of mechanics contained in Newton's equations or the integral statement embodied in Hamilton's Principle (and the resulting Lagrangian equations) have been shown to be entirely equivalent. Hence there can be no distinction between these viewpoints which are based on the description of *physical effects*. From a philosophical standpoint, however, it is possible to make a distinction. In the Newtonian formulation, a certain force on a body is considered to produce a definite motion; that is, a definite *effect* is always associated with a certain cause. According to Hamilton's Principle, however, the motion of a body may be considered to result from the attempt of Nature to achieve a certain *purpose*, namely, to minimize the time integral of the difference between the kinetic and potential energies. Clearly, the operational solving of problems in mechanics is not dependent

on adopting one or the other of these views, but historically such considerations have had a profound influence on the development of dynamics. (Marion 1972 p. 212)

It might be objected that the preceding remarks notwithstanding, it still happens to be the case that the concept of a force acting on a body to produce a definite motion, and the concept of the minimalisation of a variational energy principle are the same concept, expressed in different ways. This objection is not sustained, however, because there are genuine physical differences that distinguish the concepts of force and variational principles: in particular, the concept of a variational principle may be usefully extended to embrace quantum mechanics in a way that forces cannot:

Before proceeding, I would like to outline why I think the Lagrangian formulation in classical mechanics deserves to be treated as more than a neat reformulation of Newtonian mechanics ... The main advantage of the path integral approach is that it provides both a common language and a bridge principle between classical mechanics and quantum mechanics. When the action integral, S, is large with respect to Planck's constant, $\hbar$, as it is for macroscopic systems, only one path between initial and final co-ordinates has non-negligible probability and this is the path for which S takes an extremal value. This value gives us Hamilton's principle of least action for classical systems. At the other extreme, where $S \sim \hbar$, many paths contribute with comparable probability giving the characteristic interference effects of wave mechanics. (Allport 1993 p. 257)

Propositions relating to the interpretation of mechanics will be intelligible but disputed by adherents of the Newtonian and Hamiltonian schools. Certain claims will be held to be true relative to one account, and false relative to the other. Since the ontologies involved are substantively different, and one is not reducible to the other, this will not be an idle debate. Given their empirical equivalence, it seems there are no purely empirical reasons for choosing one account over the other. The example is a plausible case of underdetermination. To deny the significance of the debate over the consequences of the two theories is to assert a narrow empiricism, which is dogmatic and which fails to explain the historically attested impact of the choice of the alternative theories upon the subsequent development of physics:

Newton was never comfortable with the implications of the notion of attraction and the more general notion of force. Part of his uneasiness stemmed from his theology; he could not conceive that matter might of itself be active and thus in some sense independent of God's directing power ... The Cartesians, Leibniz, and later Berkeley, charged that the new mechanics did not really *explain* motion, since its central notion, *force*, could not be given an acceptable interpretation. Newton was sensitive to this charge and, in the decades following the publication of the *Principia*, kept trying to find an ontology that might satisfy his critics. He tried "active principles" that would somehow operate outside bodies. He even tried to reintroduce an ether with an extraordinary combination of properties - this despite his convincing refutation of mechanical ethers in Principia ... How should Newton's attempts at "interpretation" be regarded, after the fact? Were they an improper intrusion of 'metaphysics', the sort of thing science would bar? The term 'underlying ontology' that I have used might

> mislead here. A scientist *can* properly attempt to specify the mechanisms that underlie his equations. Newton's ether *might* have worked out; ... The metaphor of "active principle" proved a fruitful one; it was the ancestor of the notion of field, which would much later show its worth ... Scientists have never thought themselves disqualified from pursuing one of a number of physical models that, for the moment, appear empirically equivalent. As metaphors, these models may give rise to quite different lines of enquiry, leading eventually to their empirical separation. Or it may be that one of the alternative models appears undesirable on other grounds than immediate empirical adequacy (as action at a distance did to Newton). If prolonged efforts to separate the models empirically are unsuccessful, or if it comes to be shown that the models are in principle empirically equivalent, scientists will, of course, turn to other matters. But this is not a rejection of realism. It is, rather, an admission that no decision can be made in this case as to what the theory, on a realist reading commits us to. (McMullin 1984 pp. 10-11)

While it may be argued that neither of these two particular accounts (Newtonian and Hamiltonian) is correct, this does not blunt our case. It suffices for our purposes that it merely be possible for underdetermination to occur,[4] not that it actually does in this particular instance or that generally underdetermination is the case.

Other interesting candidates for underdetermination might also be cited: a physics based upon dense but not continuous numerical quantities, mixture and pure state parameters in quantum mechanics.[5] As Bergström (1993) and Hoefer and Rosenberg (1994) have suggested, these alternative accounts can be embedded as sub-theories in an all-embracing, global account of the world which records all our beliefs, which is self-contained and does not require additional hypotheses. It is precisely this type of situation that Hoefer and Rosenberg had in mind when they described Newtonian mechanics, in absolute and relative formulations, as surrogate global theories. There is sufficient plausibility to support cases of underdetermination,[6] that the onus lies with those who reject underdetermination to provide a strong refutation of all possible instances. This has not been done: Laudan and Leplin (1991) at best established that local underdetermination cannot be proved, while conceding that local underdetermination cannot be disproved, and Bergström (1993), Hoefer and Rosenberg (1994) have reiterated the case for global underdetermination. We can support Laudan and Leplin's conclusions:

> We do not deny the possibility that the world is such that equally viable, incompatible theories of it are possible. We do not deny the possibility of the world's being unamenable to epistemic investigation and adjudication beyond a certain level. But whether or not the world is like that is itself an empirical question open to investigation, The answer cannot be preordained by a transcendent, epistemic skepticism. (Laudan and Leplin 1991 p. 459)

Let us now consider how the advocates of the various accounts we have discussed might respond to underdetermination, starting with the realist.

The realist response to underdetermination

Faced by cases of undetermination, Newton-Smith advocated two postures for the traditional realist: ignorance or arrogance. Turning first to the Arrogance Response which Newton-Smith preferred, let p be a proposition which renders the two rival theories in question incompatible:

> If we cannot discover whether it is a fact that *p* or not, we do not assume that there is a matter of fact at stake. (Newton-Smith 1981 p. 42)

This has two negative aspects. First, the move in general involves compromising the standard ontological ingredient of realism, which means that it is not likely to be adopted by traditional realists. In order to limit the damage, one might advocate a limited instrumentalism with regard to alternative accounts that are deemed to be undecideable, but this is not without difficulties. While it may be argued that the occurrence of actual instances of underdetermination, which provoke this rear-guard action, is entirely in keeping with a naturalistic account of the scientific enterprise, the ability of what were genuinely held to be matters of fact to cease to be held to be matters of fact, even when we have successfully grounded the referents and meanings of terms and have put our best epistemic methods to work, suggests that the framework we have for linking language to the world, and our epistemic methods are unsatisfactory.

Proponents of the Arrogance Response may reply that, to the contrary, our epistemic methods have hereby been shown to be effective, since they have not led us to postulate a matter of fact when no such matter of fact exists. This counter is not convincing, however, because we are unable to discern clearly what it is about the evidential circumstances which made what we genuinely held to be a matter of fact not to be a matter of fact. If we cannot specify the circumstances where this loss of "matter-of-fact-ness" occurs (beyond saying, perhaps, that the circumstances relate to matters about unobservables), how can we be sure that matters of fact are matters of fact? It is not a compelling argument to say that our epistemic methods are sound because whenever they are found to lead us to mistaken beliefs, we can use them, when our error is discovered, to say that we made a mistake: this is a poor warrant of their effectiveness. We want assurances in advance, not humility after the event. We might, after all, by the same line of reasoning, accept that our subsequent conclusion that we had made a mistake could itself be wrong (so there was a matter of fact at stake after all). Equally we can imagine, before the existence of an underdetermined rival theory is established, being questioned about whether p is a fact, about the possibility of alternative theories etc. Assume we reply contemptuously that p is a fact and there are no plausible alternative theories, but that subsequently a viable alternative theory is presented. In light of the suggested subsequent adoption of the Arrogance

Response when underdetermination is brought to our attention, our arrogance in answering these earlier questions (to the effect that p is a fact, there are no alternative theories) might seem to have been misplaced. Furthermore, the situation presented by the discovery of underdetermined rivals is rare, and is not to be assimilated with the familiar one of a mistaken belief about a fact being corrected by subsequent experiments and theory. Instead, we have a situation which denies entirely the prior significance of established theoretical claims - there is no fact of the matter, either way - because of the emergence of an alternative theory. It is not that that we have got something wrong, but that it makes no sense to talk of the rightness or wrongness of this item. This has implications for why we consider theoretical statements matters of fact, beyond our particular concern about the specific situation where underdetermination has occurred.

We may be tempted to conclude that one case of underdetermination is sufficient to call into question the validity of traditional realism altogether, not because we make mistakes (which the traditional realist can hope to rectify), but because a situation has been identified which can never be resolved, never be put right: what seemed a superficial wound turns out to be fatal. Given the impossibility of defining what is decideable, or ruling out the possibility of underdetermination with regard to currently accepted theoretical sentences, we may ask why the traditional realist is not forced, because of our general suspicions concerning the reliability of the epistemic methods of traditional realists, to retreat entirely to an observational core, where "there would be nothing to be a realist about except the observational consequences on the arrogance response" (Newton-Smith 1981 p. 43) ? What then are we to make of the richness and the fertility of explanations based on non-observables? Are we not forced into constructive empiricism?

Perhaps the realist in question might reply that our methods are sound in most circumstances, but it is simply a fact that they do not work in one or two particular cases. While this possibility cannot be ruled out a priori, we may express our discomfort at the finding that two sets of circumstances, one of underdetermination and one lacking underdetermination, can be ontologically opposed. Imagine the two sets of circumstances are both fully supported by our best scientific reasoning, but in one set of circumstances the ability of our theories to predict and explain corresponds to a fact-of-the-matter, and in the other it does not, and yet we have no means of distinguishing between these two types of situation on the basis of our theories of language or of reference. We cannot explain the loss of "facticity". Whatever it is that makes the situations different, is beyond our reach. Given that is the case, it is hard not to conclude that this solution is unsatisfactory in its adhocness. If they are faulty and incomplete in this instance, how can we be sure of their soundness elsewhere?

To deal with the difficulty posed by these cases, and to address the seemingly adhoc tactics of the Arrogance Response, one might focus not upon our epistemic methods, but upon the links between language and the world. Dummett has proposed an account of meaning in which circumstances of underdetermination are held to give rise to undecidable propositions. If the proposition is undecidable, then we do not understand what it means to say that the proposition is true or false. As a consequence, it may be argued that the proposition has not been given a fully determinate meaning. While such an account of meaning, if upheld, might lead to a revision of the arguments presented concerning the Arrogance Response, the investigation of alternative accounts of meaning falls outside the scope of the present work.

Consider now the Ignorance Response to cases of underdetermination: one of our two theories is true but we shall never know which - some matter of fact, beyond our power to discover, makes one view true. Putnam, on behalf of Quine, lent support to this view:

> What this shows is that even if there should be observationally equivalent statements in Quine's sense [i.e. that accord with the past, present and future record of actual observations], which in addition to being equivalent were equally simple, etc., i.e. which would come out as equally good on all of the usual methodological canons, still it would not follow that there was no fact of the matter as to which of the two theories was right. The step from underdetermination of scientific theories by the totality of observation statements, if it is a fact, to there being no fact of the matter as to which theory is right, is not an obvious step at all ... For our present purposes it is enough to remark that there is no clear route from '(observationally) equivalent descriptions' to 'no fact of the matter' unless we are willing to assume such difficult and problematical philosophical doctrines as the holistic version of verificationism and the rejection of counterfactuals, or at least, the rejection of realism with respect to counterfactual conditionals ... Thus Quine does not believe that there is any step, in general, from the fact that the choice between theories is underdetermined, in his sense, to there being 'no fact of the matter'. (Putnam 1975 pp. 181-2)

Newton-Smith, on the other hand, argued against such a response. Let us consider his reasons:

> However, in virtue of being incompatible there will be some assertion *p* which is contained in one theory, the negation of which is contained in the other theory. In view of our inability to decide which theory is the true one, *p* will be empirically undecideable. On the ignorance response we assume that there is a matter of fact at stake with regard to *p*. However, there is nothing observable that is explained by the supposition that there is a matter of fact at stake. For *ex hypothesi* all observations are explained equally well on the theory containing *p* and on the theory containing the negation of *p*. (Newton-Smith 1981 p. 41)

Upon first inspection, it does seem that the Ignorance Response is problematic: it would seem that no evidence relating to observables would make any difference to the relative standing of the alternative theories. Closer examination suggests, however, the arguments disguises an equivocation in the use of the word 'all' in 'all observations are explained equally well". Our rival theories, T_1 and T_2, may be underdetermined in the strong sense of accommodating equally well the observable predictions that follow from all possible, including counter-factual, values of the variables which occur in those particular theories (as opposed to simply the observations, past, present and future, that actually occur). It need not be the case, however, that T_1 and T_2 each contain every variable in science necessary to make every possible observable prediction. T_1 and T_2 may be incompatible sub-theories of two alternative global theories, which are alike in other respects.

As a consequence, we may challenge the assertion that "there is nothing observable that is explained by the supposition that there is a matter of fact at stake". Were we to discover some new unobservable effect, for instance relating to the nature of some other, new theoretical entity, this finding might be accommodated by one theory and not the other. Given this might be the case, it is possible that this new theoretical entity might lead to observable consequences in a domain far removed from the domain covered by the alternative theories T_1 and T_2.[7]

Laudan and Leplin have not only provided historical examples of this type of *indirect evidential support*, but have also formalized the circumstances in which this occurs:

> What, then, is the connection that we claim our examples to establish between nonconsequential evidence and differential support of empirically equivalent theories? We propose the following exemplar. Theoretical hypotheses H_1 and H_2 are empirically equivalent but conceptually distinct. H_1, but not H_2, is derivable from a more general theory T, which also entails another hypothesis H. An empirical consequence e of H is obtained. e supports H and thereby T. Thus, e provides indirect evidential warrant for H_1, of which it is not a consequence, without affecting the credentials of H_2. Thus, one of two empirically equivalent hypotheses or theories can be evidentially supported to the exclusion of the other by being incorporated into an independently supported, more general theory that does not support the other, although it does predict all the empirical consequences of the other. (Laudan and Leplin 1991 p. 464)

So powerful did Laudan and Leplin consider this insight, that they thought it could be used to undermine the possibility of underdetermination itself. Because any particular theory is ultimately defeasible by new evidence, and by theoretical developments, Laudan and Leplin argued that there was no reason to suppose that as science progressed, as we obtained a complete picture of all observable domains, cases of (putative) underdetermination would not be resolved.

The difficulty with taking the Ignorance Response to the limits of progress, where we encompass every possible observation, is that it invites other extreme responses. If T_1 is found to be incompatible with an all-encompassing Grand Unified Theory of the Universe, (and T_2 is accordingly to be preferred), who can rule out a priori the possibility of more than one Grand Unified Theory of the Universe, with which T_2 is incompatible, i.e. underdetermination at the level of the Cosmos? This circumstance is explicitly postulated and discussed by Hoefer and Rosenberg (1994) and Bergström (1993). Laudan and Leplin have gained nothing by raising the stakes.

The defeasibility argument is perhaps better employed by Ellis, who used it to argue against van Fraassen that underdetermination is not endemic in science. The internal realist may hold that in the process of developing a complete science, local cases of underdetermination will be resolved. Constructive empiricists might then seek to maintain against Ellis that underdetermination remains by positing also more than one complete theory of science, but this time the argument will not work, according to Ellis. In the epistemic limit, where truth is held to coincide with warranted assertibility, internal realists, such as Ellis, reject the possibility of alternative complete accounts of science, on the grounds that such putative cases of underdetermination of science in its entirety are metaphysical in outlook, and for this reason they claim underdetermination collapses into skepticism. This argument hinges critically upon the notion of truth employed.

Putnam has argued against traditional realists that it is incoherent to suppose that in the epistemic limit, our ideal theory of the world T_1 could be false, and that some other theory T_2, for ever beyond our reach, could be true:

> Lifting restrictions on our actual all-too-finite powers, we can imagine T_1 to have every property *except objective truth* - which is left open - that we like ... The supposition under consideration is that T_1 might be all this *and still be* (in reality) *false* ...
>
> So, the interpretation of 'reference' ... certainly meets all *operational* constraints on reference. But the interpretation of 'reference '... certainly meets all *theoretical* constraints on reference - it makes the ideal theory, T_1, come out true. So what *further* constraints on reference are there that could single out some other interpretation as (uniquely) 'intended', and [our] interpretation as an 'unintended' interpretation (in the model-theoretic sense of 'interpretation')? The supposition that even an 'ideal' theory (from a pragmatic point of view) might really be false appears to collapse into *unintelligibility*. (Putnam 1978 p. 126)

While initially Putnam's comments might appear to support Ellis, in fact they do not. What Putnam wanted to secure was agreement that meeting our ideal epistemic constraints was sufficient to warrant the attribution of truth to our ideal theory, that there were not further criteria to be satisfied. He did not rule out the possibility of more than one acceptable interpretation of the theory within these constraints, and, as we shall see later, on occasion advocated a limited notion of pluralism.

Ellis might, nonetheless be able to sustain his argument, if he were able to give additional content to the notion of an ideal limit, beyond simply making it a definitional requirement that at this limit, there be only one complete account of nature. Putnam thought this could not be done:

> On this view (mine), then, 'truth' (idealized justification) is as vague, interest relative, and context sensitive as *we* are ... The impossibility (in practice at least) of formalizing the assertibility conditions for arbitrary sentences is just the impossibility of formalizing general

intelligence itself.

> If assertibility (in the sense of *warranted* assertibility) is not formalizable, idealized warranted assertibility (truth) is even less so, for the notion of better and worse epistemic conditions (for a particular judgement) upon which it depends is revisable as our empirical knowledge increases. That it is, nevertheless, a meaningful notion; that there are better and worse epistemic conditions for most judgements, and a fact of the matter as to what the verdict would be if the conditions were sufficiently good, a verdict to which opinion would 'converge' if it were reasonable, is the heart of my own 'realism'. It is a kind of realism, and I mean it to be a *human* kind of realism, a belief that there is a fact of the matter as to what is rightly assertible for us, as opposed to what is rightly assertible from the God's eye view so dear to the classical metaphysical realist. (Putnam 1983 xvii, xviii)

Insofar as Putnam touched upon the circumstances that might relate to underdetermination at the ideal epistemic limit, he would seem to advocate the Arrogance Response:

> The simile of frictionless planes aside, the two key ideas of the idealization theory of truth are (1) that truth is independent of justification here and now, but not independent of *all* justification. To claim a statement is true is to claim it could be justified. (2) truth is expected to be stable or 'convergent'; if both a statement and its negation could be 'justified', even if conditions were as ideal as one could hope to make them, there is no sense in thinking of the statement as having a truth-value. (Putnam 1981 p. 56)

Returning to Ellis (1985), we note that his tactic was to assert that any specific claim of empirical underdetermination is always defeasible given the openness of evidence that might be brought to bear in order to discriminate between two alternative theories. Only in cases where underdetermination is already "built-in", (for example, an alternative theory to T_1 which states that although the world is not as theory T_1 says it is, the world behaves, so far as we can ever tell, as if T_1 were true), can we be sure that the claim is not defeasible. Ellis considered such cases to be instances of a general skepticism, which neither he nor realists in general were in a position to resolve. Against van Fraassen's general claims of pervasive underdetermination, Ellis' defeasibility argument has some force, but it does not strictly rule out the possibility of two alternative empirical accounts at the epistemic limit: his argument simply prevents us from being able to show this eventuality will occur. Where he talked of alternative rational accounts, Ellis asserted that the all-embracing nature of what we would know at the epistemic limit would ensure that the alternative account of an alien culture was incommensurable, and hence not incompatible:

> What I am denying is that there is any way that the world is independently of how it is for various kinds of beings. Different beings may have different perspectives on the world, but there is no reason to think that there is any perspective which can claim priority. But perhaps if we met some aliens who had a different perspective we could explain why they see the world as they do, differently from us. So perhaps in this way we could achieve a better

understanding of how the world really is. Maybe so, but we still could not achieve any truly objective stance, for the theory we constructed to explain the belief of creatures different from us would still be a theory of ours which we should have to evaluate as we would evaluate any other theory. And, if the aliens constructed a theory about how we thought about the world and evaluated it by their standards, then there is no guarantee that it would be the same. So no objective stance which would define the way the world is independently of our epistemic values seems to be possible. (Ellis 1985 p. 72)

Be that as it may, there still remains the question of two alternative ultimate accounts within our own culture, where it would seem Ellis would be compelled to fall back upon the notion of epistemic limit itself.

Fine has scrutinised the accounts of internal realists, dubbed "truthmongers", and found the notion of an epistemic limit, once divorced from the acceptance of specific communities in favourable circumstances, to be as metaphysical as the traditional realists account of truth:

For the anti-realism expressed in the idea of truth-as-acceptance is just as metaphysical and idle as the realism expressed by a correspondence theory ... To understand this [acceptance] conception of truth we must get a sense of how things would be were they different in certain respects from what they are now. Whatever your line about counterfactuals, this understanding involves at least either the idea of truth in altered circumstances, or the idea of truth in these actual circumstances. But each alternative here folds in upon itself, requiring in turn further truths. I believe there is no grounding for this process unless we turn away from the acceptance picture at some point ... It seems to me that the acceptance idea never can get off the ground, and that we cannot actually understand the picture of truth that it purports to offer. If we think otherwise, that is probably because we are inclined to read into the truthmonger's project some truths (or ideas of truth) not having to do with acceptance at all - perhaps, even, some truths via correspondence! Thus, with respect to warrant and intelligibility, the acceptance picture emerges as quite on a par with the correspondence picture. (Fine 1986a p. 141)

Others (Jardine, for instance) have felt sensitive to this criticism, and have staunchly tried to rule out the possibility of underdetermination from the start. Either way, for the traditonal realist, this resolution of underdetermination involves an unacceptable concept of truth: is there instead a way of heading off (sub-theory) underdetermination for a traditional realist without collapsing truth into entirely an epistemic notion?

What we can learn from Laudan and Leplin is that there are situations which involve a strong form of underdetermination (i.e. one which includes counterfactual observations) between two empirically equivalent theories, which do not lead us into Grand Unified Theories of the Universe, and where the Ignorance Response is not obviously a failure. These are situations where two theories support counterfactual values for all the variables which appear in the theories, and which share all possible observational predictions for the observable phenomena covered by the theories. These theories need not cover all phenomena, and we may regard them in some sense as global, without considering them cosmic (i.e. they could be subtheories of alternative global accounts). In these situations it is possible that detailed application of some future theory T_3 to T_1 and T_2 will unlock the current impasse: our ignorance is genuine ignorance.

Unfortunately, however, we cannot rule out the opposing possibility that no new theory will come to our aid. Nor can we rule out the possibility of an Appeal Court ruling in favour of a further theory T_4, which reverses the decision between T_1 and T_2 on the basis of some future T_3. Van Fraassen, for instance, has shown how underdetermination might persist in the case of absolute and relative Newtonian mechanics even after the introduction of additional theories such as electromagnetism (van Fraassen 1980 p. 50). Laudan and Leplin (1991) have claimed nonetheless that this case of underdetermination is defeasible, but close scrutiny of their arguments by Hoefer and Rosenberg (1994) cast doubt on their claim. Even Boyd came to the same conclusions: in the case of Reichenbach's example of alternative force-cum-geometries - 'F and G' or the (universal force) alternative 'F' and G''. He noted:

> We can know that scientific research governed by the conventional adoption of 'F and G' will lead to the refutation of F, under all and only those circumstances in which scientific research governed by the conventional adoption of 'F' and G'' would lead to the refutation of F'. Thus if the scientific realist cannot show 'F and G' and 'F' and G'' to be currently distinguishable on experimental evidence despite having the same observational consequences, there is little hope of his showing that future research could distinguish them on the basis of experimental evidence. (Boyd 1973 p. 6)

Future theory development may not remove underdetermination. In these circumstances what recourse may we make to the Ignorance Response?

In his analysis of the Ignorance Response Newton-Smith suggested that the superiority of the one theory over the other must needs be predicated on the use of "inaccessible" facts, which he suggested are not discoverable and cannot be known (as opposed to being simply unobservable). Some realists are prepared to accept the metaphysics (e.g. Leplin), but is there not a version of the Ignorance Response without metaphysics which may be salvaged?

Newton-Smith made his claim about inaccessible facts because he held that evidential equivalence implies that "*Ex hypothesi* nothing will give a reason for thinking that one theory rather than the other is true" (1981 p. 41). Let us unpack the hypothesis: what did Newton-Smith have in mind in terms of evidence other than empirical evidence?

> Suppose that T_1 and T_2 are *empirically equivalent* in the sense that each has precisely the same observational consequences. Suppose further that T_1 and T_2 fare equally well under any principle other than fit with the data that is indicative of truth or approximate truth. For instance, it is sometimes supposed that simplicity is a guide to the truth. Under this latter supposition we would be assuming that T_1 and T_2 are equally simple. If a pair of rival, observationally equivalent theories fare equally well on any justifiable principles of evidence I shall say that they are evidentially equivalent. (Newton-Smith 1981 p. 40)[8]

In fact, evidential equivalence in terms of these principles together with empirical equivalence, does not imply that we could not have reasons for thinking one theory rather than another is true, (as Newton-Smith implicitly acknowledged when he subsequently contemplated compatibility with a unique total theory of nature as a criterion for choosing one theory over the other, 1981 p. 41). Boyd, a convergent realist like Newton-Smith, has argued strongly that purely *theoretical* considerations involving inductive inferences from previously established theoretical knowledge (as contrasted with indirect evidential support based upon the observable consequences of theories other than T_1 and T_2 which we have just considered) can be brought to bear on choice of theories which are empirically indistinguishable.

> The point here is that, if the realist and dialectical conception of scientific methodology is right, then considerations of the theoretical plausibility of a proposed theory in the light of the *actual* (and approximately true) theoretical tradition are *evidential* considerations: results of such assessments of plausibility constitute evidence for or against proposed theories. Indeed, such considerations are a matter of theory-mediated empirical evidence, since the background theories with respect to which assessments of plausibility are made are themselves empirically tested (again in a theory-mediated way). Theory-mediated evidence of this sort is no less empirical than more "direct" experimental evidence - largely because the evidential standards which apply to so-called direct experimental tests of theories are theory-determined in just the same way that judgements of plausibility are. In consequence, the *actual* theoretical tradition has an epistemically privileged position in the assessment of *empirical* evidence. (Boyd 1983 pp. 69,70)

If Boyd is to be believed, new theory might enable us, via the use of theoretical inductive evidence, to make a choice between rivals in some situations.[9] But a stronger case might be made: theoretical considerations would never allow us to have two competing, empirically equivalent theories that are equally supported by available theory unless the theories were notationally equivalent - hypothetical evidential equivalence would never arise.

Unfortunately, even if we can fashion ourselves a finely meshed theoretical sieve using wire drawn from the existing tradition, both in terms of the entities and theoretical mechanisms of current science, and in terms of the methodological principles (abduction, confirmation, testing etc.) we accept, this approach would not resolve the problem posed by alternative, empirically equivalent theories.

Boyd proposed that the realist defend his choice of 'F and G' on the grounds of the high implicit plausibility accorded to 'F and G' by the causal mechanisms posited by existing theory. This takes the argument one step further back, for the radical underdeterminationist may make a parallel case for 'F' and G'' based upon prevailing alternative theory (i.e. indirect evidential support). To overcome this deadlock, Boyd employed the existing theoretical tradition: he suggested that only realism could provide an adequate explanation of why reliance on traditional causal mechanisms, in choosing between empirically equivalent theories, worked. But imagine that at the outset of science, man faced an initial choice between underdetermined alternatives. The fact, that man made a choice, and subsequently developed a successful scientific tradition, cannot then be used to decide between alternative empirically equivalent theories, where one of them is incompatible with the tradition, on other than pragmatic grounds. There could, the underdeterminationist will assert, have been alternative traditions. Boyd's argument merely begs the question as far as the underdetermination of theory choice is concerned.

If there is no a priori defence for the traditional realist without metaphysics, the answer probably lies in a more practical approach. Given that many realists have been made to accept the negative induction concerning the truth of theories, we can use the same inductive ploy to establish either (1) induction on past instances shows there are in fact no genuine cases of underdetermination that do not involve notational variants,[10] or (2) the "negative induction" itself implies that we will never arrive at a situation where we have two stable side-by-side notationally distinct alternative theories which are both held to be true, and which might act as sub-theories in alternative, incompatible world views. Another approach would be to prevent the launch of underdetermination by establishing an empirically based, empirically testable abductive argument to the effect that the supposition that there is only one true account of science is the best explanation of our systematic failure to find stable, viable competing hypotheses. Either of these approaches seems preferable for a traditional realist to the metaphysics of the Ignorance Response, or the weakened ontology that is part of the Arrogance Response.

Instrumentalist and constructive empiricist responses

Neither the traditional instrumentalist nor constructive empiricist is troubled by underdetermination. Traditional (semantic) instrumentalists do not hold the theories of science to be true or false: other pragmatic measures are chosen to evaluate theories which relate to their predictive capability and reliability. Epistemic instrumentalists like Laudan believe that theories are capable of being true or false, indeed they are all false, but the truth or falsity of a theory is an irrelevant factor when we assess the appropriate cognitive attitude the theory should command. Either type of instrumentalist will see the choice between underdetermined rivals as a straightforward practical choice, lacking philosophical significance.

The constructive empiricist positively courts underdetermination: one of the major factors underlying van Fraassen's endorsement of empirical adequacy, as opposed to truth, is his recognition and acceptance of underdetermination as a fact of life. Theoretical statements do not warrant commitment to truth. As Boyd pointed out:

> According to this thesis [of evidential indistinguishability], two empirically equivalent theories must always be equally well supported or refuted by any possible body of observational data; it is just this thesis that underwrites the empiricist claim that knowledge of unobservables is impossible. (Boyd 1991 p. 20)

Van Fraassen himself provided a number of examples of underdetermination in physics. Where underdetermination occurs, van Fraassen advocated the adoption of pragmatic considerations such as those of the instrumentalist.

If the constructive empiricist can be said to have a weakness with regard to underdetermination, it is in allowing too much underdetermination. As we have seen, Ellis has argued (1985 p. 65) that constructive empiricism relies on the possibility of underdetermination in all circumstances where we talk of unobservables. Given the openness of new evidence, Ellis maintained that one could not establish general undefeasible underdetermination without falling into skeptical metaphysics. Laudan and Leplin have similarly argued against a general thesis of underdetermination to support partial skepticism (see above):

> We maintain not that there are no cases of empirical equivalence, but that the claim that there are is defeasible. And we deny the omnibus a priori claim that every theory has empirically equivalent rivals. (Laudan and Leplin 1991 p. 459)

These arguments need not concern us, however, since all we seek to establish is the possibility of specific cases of underdetermination.

NOA and underdetermination

Relative to his colleagues, it seems the NOAer (and the scientific realist) has difficulty responding to underdetermination. The customary responses of the traditional realist are not at his or her disposal. The Ignorance Response is not available because NOA employs a minimalist account of truth and does not posit facts of the matter true or false in a noumenal world beyond our epistemic reach. Since the NOAer believes that there is no epistemic discontinuity between observational and non-observational claims, all of which are theory-dependent, it is not possible for him or her to borrow from the constructive empiricist or the Arrogance Response in order to build a case around a notion akin to empirical adequacy. Internal realism, on the other hand, involves an unacceptable inflation of the concept of truth relative to a purely disquotational account (Fine 1986b), and instrumentalist ploys are clearly impossible given the NOAer's ontological commitment to the truth of theories. Two possible options are to modify the Ignorance Response, or to accept some degree of relativity in the concept of truth employed.[11]

Let us consider first the case of the Ignorant NOAer. Confronted by underdetermination, a NOAer may fall back on her logical convictions in order to formulate a modified Ignorance Response without metaphysics. Logic tells us 'p or not p', but we do not know which: we are ignorant.

In reply, we might ask her whether there is a fact of the matter, p, at stake given that T_1 and T_2 are incompatible. But given a purely disquotational account of truth, that there is a fact of the matter at stake has no significance: nothing is being added by stating that there is a fact of the matter. The Ignorant NOAer can but chant "p or not p. There is nothing more to say!" Without some additional ingredient above Tarski's T schema to provide interpretation for truth, without some inflation, as Quine put it, "There is no fact of the matter as to whether there is a fact of the matter".

This modified Ignorance Response is one behavioural response to how we react to underdetermination: it is the *sectarian* attitude, introduced by Quine, and clarified by Bergström:

> Suppose, then, that T_0 is our ordinary global theory of the world, and let T_r be a rival theory that is radically different from and irreducible to T_0 but empirically equivalent to it and equally good. Now, if we happened to come across T_r, how should we react to it? This is a problem that has been discussed by Quine in many of his writings. In one place, he refers to it as "the cosmic question whether to call two such systems true."
>
> Over the years, Quine has given different and even incompatible answers to this question. In a reply to a paper by Roger F. Gibson, where the incompatibility is noted, Quine says:
>
>> *In the first passage I had held that one of the two systems of the world must be deemed false even if we know them to be empirically equivalent. I shall call this the sectarian position. My reason for it was naturalism: my disavowal of any higher tribunal than science itself. In the latter and conflicting passage, as Gibson relates, I opted for truth of both systems, finding it offensive to my empiricist sensibilities to declare otherwise. This I call the ecumenical position.*
>
> Notice that Quine's problem is whether different systems should be called or declared true, not - at least, not primarily - whether they are true. The question of whether or not a given theory is true can hardly be decided on the basis of philosophical considerations of the kind to which Quine refers. Rather, it is a question for science to answer.
>
> Quine is presupposing that we accept one system already, and hence call it true. The question is what to say about its empirically equivalent rivals. Thus, for example, in one place he formulates his ecumenical position as follows : "If we subscribe to one of them as true, we can call them all true." (Bergström 1993 p. 341)

By eschewing the means to explain in what the facticity of the statement "p or not p" resides, the Ignorant NOAer, perhaps unwittingly, becomes an advocate of the sectarian attitude:

> In order to understand Quine's problem, one must appreciate the fact that Quine accepts a purely disquotational view of truth [just like the NOAer; PJ]. The term 'true' is a device for semantic assent; " to call a statement true is just to reaffirm it". If this is taken seriously, however, there seems to be a very straighforward solution to Quine's problem. The solution should be sectarian. By hypothesis, T_0 is our system, the system we accept and affirm. Therefore T_0 (and its parts) is the only system we can reaffirm. We can call T_0 true, for to say that T_0 is true is just to reaffirm it. But we should not say that T_r is true, for by hypothesis T_r is not a system we affirm or accept and is not logically equivalent to anything we accept. (Bergström 1993 p. 342)

Are there reasons to think this might not be an entirely happy situation for a NOAer?

It might be argued that the sectarian attitude places narrowing constraints on science which a NOAer is likely to find uncomfortable, given the liberalism and non-intervention which the NOAer believes should characterise the relationship between philosophy and science. If science is not in need of interpretation, why should it be left to the NOAer to assert of two rival, incompatible but empirically equivalent theories, that one is true and the other is false? Is this not a case of philosophy dictating to science?

In response, it might be objected, that in adopting the sectarian attitude, the Ignorant NOAer does not seek to impose a philosophical outlook upon science, and merely respects the laws of logic. The Ignorant NOAer does, nonetheless, prepare the ground for an asymmetric choice between alternatives, while recognizing the impossibility of having legitimate reasons for making such a choice. As a conservative philosopher, one may be inclined to feel that the value of a promissory note which can never be repaid is zero, and that we would be better off had the note never been issued. We may feel dissatisfied with the account offered and wish to consider the alternatives.

To be agnostic about the truth or falsity of the two theories is not an attractive option for a NOAer. Both theories T_1 and T_2 will satisfy the canons of reasoning that legitimise this commitment and belief. To set aside cases of underdetermination into a special agnostic category, would appear to invoke additional, metaphysical principles of evidence that rule against T_1 and T_2 ; hardly a move which will appeal to a NOAer, given Fine's criticism of internal realism.

A more appealing option, perhaps, that is consonant with NOAer's non-prescriptive attitude to science, is Quine's *ecumenical* alternative:

> The opposing attitude is the *ecumenical* one, which would count both theories true. Its appeal is empiricism: reluctance to discriminate invidiously between empirically equivalent and equally economical theories. (Quine 1990 p. 99)

The pluralism that the ecumenical attitude fosters would fit well with the NOAer's belief in encouraging the creativity of science by removing the oppressive burdens placed on scientific activity by traditional realism. It might be argued, however, that in advocating the ecumenical attitude, we are in fact imposing philosophical reasoning upon science, contrary to the practice of scientists who maintain their existing theoretical traditions and spurn alternative theoretical traditions which produce equally good results, in keeping with the sectarian attitude. If this were true, this would indeed be contrary to the non-interventionist posture of NOA with regard to science.

Two reasons may be advanced to support the adoption of the ecumenical rather than the sectarian attitude by a NOAer. First, a pre-occupation with settling matters of fact as they might pertain to unobservable theoretical entities, (as opposed to investigating the empirical consequences of new alternative, radical theories) stemming from a commitment to traditional realism, was held to be restrictive and damaging to science in the early twentieth century, and to be contrary to the practices of the best scientists of that time (for example, Einstein and Bohr). The reluctance to contemplate incompatible alternatives that explained phenomena at least as well as prevailing theories (for instance, special relativity vs. ether-drift accounts of the Fitzgerald electromagnetic contraction) appears to be characteristic of the sectarian attitude not the ecumenical attitude. An open-minded attitude to alternatives has been endorsed by Fine who wrote:

> A study of [Einstein's] tortured path to general relativity shows the repeated use of this Machist line, always used to deny that some concept has a real referent. Whatever other competing strains there were in Einstein's philosophical orientation (and there certainly were others), it would be hard to deny the importance of this instrumentalist / positivist attitude in liberating Einstein from various [traditional] realist commitments. Indeed, on another occasion, I would argue in detail that without the "freedom from reality" provided by his early reverence for Mach, a central tumbler necessary to unlock the secret of special relativity would never have fallen into place. (Fine 1986a p. 123)
>
> One can hardly doubt the importance of a nonrealist attitude for the development and practically infinite success of the quantum theory. Historical counterfactuals are always tricky, but the sterility of actual realist programs in this area at least suggests that Bohr and company were right in believing that the road to scientific progress here would have been blocked by realism. (Fine 1986a p. 125)

The second reason why the ecumenical attitude is appropriate is that NOA does not have the resources for settling questions of truth, and when faced by such questions, NOA defers to science in a responsive and unrestrictive way. Where we confront a specific pair of underdetermined alternatives, the most likely attitude of scientists is to work actively on both theories: an ecumenical attitude is consistent with this. We again find support for these arguments in the work of Fine:

> As with the use of other concepts, other disagreements are bound to arise over what is true (for instance, as to whether inference to the best explanation is always truth-conferring). NOA pretends to no resources for settling these disputes, for NOA takes to heart the great lesson of twentieth-century analytic and continental philosophy, namely, that there are no

general methodological or philosophical resources for deciding such things. The mistake common to realism and all the antirealisms alike is their commitment to the existence of such non-existent resources. If pressed to answer the question of what, then, does it *mean* to say that something is true (or to what does the truth of so-and-so commit one), NOA will reply by pointing out the logical relations engendered by the specific claim and by focusing, then, on the concrete historical circumstances that ground that particular judgement of truth. For, after all, there is nothing more to say. (Fine 1986 p. 134)

NOA is fundamentally a heuristic attitude, one that is compatible with quite different assessments of particular scientific investigations, say, investigations concerning whether or not there are magnetic monopoles. At the time of this writing the scientific community is divided on this issue. There is a long history of experimental failure to detect monopoles, and one recent success - maybe. I believe that there are a number of new experiments under way, and considerable theoretical work that might narrow down the detectable properties of monopoles. In this context various ways of putting together the elements that enter into a judgement about monopoles will issue in various attitudes toward them, ranging from complete agnosticism to strong belief. NOA is happy with any of these attitudes. All that NOA insists is that one's ontological attitude toward monopoles, and everything else that might be collected in the scientific zoo (whether observable or not), be governed by the very same standards of evidence and inference that are employed by science itself. The attitude tolerates all the differences of opinion and all the varieties of doubt and skepticism that science tolerates. It does not, however, tolerate the prescriptions of empiricism or of other doctrines that externally limit the commitments of science [PJ: the sectarian attitude?]. Nor does it overlay the judgements, say, that monopoles do exist, with the special readings of realism or of the truth-mongering antirealisms. NOA tries to let science speak for itself, and it trusts in our native ability to get the message without having to rely on metaphysical or epistemological hearing aids. (Fine 1986 p. 150)

If we accept that the ecumenical attitude is more appropriate for a NOAer than the sectarian attitude, what sense are we to make of the parallel truths of the two rival theories? Quine considered the consequences of adopting the type of ecumenical attitude developed by Davidson, which involved the rewriting of theoretical terms in one of the two theories so as to remove incompatibility. Quine wrote:

But a different ecumenical line has been urged by Donald Davidson: that we account both theories separately true, the truth predicate being understood now as disquotation in an inclusive and theory-neutral language in which both theories are couched. In recent years I have vacillated among these alternatives, which are now down to two: the sectarian line and the ecumenical line à la Davidson.

The latter alternative raises questions regarding the inclusive language. It would include all terms of both of the rival systems of the world, and its variables would range over both ontologies. Distinctive predicates would serve to delimit values of the variables to the one ontology or the other as needed. How much more widely should the variables range? And what of truth: will there be a hierachy of truth predicates and a matching hierachy of styles of variables, as at the end of § 37? We must call a halt. We sought only an inclusive language, not a third theory. (Quine 1990 pp. 99-100)

For these reasons Quine advocated the sectarian attitude, but recognised that this was at the expense of foregoing evenhandedness of truth in dealing with the alternative theories. His attempt to recapture this even handedness by allowing the sectarian advocate to hop at will between the two competing accounts T_1 and T_2 is not convincing. Instead, a more natural account of truth for two ecumenical alternatives might arise from a relative notion of truth.

Quine gave a clue as to how this might be done in talking about relativity in the context of the indeterminacy of reference:

> But I can now say what ontological relativity is relative to, more succinctly than I did in the lectures, paper, and book of that title. It is relative to a manual of translation. To say that 'gavagai' denotes rabbits is to opt for a manual of translation in which 'gavagai' is translated as 'rabbit', instead of opting for any of the alternative manuals. (Quine 1990 p. 51)

Consider the case of two empirically equivalent, incompatible theories T_1 and T_2 which share much scientific language, but which each employ some distinct theoretical terms. Let L_1 be the language in which T_1 is formulated, and L_2 be the language in which T_2 is formulated. Much of the translation between L_1 and L_2 will be homophonic, but the distinct theoretical terms need not be intertranslateable or inter-reducible. We may then formulate in each language a T schema for disquotation relative to that language. In this way it will be possible for T_1 to be true in L_1, and for T_2 to be true in L_2. We will also be able to say that a proposition p is true in L_1 but false in L_2.

To summarise the argument to this point: a NOAer cannot adopt any of the traditional responses of realists to deal with underdetermination. A modified version of the Ignorance Response, akin to Quine's sectarian attitude, may be available to an Ignorant NOAer, but a version of the ecumenical attitude, which incorporates a relative notion of truth may be preferred because of the methodological and heuristic benefits it confers to science.

That underdetermination should give rise to relativity of truth is not new. In "Two Philosophical Perspectives" (1981) Putnam endorsed a relativity of truth pertaining to a case of underdetermination in physics similar to the one we have described:

> The Maxwell field theory and the retarded potential theory are incompatible from a metaphysical point of view, since either there are or there aren't causal agencies (the 'fields') which mediate the action of separated particles on each other (a realist would say). But the two theories are mathematically intertranslatable. So if there is a 'correspondence' to the noumenal things which make one of them true, then one can define another correspondence which makes the other theory true. If all it takes to make a theory true is abstract correspondence (never mind which), then incompatible theories can be true.
>
> To an internalist this is not objectionable: why should there not sometimes be equally coherent but incompatible conceptual schemes which fit our experiential beliefs equally well? If truth is not (unique) correspondence then the possibility of a certain pluralism is opened

up. But the motive of the metaphysical realist is to save the notion of the God's Eye Point of View, i.e. the One True Theory. (Putnam 1981 p. 73)

In "Models and Reality" (1980) Putnam explored a particular instance of underdetermination with regard to set theory. There are clear parallels between the account developed by Putnam and the one here proposed, as the following passage illustrates:

> Yet, it seems to me that if we encountered an extra-terrestrial species of intelligent beings who had developed a high level of mathematics, and it turned out that they *rejected* the axiom of choice (perhaps because of the Tarski-Banach Theorem), it would be wrong to regard them as simply making a *mistake*. To do *that* would, on my view, amount to saying that acceptance of the axiom of choice is built into our notion of rationality itself; that does not seem to me to be the case. To be sure, our acceptance of the axiom of choice is not arbitrary; all kinds of "intuitions" (based, most likely, on experience with the finite) support it; its mathematical fertility supports it; but none of this is so strong that we could not say that an equally successful culture which based its mathematics on principles *incompatible* with choice (e.g., on the so-called "axiom of determinacy") was *irrational*.
>
> But if both systems of set theory - ours and the extra-terrestrials' - count as *rational*, what sense does it make to call one *true* and the others *false*? From the Platonist's point of view there is no trouble in answering this question. "The axiom of choice is true - true in the model", he will say (if he believes the axiom of choice). "We are right and the extra-terrestrials are wrong". But where is the model? If the intended model is singled out by theoretical and operational constraints, then, first, "the" intended model is plural not singular (so the "the" is inappropriate - our theoretical and operational constraints fit many models, not just one, and so do those of the extra-terrestrials as we saw before.) Secondly, the intended models for us do satisfy the axiom of choice and the extra-terrestrially intended models do not; we are not talking about the same models, so there is no question of a "mistake" on one side or the other.
>
> The Platonist will reply that what this really shows is that we have some mysterious faculty of "grasping concepts" (or "intuiting mathematical objects") and it is *this* that enables us to fix a model as *the* model, and not just operational and theoretical constraints; but this appeal to mysterious faculties seems both unhelpful as epistemology and unpersuasive as science ...
>
> Now, suppose this is right and the axiom of choice is true when taken in the sense that it receives from *our* embedding theory and false when taken in the sense that it receives from extra-terrestrial theory. Urging this relativism is not advocating *unbridled* relativism; I do not doubt there are some objective (if evolving) canons of rationality; I simply doubt that we would regard them as settling this sort of question, let alone as singling out *one* unique "rationally acceptable set theory". If this is right, then one is inclined to say that the extra-terrestrials have decided to let the axiom of choice be false and we have decided to let it be true; or that we have different "conventions"; ... (Putnam 1980 pp. 470-71)

Putnam's key message is that constrained relativity occurs.

In Putnam's examples, T_1 and T_2 are similar in certain respects and share a number of theoretical terms as well as their observational vocabularies (or at least there exist reliable translation manuals between terms that share the same referent), but T_1 and T_2 are incompatible in respect of some proposition p. This may lead us to incorporate an indexical element into our notion of what constitutes meaning: in addition to Putnam's four components of meaning (syntactical marker, semantical marker, stereotype, reference) let us add an identity marker that links a term to the theory or context in which it is introduced: a subscript, say, as epitomized by Oscar_1 and Oscar_2. It would then be possible for two words or propositions to be identical in respect of all elements of meaning save this indexical element. We would then be able to assert that p strictly has different meanings in T_1 and T_2, hence avoiding the threat of contradiction, without doing violence to our intuition that in all other respects p has the same meaning in the two theories. Putnam anticipated something of this sort when he proposed in Lecture 3 of Meaning and the Moral Sciences, that interest-relativity of explanation was often the source of the indeterminacy of translation: a person's interests settle the intended interpretation of terms. Quine similarly emphasized the critical role of a background language, and in particular the use of pronouns and other indexicals, in resolving questions of ontological relativity in practice.

The use of the indexical fulfils a similar function to the syntactic device Quine borrowed from Davidson to render alternative accounts compatible: for example, if T_1 and T_2 are incompatible and both theories talk conflictingly about the universe, the conflict between T_1 and T_2 can be removed by replacing 'universe' in one of the theories by 'yuniverse'. The merit of the indexical element is that the common core comprising the other elements of meaning, is explicitly recognized, and the syntactic artificiality of Davidson's and Quine's manoeuvre is avoided.

In this way, our approach to indexicality, attempts to avoid what seems to be a dilemma. For it may be objected that the indexical element either does some useful work or it does not. If it does useful work, then one might argue that the account of meaning which it supports is holistic, resulting in incommensurability. On the other hand, if the indexicality does no more than flag T_1 and T_2, it may be held to be an approach which adds nothing to Quine. The dilemma argument, however, is not telling. Both horns require us to abandon entirely the notion of common elements of meaning between T_1 and T_2 i.e. to deny the existence of an invariance class of referents common to the two languages, in order to preserve synonymy based upon truth values. Doing so conflicts with the theories of usage, reference and meaning which we customarily use to ground terms: according to these theories, the grounding of the invariance terms which comprise the invariance set between T_1 and T_2 is legitimate. By recognizing the shared components of meaning (syntactical and semantical markers, stereotype and reference in Putnam's account) we can establish an unproblematic notion of the invariance class of terms shared between T_1 and T_2, without running into problems with the law of contradiction.

Some might object that the role of the identity marker is already played by the reference, and to some extent they are correct. The introduction of the identity marker helps, however, in the circumstance where an imaginary bilingual NOAer, along the lines of Putnam's causal account of reference, witnesses one single introductory event for each ostensive term that is introduced into both T_1 and T_2 and which belongs to the invariant set for L_1 and L_2. It is presumptious to think that the NOAer is wrong when she asserts that these terms have the same referents. The marker also helps us to understand how we may have competing theories which are strongly (but not strictly) incompatible, and yet are commensurable. The theories are not strictly incompatible because the meaning of p in 'p is true' in L_1, is different from the meaning of p in 'p is false' in L_2, because of the identity markers: we have marked a syntactic distinction. Yet, since all other elements of meaning are the same in the two languages, T_1 and T_2 may be compared and sense can be made of their competing claims: we have recognised a semantic overlap. In this way, we have introduced a technical incommensurability to satisfy the constraints of logic, while retaining a commensurability of content. Perhaps this approach could be described as one of *partial* or *fuzzy contradiction*. Using it, we contend that an account of relativism can be given that is not incoherent, trivial or lacking significance.

Nonetheless, we must recognise that a general theory of meaning has not been provided to justify the use of indexicality in a context where it is now legitimate to say that p has the same meaning in L_1 and L_2 : we might be accused of formal contradiction, since indexicality implies the strict opposite. Such an account is beyond the scope of the present work, but a number of observations are in order.

First, the difficulty we find with traditional truth-conditional accounts of meaning arises not from the belief that the meaning of a sentence is conveyed by an understanding of its truth conditions, but by the customary rider that this implies that two sentences may only have the same meaning for a speaker if they have the same truth values. Lurking behind this second step, we believe, is a serruptitious traditional realism: there is only one real world, one intended interpretation for reference. For a NOAer, who accepts a purely disquotational account of truth, and who advocates an ecumenical attitude to underdetermined alternatives, the supposition of One True Account is not warranted. Without this supposition, however, we cannot make the step to truth values from truth conditions.

Second, it is not necessary to abandon the central emphasis of traditional accounts of meaning on truth conditions in favour of, say, a behaviourist approach, to accommodate the ecumenical NOAer. It suffices to break the link between truth conditions and truth values. We could articulate a theory of meaning based upon truth conditions where, for the sentences which are not empirically decideable, a sentence is true if and only if it is entailed as a consequence by an empirically adequate theory. In this way, many of the difficulties associated with alternative theories of meaning may be avoided, if we preserve the core link between meaning and truth conditions. Leaving aside the need to complete this account, let us return to the mainstream of the argument.

If we are not, as NOAers, allowed to draw a distinction between observational and theoretical terms, then both T_1 and T_2 warrant a (moderate) realist interpretation. This would seem to suggest an ecumenical pluralism that is significant, and which reflects the different ways that we focus on a particular phenomenon, each providing a complete, but mutually exclusive predictive picture. Some critics say that such alternatives are "merely" notational variants, but unless we adopt a positivist account of theoretical terms, where terms are partially defined by meaning postulates, the differences between empirically equivalent theories in terms of ontology are meaningful and significant, certainly to a NOAer who accepts the literal truth of theoretical dialogue. In other words, we take complementarity at face value.

Such a view is consistent with the existence of an overabundance of operational procedures for interacting with the world as reflected, for instance, in the availability of multiple alternative measuring procedures. Of course, a traditional realist will claim that these different complementary theories add weight to his search for the noumenal constitution of the world, but this nether world is explicitly rejected by a NOAer. In response to a genuine case of underdetermination, the NOAer must embrace a relativism that anchors alternative accounts, but which precludes the assertion of a statement and its negation within a common language at the same time (thus avoiding contradiction and incoherence). This may be achieved by indexicality.

The modest relativity introduced by underdetermination is not likely to be a common problem in practice. The continuity of reference between theories itself imposes considerable constraints on the significance of any relativity established. If the two underdetermined rivals involved radically different approaches, it is unlikely that the key concepts and theoretical terms involved would justify continuity of reference: a radical shift of meaning would be deemed to have occurred. The theories in question would not be held to be rivals in conflict. Given the established rarity of incommensurability, such instances of radical relativity, if they ever occur, are not likely to be pernicious and need not worry the NOAer unduly. In the case of more modest relativity, current science is not likely to give rise to many instances, in the same way that CSR does not give much, if any, scope for relativity at the level of everyday objects. The recognition of an element of relativity in assessing the claims and merits of alternative, equally supported theories, seems to fit the language and behaviour of scientists better than a rigid doctrinaire insistence on "absolute truth or falsity at all costs", or a complete rejection of both these notions as applied to the two rival theories in question. Faced by a case of underdetermination (even one held by some to involve notational equivalents), an ecumenical posture is prevalent. As Horwich has observed:

> There is nothing to prevent a semantic realist [NOAer] who endorses the redundancy theory of truth from supposing that various theoretical truths might be underdetermined by all possible evidence and, therefore, impossible to establish with certainty. (Horwich 1982 p. 188)

Summary

In this chapter we have reviewed some of the arguments which seek to establish the possibility of cases of underdetermination, and have concluded that the case for underdetermination is sufficiently plausible that philosophers of science must be prepared to tackle this issue.

Traditional realists have responded to underdetermination in two ways, both of which are problematic. According to the Arrogance Response, there is no matter of fact at stake between two empirically equivalent theories, a view which conflicts strongly with the customary ontological commitments of the traditional realist. The Ignorance Response fares no better: we preserve the ontological commitment of the realist, but only by divorcing the realist's ontology from his epistemology.

To overcome the problems associated with the Ignorance Response, internal realists have argued that in the epistemic limit, two alternative, empirically equivalent theories could not both be warranted and hence both be true. Unfortunately, such arguments presuppose an epistemic notion of truth, which incorporates inflationary, metaphysical assumptions comparable to those of the traditional realist.

Underdetermination, by contrast, does not pose a problem for instrumentalists, and constructive empiricists use underdetermination as an argument to support their notions of empirical adequacy.

Turning to NOA and similar moderate realist positions, we cannot adopt either of the traditional realist responses to underdetermination: NOA rejects the noumenal world traditionally used to support the Ignorance Response, and the Arrogance Response is not available since a NOAer has no grounds for drawing an epistemic veil over the unobservable. The internal realist response is also ruled out because of the notion of truth employed.

Instead a NOAer may advocate a modified Ignorance Response, relying simply on a disquotational account of truth, similar to the sectarian attitude outlined by Quine, as a way of dealing with underdetermination. Such a view sits less comfortably, however, with NOA's non-prescriptive attitude to science than Quine's alternative ecumenical attitude, but the pluralism the latter involves leads to a notion of relativity of truth.

Relativity of truth need not collapse into incoherence because traditional theories of meaning are held to require identical truth values for sentences which have the same meaning in incompatible rival theories. Indexicality allows us to preserve the sense in which sentences in the rival theories have the same meaning, while allowing the truth values of these sentences to be contraries. Putnam has offered examples of sentences that have relative truth values. Such relativity need not be unlimited, and can be highly constrained by the embedding theories employed and by the sharing of reference. Furthermore modest relativity seems to fit the language and behaviour of scientists. In the next chapter we will explore how this relativity can help NOA accommodate the underdetermination which arises in the case of the alternative empirical systems used to anchor primitive derived constants.

Notes

1 *Suppose we formulate* [the relativist picture] *in terms of sentences*:

> *It is possible that sentence S is true in Θ and false in Ψ,*

where 'Θ' and 'Ψ' are to be replaced by specifications of whatever it is that truth is supposed to be relative to; say, a particular social group or a particular theory. In this formulation the thesis is trivial and completely devoid of interest. For it reveals the commonplace and humble fact that the same sentence can be ascribed different meanings and, hence, ascribed under those different meanings different truth-values. We will call this thesis of relativity trivial semantical relativism *or TSR.* (Newton-Smith 1981 p. 35)

2 Horwich (1982) has argued that because of difficulties that may arise in defining the empirical content of theories without a strict observational / theoretical distinction, we can only give sense to evidential indistinguishability in the case of notationally equivalent theories, where underdetermination loses much of its philosophical interest. In fact, there is no reason to suppose that defining the empirical consequences for underdetermined theories is especially problematic. If we believe in the possibility of testing and confirmation of theories in general, as a NOAer surely does, then it follows that we can establish what the empirical consequences of a theory are in a practical, workable way. We need not be concerned by the fact that any theory can support a limitless choice of auxiliary hypotheses so as to render any possible observational conclusion. Instead, we should employ the same procedures and methods to define the empirical consequences of pairs of underdetermined theories that we do normally.

3 We may be guided in our notion of a causal account of reference by Putnam: *To have linguistic competence in connection with a term it is not sufficient, in*

general, to have the full battery of usual linguistic knowledge and skills; one must in addition, be in the right sort of relationship to certain distinguished situations (normally, though not necessarily, situations in which the referent *of the term is present). It is for this reason that this sort of theory is called a "causal theory" of meaning ... If I teach the word to some one else by telling him that the word 'electricity' is the name of a physical magnitude, and by telling him certain facts about it which do not constitute a causal description ... even if the facts I tell him do not constitute a definite description of any kind, let alone a causal description - still, the word's being in his vocabulary will be causally linked to its being in my vocabulary, and hence, ultimately, to an introducing event ... Now then, if anyone knows that 'electricity' is the name of a physical quantity, and his use of the word is connected by the sort of causal chain I described before to an introducing event in which the causal description given was, in fact, a causal description of electricity, then we have a clear basis for saying that he uses the word to refer to electricity ... This account stresses causal descriptions because physical magnitudes are invariably discovered through their effects, and so the natural way to first single out a physical magnitude is as the magnitude responsible for certain effects.*(Putnam 1975 pp.199-202)

4 Newton-Smith distinguished (1978 p. 74) between a strong and a weak underdetermination thesis. According to the former, underdetermination is always possible; according to the latter, underdetermination occurs in some instances. We are interested in defending the weak thesis.

5 Van Fraassen 1980 p. 63.

6 In a similar fashion Putnam (1975 p. 185), on behalf of Quine, has argued that whether there are cases of indeterminacy of translation, is an empirical question: while the existence of such cases has not been proved, neither has their impossibility been established.

7 One can also imagine a situation where the model associated with one of two empirically equivalent theories is isomorphic to a third model where the empirical substructures are more extensive than in the first model. Based upon the testability of parts of the empirical substructure of the third model, it may be possible to provide convincing reasons to reject the theory which does not have a model isomorphic to the third model.

8 Putnam explicitly advocated simplicity and agreement with intuition as relevant evidential criteria (1975 pp. 165-6) Churchland (1985 p. 40) has similarly argued for the importance of super-empirical virtues (simplicity, coherence

etc.) in the context of choice between holistic theoretical alternatives which each incorporate their own construal of the observational evidence to be explained.

9 One instance of underdetermination where theory may be brought to bear is the case of Goodmanesque predicates, one of which is projectible, the other not.

10 In these circumstances one would argue that the example of Newtonian and Hamiltonian mechanics fails because neither theory is now held to be (strictly) true.

11 Insofar as Fine has said that NOA is compatible with incommensurability, he must be counted as a relativist with regard to truth: (1) *As a scientist, say, within the context of the tradition in which he works, the NOAer of course, will believe in the existence of those entities to which his theories refer. But should the tradition change, say, in the manner of the conceptual revolutions that Kuhn dubs "paradigm shifts", then nothing in NOA dictates that the change be assimilated as being progressive, that is, as a change where we learn more accurately about* the same things. *NOA is perfectly consistent with the Kuhnian alternative, which counts such changes as wholesale changes of reference* (Fine 1986a p. 130); (2) *Finally, if our subjects are immersed in the matrix of some paradigm and the circumstances are those encompassed by the values and rules of the paradigm, then we get the specifically paradigm-relative concept of truth (and of reference) that is charcteristic of Thomas Kuhn's (1970) antirealism.* (Fine 1986a p. 138)

7 Constants and NOA

Introduction

In the early chapters of this work, an account of constants has been provided which is realist in outlook. Constants measured by fundamental and derived means have been carefully characterised and sorted.

The primitive fundamental constants identified are properties of elementary particles which may function as standard objects in a formal system of fundamental measurement. This account of fundamental measurement has been defended against conventionalist attacks which aim to undermine the distinction between fundamental and derived measurement.

An account of primitive derived constants has similarly been developed. Primitive derived constants describe the interactions that take place between elementary particles, where those interactions are captured by laws involving the fundamentally measurable properties of the particles concerned. Careful examination of the arguments made by conventionalists against the significant status of derived constants has shown that these arguments conflate aspects of the numerical representation of measurement systems with aspects of the empirical systems themselves. As a consequence these arguments are not telling, and to support further the substantive nature of primitive derived constants, a notion of empirical dimensions, grounded in the relational systems which give rise to derived measurements, has been presented.

In the second half of this book, the relative strengths and weaknesses of a number of the major philosophical traditions in the philosophy of science have been briefly reviewed in order to explain the origins and relative appeal of NOA. Further discussion of the need for such accounts to be able to deal with underdetermination has taken place, and particular attention has been paid to the responses a NOAer might make. Both sectarian and ecumenical attitudes for an

Ignorant NOAer have been considered, and methodological and heuristic reasons may be advanced in order to support the preferred ecumenical line. The pluralism inherent in the ecumenical attitude is not held to be incoherent or trivial, and it supports a limited relativism of truth which is not considered to be damaging.[1]

It is now time to draw together these two threads in support of our modestly realist account of constants.

Alternative Empirical Systems

In Chapter 4, it was shown that a non-conventionalist account of primitive derived constants could be constructed from the relational complexes of particle systems produced under the measurement operations of certain fundamental quantities according to a defining law. Consideration of the affine vector space which may be used to represent quantities, in particular the known rotational characteristics of the axes in this space, suggests that a particular derived constant may be characterised by more than one empirical system. Meaningful questions may be asked in relation to the particular choice of empirical system, (as exemplified, for instance, by the choice of empirical systems which ground the speed of light or the gravitational constant). How may this account be accommodated by NOA?

In general terms, insofar as NOA advocates the application of the standards and procedures of rational inquiry seen in the realm of everyday objects, to the realm of scientific inquiry, a NOAer will be strongly committed to the existence of the fundamentally measurable quantities of elementary particles, and to the existence of those primitive derived quantities that characterise the interactions of these particles. Constants, then, will be treated as being on the same evidential footing as atoms, nuclei, and particles (though we recognise that constants are invariant quantities which are properties of objects, whereas atoms and the like are objects). This is entirely consistent with the positive stance in general of a NOAer to entity realism (though the NOAer does not restrict his beliefs simply to entities).

It remains to be asked, however, whether the possibility of alternative empirical systems for primitive derived constants has any awkward consequences for the NOAer's general responses to underdetermination.

Let us return to the example given in Chapter 4 where we showed how it was possible to account for primitive derived constants as the characteristic feature of empirical systems comprising particles under combinations of fundamental measuring operations described by a covering law: the example given was for the gravitational constant, relying upon the fundamental measurement operations of mass, length and force.

Consider now the set of empirical systems which would arise under a different set of fundamental measurement operations, which might now include period or time measurements in order to eliminate the use of the fundamental measurement of force. These systems would again be characterised by an invariant feature of interaction, namely the gravitational constant. Thus it is possible that we may establish more than one set of empirical systems for the gravitational constant.

As an example of such an alternative system, imagine an empirical system comprising two sets of massive objects, one of equal light objects, the other of heavy objects of different masses. If these objects are paired from each set, we may construct orbital systems comprising pairs of masses governed by Kepler's Third Law:

$$GM = 4\pi^2 r^3 T^{-2}$$

The form of this law is similar to that used to support an empirical notion of dimensions, and to ground G, given in Chapter 4. The measuring operations involved are all fundamental, but are different to those previously used to obtain G.[2] The situation may be likened to the equivalence of Newtonian and Hamiltonian formulations of mechanics.

Given that we enjoy a surplus of fundamentally measurable quantities relative to the number of fundamental quantities we require for the optimal representation of much of current physics (probably five), it will be possible to describe a large number of instances of empirically equivalent systems which ground our chosen primitive derived constants. We could, for instance, consider c defined by empirical systems in which the fundamental measurement operations are mass and energy, as opposed to being defined by empirical systems in which the fundamental quantities are period and length. Significant cases of underdetermination will occur.

> Any universal constant may be so described as a "concept synthesizer", expressing the unification of two previously unconnected physical concepts into a single one of extended validity ... Of course, any one universal constant usually brings about several such synthetical concepts. Planck's constant also unifies momentum and wave number through the de Broglie relationship $\boldsymbol{p} = \hbar\boldsymbol{k}$, while c unifies mass and energy through the Einstein relationship $\Delta E = c^2\Delta m$ ... From this abstract point of view, the various specific syntheses expressed through a universal constant between various pairs of concepts belonging to two theoretical frameworks (for instance the three formulae $E = \hbar\omega$, $\boldsymbol{p} = \hbar\boldsymbol{k}$, $L = \hbar m$) are but equivalent consequences of the general theoretical unification of these frameworks. Nevertheless, because of historical considerations and epistemological motivations, they are not actually given an equal status, especially in educational practice. Some of them are taken as a starting point of fundamental hypothesis, such as $E = \hbar\omega$ or $\Delta s^2 = \Delta t^2 - c^{-2}\Delta x^2$, while other ones are considered as derived relations, or consequences, such as $\boldsymbol{p} = \hbar\boldsymbol{k}$, or $\Delta E = c^2\Delta m$. (Levy-Leblond 1977 pp 193-4)

Levy-Leblond highlighted the types of conceptual debate that can occur with regard to Planck's constant. This is entirely similar to the conceptual discusssion of the role of forces and energies which occurred in mechanics. Given the impossibility of realizing the alternative idealized empirical systems that may be used to anchor particular primitive derived constants, and the numerical consistency of the measurements obtained by these alternative empirical systems, we will not be able to settle the conceptual debate. Our failure to resolve the debate does not, however, render the debate meaningless or insignificant. Rather, we must recognize that we are faced by an interesting and non-trivial case of underdetermination.

The use of alternative sets of fundamentally measured quantities (i.e. not the customary M, L, T, q, θ) will also give rise to some entirely new constants which directly relate these alternative quantities. For instance, resistance, capacity, self-inductance, thermal capacity and monochromatic illumination are all fundamentally measurable quantities which we might use to investigate the world. There may, of course, exist other fundamentally measurable quantities which have hitherto failed to detect. Using any of these alternative fundamental quantities as our tools of inquiry might not only lead to alternative empirical systems used to ground, say, Planck's constant or the gravitational constant, but might also give rise to new constants which have yet to be discovered. Historically, we have chosen not to investigate or apply them. In other words, there are many different choices of colour for those who wish to paint the canvass of Nature other than the ones we customarily use.

Our investigation of underdetermination in the case of the measurement of constants leads us naturally to contemplate a further possibility of underdetermination in the broader context of fundamental measurement. In the case of fundamental measurements where the measurement operation does not obey Hölder's customary axioms, the choice of representation will not obey the conditions described in Chapter 3, (i.e. non-standard, and even what Suppes called "pathological" representations will be allowed). Situations will occur where the alternative physical picture is not reducible to the one we normally adopt, which incorporates Campbell's Second Axiom. An obvious example would be where the alternative representation was dense but not continuous. The alternative representations will not simply be notational variants. Further scientific and philosophical appraisal of this general possibility of underdetermination, resulting from the choice of non-standard fundamental measurement operations and associated representations, is beyond the scope of the present work.

This redundancy in our framework of measurement may seem at first sight to be similar to, if not the same as, the multiplicity of mathematical representations available to us for our physical laws as a consequence of the unlimited choice of reference axes for dimensions in the affine representation space for quantities. The key difference is that the plurality of alternative empirical systems that may be chosen for the underpinning of our primitive derived constants is a *feature of the world* that arises as a consequence of the fundamental measurement operations that are actually available to us - we have several possible conceptual definitions, in Reichenbach's terminology. In the case of alternative mathematical representations, this is a redundancy that arises from the particular representation theorems we have chosen to employ for our measurement operations - we have a choice of several different co-ordinative definitions. The former gives rise to underdetermination; the latter to conventionalism of representation.

The accommodation of NOA

The underdetermination of empirical systems that define primitive derived quantities associated with the basic interactions of matter has significance in its own right, and may serve as a counter-example to the arguments of Laudan and Leplin against the possibility of meaningful underdetermination.

Furthermore, this underdetermination can be accommodated in NOA, if we adopt the preferred ecumenical attitude, through the introduction of a degree of relativity that is useful and advantageous. Rather than being required to assert or deny that the universal gravitational constant, say, arises from the action of gravitational force upon massive bodies that are separated (as opposed to being, say, a characteristic of rotating bodies in a gravitational field), we can refer judgements of the truth or falsity of this statement to the particular empirical system of fundamental measurements which is employed to give sense of the law of gravitation. In other words, these *claims can be relativized to the particular choice of empirical system which has been made in order to ground a given primitive derived constant.*

Quine (1969) spoke of the anchoring of reference to a coordinate system. In a similar way, we may choose to anchor a constant to a particular measurement system. We may then consider the question of whether such reference is absolute given that we may analogously speculate about the position of our coordinate system: this could lead to regress. Quine replied:

> Very well; in the case of position and velocity, in practice, pointing breaks the regress. But what of position and velocity apart from practice? what of regress then? The answer, of course, is the relational doctrine of space; there is no absolute position or velocity; there are just the relations of coordinate systems to one another, and ultimately of things to one another. And I think that the parallel question regarding denotation calls for a parallel answer, a relational theory of what the objects of theories are. What makes sense is to say not what the objects of a theory are, absolutely speaking, but how one theory of objects is interpretable or reinterpretable in another. (Quine 1975 p. 50)

In the same way, according to this account we will not have an absolute notion of a primitive derived constant, but a relative one that is accommodated by NOA: an aspect of NOA that might be considered a vulnerability, has turned out to be a virtue.

It may be objected at this point that realism has been abandoned, and that the account of derived constants is not a realist one. If we understand realism to involve a traditional, noumenal One-True-Story account, realism has been abandoned, but such abandonment occurred long before with regard to fundamentally measured constants and everyday objects. On the other hand, if we take NOA to be a modestly realist account, relying upon a weak correspondence notion of truth, then we may argue that in certain unusual situations where underdetermination occurs, our methods do not give rise to a unique set of satisfaction relations between predicates and objects used to define truth, but to a plurality of sets, which we cannot choose between. The recognition of such sets sanctions existence claims which are of the same kind as we familiarly use for other objects in science and the world: in this way, our account of derived constants permits a realist construal. Such considerations reflect the interdependence which exists between the organisation of the world in terms of objects and the language which we use to describe these objects.

Alternatively, if we insist on the adoption of the sectarian rather than the ecumenical attitude, we might maintain that we are Ignorant NOAers, and that only one empirical system entails a true set of conceptual claims about the primitive derived constant concerned, but we are unable to say which. The Law of the Excluded Middle will come to our aid, if we cannot accept the possibility of more than one true account.

Whichever attitude is accepted, using NOA, we have been able to give an account of constants that is largely realist, but which involves some elements of underdetermination that can be usefully accommodated by NOA and are not problematic. Underdetermination in the case of primitive derived constants does not pose a particular challenge to NOA once we have recognised the general strategies a NOAer must adopt when confronted by cases of underdetermination.

The same methods of reasoning which support the existence claims for chairs, integrated circuits and atoms support the existence claims for constants. This is not to say that our understanding of constants is not immune to revision, or even that there is no possibility that we might be mistaken in our existence claims in the light of further knowledge. We might best consider constants as well entrenched entities in a worldview that is not an externalised, inaccessible metaphysical posit, but the worldview of people and things of varying degrees of complexity and foundation.

Principal findings

It is hoped that the reader will, after considering the detail of the arguments presented, agree the principal findings of this research, as first revealed in the introductory chapter:

1 It is possible to distinguish between two separate categories of universal constants: those measured by fundamental means and those given by derived

measurement relying on a supporting law.

2 The most primitive fundamental universal constants are the charge, mass and magnetic moments of elementary particles; the most primitive derived constants are c, h, G, ϵ, and k.

3 All other universal constants customarily regarded as significant can be obtained from this set of primitive constants.

4 The fundamental universal constants can function as the standard objects within a formal axiomatic system of extensive measurement, and are properties of particles.

5 The derived universal constants can be defined within a formal system of derived measurement and characterise the interactions of particles.

6 The distinction between fundamental and derived quantities is not undermined by substitution of derived for fundamental quantities nor the possibility of alternative representations of fundamental quantities.

7 The conventionality that extends to the dimensional representation of derived quantities does not undermine the status of primitive universal derived constants, which can be grounded in an alternative empirical notion of dimensions.

8 NOA seems to offer a number of advantages compared with traditional and internal realism, instrumentalism and constructive empiricism. The potential vulnerability of NOA to problems arising from undetetermination can be overcome by employing a notion of relativism that finds its origins in Quine's work on the indeterminacy of translation.

9 The choice of alternative empirical systems to ground primitive derived constants represents a case of underdetermination that can be happily accommodated by NOA.

10 NOA provides a modestly realist account of science in which we may embed our notions of primitive constants.

Future research

At many points in the present work further incremental analysis to strengthen and enhance the arguments presented would be warranted, but in addition a number of key topics of broad scope deserve separate, detailed scrutiny. They include:

1 The formal generalisation of the representation framework developed for empirical systems which give rise to derived constants.

2 The linking and integration of a formal representation theorem for derived constants with existing work on the automorphic structure of relational systems in general, and with the generalised findings relating homogeneous linear equations of standard mathematical representations and the Maxwellian concept of dimensions embodied therein.

3 An investigation of the underdetermined aspects of alternative fundamental measurement.

4 Revision of the account presented to accommodate the constants that arise in the current standard model of particle physics.

Conclusion

Strong views have been traditionally expressed concerning the status and nature of the fundamental constants of physics. They have ranged from views, steeped in the manipulative conventionality of the representation of equations, that claimed that constants had a capricious, eliminable status, to views that endorsed the investigation of these constants as the acme of scientific inquiry. Through a careful examination of the formal underpinnings of these views, we have been able to make sense of these competing claims. The representational nature of constants is, indeed, entirely a matter of convention, and were we able to measure the world non-extensively, this would be all there is to be said. But we cannot, and it is clear that physicists are right to attribute a substantive nature to the constants that they so painstakingly investigate. We may still question the foundations of such a view, but there is no basis for dealing with constants on a discriminative basis compared to atoms, neutrinos and other members of the particle zoo, whose properties and interactions are captured by the constants we employ.

Notes

1 It may be held that the ecumenical attitude does not differ significantly from a form of limited conventionalism which realists might adopt to deal with the rare cases of underdetermination: the conventionalist suggests that when faced by

alternative empirical systems used to ground a particular derived constant, which are underdetermined, we agree by convention to accept all the alternatives as a suitable anchor, but maintain in our hearts that there is only one true "real" foundation. While seeming to be similar, the conventionalist and ecumenical accounts are, however, philosophically far apart. The conventionalist is likely to assert that there is only one feature of the world in question, but we do not know which of the proposed alternative empirical systems corresponds to this feature. In contrast, the ecumenical account asserts that there are in fact several features of the world, all exist and are truthfully described by the appropriate empirical system. At the periphery of our epistemological reach, where we encounter underdetermination, our methods lead us to assert alternative accounts, each of which has an equal footing. The methods we have used to arrive at this conclusion are those which we use to support the existence of objects in general, and there is no discontinuity in the application of these methods as we move from the world of everyday objects to unobserved entities. Unless we wish to embrace a general scepticism, we will be inclined to place faith in the reliability of our methods which leads us to the conclusion that, in certain unusual situations, the world exhibits a degree of pluralism that may be understood within a framework of constrained relativism. In other words, it does not seem possible for a NOA to detach the ontological aspects of truth entirely from the epistemological aspects, (but this does not require us to collapse the ontological aspect altogether, as is required by the internal realist).

2 The idealization introduced by light objects need not be problematic and a more accurate result taking into account the light masses might be obtained using a Taylor expansion of multinomial terms, which might be operationally defined as in Chapter 4 in terms of the same fundamentally measured quantities mass, length and time.

Bibliography

Aronson J.L., Harré R., Way E.C., *Realism Rescued*, 1994, Blackwell, Oxford.

Allport P. P., Are the Laws of Physics 'Economical' with the Truth?, 1993, *Synthese*, **94**, 245-290.

Barrow J.D., *The World within the World*, 1988, Oxford University Press, Oxford.

Barrow J.D., *Theories of Everything*, 1990, Oxford University Press, Oxford.

Bergström L., Quine, Underdetermination, and Skepticism, 1993, *J. Phil.*, **XC**, 331-358.

Birkhoff G., *Hydrodynamics*, 1960, Princeton University Press, Princeton.

Boyd R.N., Realism, Underdetermination and a Causal Theory of Evidence, 1973, *No us*, 7, 1-12.

Boyd R.N., On the Current Status of Scientific Realism, 1983, *Erkenntnis*, **19**, 45-90.

Boyd R.N., Lex Orandi est Lex Credendi, in *Images of Science*, ed. Churchland P.M. and Hooker C.A., 1985, University of Chicago Press, Chicago.

Boyd R.N., Confirmation, Semantics, and the Interpretation of Scientific Theories, in *The Philosophy of Science*, ed. Boyd R.N., Gasper R., and Trout J.D., 1991, MIT Press, Cambridge.

Bridgman P.W., Dimensional Analysis, 1926, *Phil. Mag.*, **2**, § 12, 1263-1266.

Bridgman P.W., *Dimensional Analysis*, 1931, Yale University Press, New Haven.

Bridgman P.W., *The Logic of Modern Physics*, 1960, Macmillan, New York.

Bridgman P.W., The Operational Character of Scientific Concepts, in *The Philosophy of Science*, ed. Boyd R.N., Gasper R., and Trout J.D., 1991, MIT Press, Cambridge.

Buckingham E., On Physically Similar Systems; Illustrations of the Use of Dimensional Equations, 1914, *Phys. Rev.*, **4**, § 4, 345-376.

Buckingham E., Dimensional Analysis, 1924, *Phil. Mag.*, **48**, § 283, 141-145.

Bunge M., *Springer Tracts in Natural Philosophy*, 1966, Volume 10.

Burniston Brown G., A new treatment of the Theory of Dimensions, 1941, *Pro. Phys. Soc.*, **53**, 418-432.
Burniston Brown G., A note on W. Wilson's 'Dimensions of Physical Quantities', 1942, *Phil. Mag.*, **33**, § 220, 367-368.
Campbell N.R., *Physics - The Elements*, 1920, Cambridge University Press, Cambridge.
Campbell N.R., Ultimate Rational Units, 1924a, *Phil. Mag.*, **47**, § , 159-172.
Campbell N.R., Dimensional Analysis, 1924b, *Phil. Mag.*, **47**, § 279, 481-494.
Campbell N.R., Dimensional Analysis, 1926, *Phil. Mag.*, **1**, § 5, 1145-1151.
Campbell N.R., *An Account of the Principles of Measurement and Calculation*, 1928, Longmans, London.
Campbell N.R., Measurement and Its Importance for Philosophy, 1938, *Aristotelian Soc. Supp.*, 121-142.
Campbell N.R., Dimensions, 1942*a*, *Phil. Mag.*, **33**, § 220, 398.
Campbell N.R., Dimensions and the Facts of Measurement, 1942*b*, *Phil. Mag.*, **33**, § 225, 761-771.
Carnap R., *Meaning and Necessity*, 1956, University of Chicago, Chicago.
Carnap R., Empiricism, Semantics, and Ontology, in *The Philosophy of Science*, ed. Boyd R.N., Gasper R., and Trout J.D., 1991, MIT Press, Cambridge.
Cartwright N., *How the Laws of Physics Lie*, 1983, Oxford University Press, Oxford.
Cartwright N., *Nature's Capacities and Their Measurement*, 1989, Oxford University Press, Oxford.
Cartwright N., Is Natural Science 'Natural' Enough? A Reply to Philip Allport, 1993, *Synthese*, **94**, 291-301.
Churchland P.M., The Ontological Status of Observables: In Praise of the Superempirical Virtues, in *Images of Science*, ed. Churchland P.M. and Hooker C.A., 1985, University of Chicago Press, Chicago.
Clerk Maxwell J., *A Treatise on Electricity and Magnetism*, 1892, Oxford University Press, Oxford.
Clerk Maxwell J., On the Mathematical Classification of Physical Quantities, 1871, *London Math. Soc.*, Vol. III, **34**, 224 -232.
Cohen E.R., Crowe K.M. and Dumond J.W.M., *Fundamental Constants of Physics*, 1955, Interscience Publishers, New York.
Corrsin S., A simple geometrical proof of Buckingham's Π Theorem, 1951, *Am. J. Phys.*, **19**, 180-181.
Dalzell D.P., Remarks on Electrical Units, 1944, *Phil. Mag.*, **35**, § 242, 188-191.
Dalzell D.P., A summary statement of the Principles of Measurement, 1945, *Phil. Mag.*, **36**, § 258, 485-490.
Dingle H., On the Dimensions of Physical Magnitudes, 1942*a*, *Phil. Mag.*, **33**, § 220, 321-344.
Dingle H., On the Dimensions of Physical Magnitudes (second paper), 1942*b*,

Phil. Mag., **33**, § 224, 692-697.

Dingle H., On the Dimensions of Physical Magnitudes (third paper), 1943, *Phil. Mag.*, **34**, § 236, 588-599.

Dingle H., On the Dimensions of Physical Magnitudes (fourth paper), 1944*a*, *Phil. Mag.*, **35**, § 244, 296-300.

Dingle H., On the Dimensions of Physical Magnitudes (fifth paper), 1944*b*, *Phil. Mag.*, **35**, § 248, 616-618.

Dingle H., On the Dimensions of Physical Magnitudes (sixth paper), 1946, *Phil. Mag.*, **37**, § 264, 64-66.

Dingle H., On the Dimensions of Physical Magnitudes (seventh paper), 1949, *Phil. Mag.*, **40**, § 300, 94-99.

Dingle H., A Theory of Measurement, 1950, *Brit. J. Phil. Sci.*, **1**, 5-26.

Dirac P.A.M., The Cosmological Constants, 1937, *Nature*, **139**, 323.

Douglas J.F., *Dimensional Analysis for Engineers*, 1969, Pitman, London.

Drazil J.V., *Quantities and Units of Measurement,* 1983, Mansell Publishing, London.

Dresner S., *Units of Measurement*, 1971, Harvey Miller and Metcalf, Aylesbury.

Dummett M., Truth in *Philosophical Logic* ed. Strawson P.F., 1967, Oxford University Press, Oxford.

Duncan W.J., *Physical Similarity and Dimensional Analysis*, 1953, Arnold, London.

Duncanson W.E., The Dimensions of Physical Quantities, 1941, *Pro. Phys. Soc.*, **53**, 432-448.

Duncanson W.E., Note on some recent papers on Physical Quantities and their Dimensions, 1942, *Pro. Phys. Soc.*, **54**, 504-509.

Eddington A.S., *The Nature of the Physical World*, 1930, Cambridge University Press, Cambridge.

Eddington A.S., *The Philosophy of Physical Science*, 1939, Cambridge University Press, Cambridge.

Eddington A.S., *Relativity Theory of Protons and Electrons*, 1936, Cambridge University Press, Cambridge.

Eddington A.S., The Theoretical Values of the Physical Constants, 1942, *Pro. Phys. Soc.*, **54** , 491-504.

Eddington A.S., *Fundamental Theory*, 1946, Cambridge University Press, Cambridge.

Ellis B.D., *Basic Concepts of Measurement*, 1966, Cambridge University Press, Cambridge.

Ellis B.D., On the Nature of Dimensions, 1964, *Phil. Sci.*, **31**, 357-380.

Ellis B.D., What Science Aims to Do, in *Images of Science*, ed. Churchland P.M. and Hooker C.A., 1985, University of Chicago Press, Chicago.

Ehrenfest-Afanessjewa, Dimensional Analysis viewed from the standpoint of the Theory of Similitude, 1926, *Phil. Mag.*, **1**, § 1, 257-272.

Esnault-Pelterie R., *Dimensional Analysis*, 1945, Rouge, Lausanne.
Fine A., How to Compare Theories: Reference and Change, 1975, *NoUs*, **9**, 17-32.
Fine A., *The Shaky Game*, 1986a, University of Chicago Press, London.
Fine A., Unnatural Attitudes: Realist and Instrumentalist Attachments to Science, 1986b, *Mind*, **XCV**, 149-179.
Fine A., Piecemeal Realism, 1991, *Phil. Stud.*, **61**, 79-96.
Focken C.M., *Dimensional Methods and their Application*, 1953, Arnold, London.
Fourier J., *Analytical Theory of Heat* , 1822, (trans. A. Freeman), 1955, Dover, New York.
Giere R.N., *Explaining Science*, 1988, University of Chicago Press, Chicago.
Glymour C., Realism and the Nature of Theories, in *Philosophy of Science*, ed. Salmon M.H., 1992, Prentice-Hall, New Jersey.
Goodman N., *Ways of Worldmaking*, 1978, Harvester, Sussex.
Guggenheim E.A., Units and Dimensions, 1942, *Phil. Mag.*, **33**, § 222, 479-496.
Hacking I., *Representing and Intervening*, 1983, Cambridge University Press, Cambridge.
Hacking I., Experimentation and Scientific Realism, in *Scientific Realism*, ed. Leplin J., 1984, University of California, Berkeley.
Hacking I., Do We See through a Microcope?, in *Images of Science*, ed. Churchland P.M. and Hooker C.A., 1985, University of Chicago Press, Chicago.
Hacking I., Experimentation and Scientific Realism, in *The Philosophy of Science*, ed. Boyd R.N., Gasper R., and Trout J.D., 1991, MIT Press, Cambridge.
Hardin C.L. and Rosenberg A., In Defense of Convergent Realism, 1982, *Phil. Sci.*, **49**, 604-615.
Harré R., *Varieties of Realism*, 1986, Blackwell, Oxford.
Hempel C.G., Empiricist Criteria of Cognitive Significance: Problems and Changes, in *The Philosophy of Science*, ed. Bord R.N., Gasper R., and Trout J.D., 1992, MIT Press, Cambridge.
Hempel C.G., *Aspects of Scientific Explanation*, 1965, Free Press, New York.
Hoefer C. and Rosenberg A., Empirical Equivalence, Underdetermination, and Systems of the World, 1994, *Phil. Sci.*, **61**, 592-607.
Hölder O., Die Axiome der Quantität und die Lehre vom Mass, *Berichte Uber die Verhandlungen der königlich Sächsischen Gesellschaft der Wissenschaften zu Leipzig (Math.-Phys. Klasse)*, **53**, 1-64.
Horwich P., Three Forms of Realism, 1982, *Synthese*, **51**, 181-201.
Horwich P., How to Choose Between Empirically Indistinguishable Theories, 1982, *J. Phil.*, **79**, 61-77.
Huntley H.E., *Dimensional Analysis*, 1952, Macdonald, London.
Isaacson E. de St Q. and Isaacson M. de St Q., *Dimensional Methods in*

Engineering and Physics, 1975, Arnold, London.
Jeffreys H., Units and Dimensions, 1943, *Phil. Mag.*, **34**, § 239, 837-842.
Jerrard H.G. and McNeill D.B., *Dictionary of Scientific Units*, 1963 & 1986, Chapman and Hall, London.
Johnson P., Causes, Spooks and Glitches, 1993, unpublished paper.
Kaye G.W.C. and Laby T.H., *Tables of Physical and Chemical Constants and some Mathematical Functions*, 15th Edition 1986, Longman, Harlow.
Krantz D.H., Luce R.D., Suppes P., and Tversky A., *Foundations of Measurement*, 1971, Volume 1, Academic Press, New York; 1990, Volume 3, Academic Press, San Diego.
Kuhn T.S., *The Structure of Scientific Revolutions*, 1962, University of Chicago Press, Chicago.
Lanchester F.W., *The Theory of Dimensions and its Application for Engineers*, 1936, Crosby Lockwood, London.
Langhaar H.L., *Dimensional Analysis and Theory of Models*, 1951, Chapman and Hall, London.
Laudan L., *Progress and Its Problems*, 1977, University of California Press, Berkeley.
Laudan L., A Confutation of Convergent Realism, 1981, *Phil. Sci.*, **48**, 19-48.
Laudan L., Explaining the Success of Science: Beyond Epistemic Realism and Relativism, in *Science and Reality*, 1984, ed. Cushing J.T., Delaney C.F., Gutting G.M., University of Notre Dame, Notre Dame.
Laudan L. and Leplin J., Empirical Equivalence and Underdetermination, 1991, *J. Phil.*, **88**, 449-472.
Laymon R., The Path from Data to Theory, in *Scientific Realism*, ed. Leplin J., 1984, University of California, Berkeley.
Leplin J., *Scientific Realism*, 1984, University of California, Berkeley.
Leplin J., *A Novel Defense of Scientific Realism*, Forthcoming.
Levin M., What Kind of Explanation is Truth?, in *Scientific Realism*, ed. Leplin J., 1984, University of California, Berkeley.
Levy-Leblond J.M., On the Conceptual Nature of the Physical Constants, 1977, *Rivista del Nuovo Cimento,* 7, 187-206.
Lewis G.N. and Adams E.Q., A Theory of Ultimate Rational Units, 1914, *Phys. Rev.*, **3**, 92-102.
Lewis G.N., Some new consequences of the Theory of Ultimate Rational Units, 1921, *Phys. Rev.*, **18**, 121.
Lewis G.N., Ultimate Rational Units and Dimensional Theory, 1925, *Phil. Mag.*, **49**, § 292, 739-750.
Lipton P., *Inference to the Best Explanation*, 1991, Routledge, London.
Luce R.D., Similar Systems and Dimensionally Invariant Laws, 1971, *Phil. Sci.*, **39**,157-169.
Luce R.D., Dimensionally Invariant Numerical Laws Correspond to Meaningful

Qualitative Relations, 1978, *Phil. Sci.*, **45**, 1-16.
Mackie J.L., *Truth, Probability and Paradox*, 1973, Oxford University Press, Oxford.
Marion J.B., *Classical Dynamics*, 1970, Academic Press, New York.
Massey B.S., 1971, *Units, Dimensional Analysis and Physical Similarity*, Van Nostrand Reinhold, London.
McMullin E., A Case for Scientific Realism in *Scientific Realism* ed. J. Leplin, 1984, University of California, Berkeley.
McMullin E., Comment: Selective Anti-Realism, 1991, *Phil. Stud.*, **61**, 97-108.
Miller R.W., *Fact and Method*, 1987,Princeton University Press, Princeton.
Moon P. and Spencer D.E., The Dimensions of Physical Concepts, 1949, *Am. J. Phys*, **17**, § 4, 171-177.
Musgrave A., NOA's Ark - Fine for Realism, 1989, *Phil. Qly.*, **39**, 383-398.
Nagel E., *The Structure of Science*, 1961, Routledge and Kegan Paul, London.
Newton-Smith W.H., The Underdetermination of Theory by Data, 1978, *Aristotelian Soc. Sup.*, **LII**, 71-91.
Newton-Smith W.H., *The Rationality of Science*, 1981, Routledge, London.
Newton-Smith W.H. Relativism and the Possibility of Interpretation, in *Rationality and Relativism*, ed. Hollis M. and Lukes S., 1982, Blackwell, Oxford.
Newton-Smith W.H., Modest Realism, 1988, *PSA*, **2**, 179-189.
Palacios J., *Dimensional Analysis*, 1964, Macmillan, London.
Pankhurst R.C., *Dimensional Analysis and Scale Factors*, 1964, Chapman and Hall, London.
Petley B.W., *The Fundamental Physical Constants and the Frontier of Measurement*, 1985, Adam Hilger, Bristol.
Psillos S., Scientific Realism Is (Still) Fine, 1996, *Phil. Rev.* forthcoming.
Planck M., *The Theory of Heat Radiation*, 1913, (trans. M. Masius), 1959 Dover, New York **§ 164**.
Planck M., *General Mechanics*, 1916, (trans. H.L. Brose), Vol. I, 1933, Macmillan, London.
Popper K.R., *The Logic of Scientific Discovery*, 1959, Hutchinson, London.
Putnam H., Meaning and Reference, 1973, *J. Phil.*, **70**, 699-711.
Putnam H., *Mind, Language and Reality*, 1975, Cambridge University Press, Cambridge.
Putnam H., *Meaning and The Moral Sciences*, 1978, Routledge and Kegan Paul, London.
Putnam H., Models and Reality, 1980, *J. Symb. Logic*, **45**, 464-482.
Putnam H., *Reason, Truth and History*, 1981, Cambridge University Press, Cambridge.
Putnam H., Why There Isn't A Ready Made World, 1982, *Synthese*, **51**, 141-167.
Putnam H., *Realism and Reason*, 1983, Cambridge University Press, Cambridge.
Putnam H., What is Realism?, in *Scientific Realism*, ed. Leplin J., 1984, University

of California, Berkeley.
Putnam H., The 'Corroboration' of Theories, in *The Philosophy of Science*, ed. Boyd R.N., Gasper R., and Trout J.D., 1991, MIT Press, Cambridge.
Putnam H., Explanation and Reference, in *The Philosophy of Science*, ed. Boyd R.N., Gasper R., and Trout J.D., 1991, MIT Press, Cambridge.
O'Rahilly A., *Electromagnetics*, 1938, Longmans, London.
Quine W.V., *From a Logical Point of View*, 1953, Harvard University Press, Cambridge.
Quine W.V., *Ontological Relativity and Other Essays*, 1969, Columbia University Press, New York.
Quine W.V., *Pursuit of Truth*, 1990, Harvard University Press, Cambridge.
Quine W.V., Natural Kinds, in *The Philosophy of Science*, ed. Boyd R.N., Gasper R., and Trout J.D., 1991, MIT Press, Cambridge.
Rosenberg A. and Hardin C.L., In Defense of Convergent Realism, 1982, *Phil. Sci.*, **49**, 604-615.
Rosenberg A. and Hoefer C., Empirical Equivalence, Underdetermination, and Systems of the World, 1994, *Phil. Sci.*, **61**, 592-607.
Rosenthal Schneider I. in *A. Einstein Philosopher Scientist*, ed. Schilpp A., 1949, Tudor, New York.
Rossini F.D., *Fundamental Measures and Constants for Science and Technology*, 1974, CRC Press, Cleveland.
Rücker A.W., On the Suppressed Dimensions of Physical Quantities, 1889, *Phil. Mag.*, **27**, § 165, 104-114.
Salmon M.H., *Philosophy of Science*, 1992, Prentice Hall, New Jersey.
Sankey C.H., *The Incommensurability Thesis*, 1994, Avebury, Aldershot.
Schlick M., Positivism and Realism, in *Philosophical Papers Volume II*, ed. Mulder H., Van de Velde-Schlick B.F.B., 1979, D. Reidel, Dordrecht.
Sedov L.I., *Similarity and Dimensional Methods in Mechanics*, 1959, Infosearch, London.
Shapere D., The Concept of Observation in Science and Philosophy, 1982, *Phil. Sci.*, **49**, 485-525.
Slater N.B., *Eddington's Fundamental Theory*, 1957,Cambridge University Press, Cambridge.
Suppes P. and Zinnes J.L., 1963, *Basic Measurement Theory*, in Handbook of Mathematical Psychology Vol.1, ed. Luce R.D., Bush R.R. and Galanter E., Wiley, New York.
Synge J.L., A Plea for Chronometry, *New Scientist*, 19 February 1959.
Taylor C., Rationality in *Rationality and Relativism*, 1982, ed. Hollis M. and Lukes S., Blackwell, Oxford.
Thun R.E., On Dimensional Analysis, 1960, *IBM J. Res.*, **4**, 349-356.
Tolman R.C., The Principle of Similitude, 1914, *Phys. Rev.*, **3**, 244-253.
Tolman R.C., The Measurable Quantities of Physics, 1917, *Phys. Rev.*, **9**, 237-

253.
Van Fraassen B.C., *The Scientific Image*, 1980, Oxford University Press, Oxford.
Van Fraassen B.C., Empiricism in the Philosophy of Science, in *Images of Science*, ed. Churchland P.M. and Hooker C.A., 1985, University of Chicago Press, Chicago.
Van Fraassen B.C., *Laws and Symmetry*, 1989, Oxford University Press, Oxford.
Van Fraassen B.C., To Save the Phenomena, in *The Philosophy of Science*, ed. Boyd R.N., Gasper R., and Trout J.D., 1992, MIT Press, Cambridge.
Whittaker E., Eddington's Theory of the Constants of Nature, 1945, *Math. Gaz.*, **29**, § 286, 137-144.
Whyte L.L., Fundamental Physical Theory, 1950, *Brit. J. Phil. Sci.*, **1**, 303-327.
Whyte L.L., A Dimensionless Physics, 1954, *Brit. J. Phil. Sci.*, **5**, 1-17.
Williams W., On the Relation of the Dimensions of Physical Quantities to Directions in Space, 1892, *Phil. Mag.*, **34**, § 208, 234-271.
Wilson W., Dimensions of Physical Quantities, 1942, *Phil. Mag.*, **33**, § 216 26-33.
Wilson W., Dimensions, 1942, *Phil. Mag.*, **33**, § 223, 631-637.
Wilson W., Dimensions, 1944, *Phil. Mag.*, **35**, § 245, 420-425.